Goddess Beyond Boundaries

Bodies beyond boundaries

Goddess Beyond Boundaries

Worshipping the Eternal Mother at a North American Hindu Temple

TRACY PINTCHMAN

OXFORD
UNIVERSITY PRESS

OXFORD
UNIVERSITY PRESS

Oxford University Press is a department of the University of Oxford. It furthers
the University's objective of excellence in research, scholarship, and education
by publishing worldwide. Oxford is a registered trade mark of Oxford University
Press in the UK and certain other countries.

Published in the United States of America by Oxford University Press
198 Madison Avenue, New York, NY 10016, United States of America.

CIP data is on file at the Library of Congress

ISBN 978–0–19–067302–4 (pbk.)
ISBN 978–0–19–067301–7 (hbk.)

DOI: 10.1093/oso/9780190673017.001.0001

Paperback printed by Marquis Book Printing, Canada
Hardback printed by Bridgeport National Bindery, Inc., United States of America

*for the Parashakthi Temple community
with extreme gratitude*

Contents

Acknowledgments

I could not have written this book without the help and support of numerous individuals affiliated with the Parashakthi Temple. I wish to express my deepest gratitude to Dr. G. Krishna Kumar, who spent countless hours with me patiently answering my questions, introducing me to devotees, and helping integrate me into the Parashakthi Temple community. I am also indebted to the other members of the temple board, who always greeted me with a smile and a warm welcome whenever I visited the temple. My heartfelt thanks go as well to the numerous devotees who embraced my research efforts and supported my investigation into their beloved goddess and her Western "house." Asha (not her real name) opened her home to me for more than ten years; she sheltered me, fed me, and offered me friendship and comfort whenever I came to Pontiac to conduct research on the temple and its community. I cannot thank her enough for making me feel completely at home. I am grateful as well to all the individuals in Tamil Nadu who helped me during my time there in 2009. I offer thanks posthumously to Thavamani, my Tamil research associate, who is no longer with us. May he rest in peace. John S. ("Jack") Hawley and an anonymous peer reviewer made enormously helpful suggestions, which I took; many thanks to these scholars for helping me improve the manuscript. Without the amazing team at Oxford University Press, this book would not have seen the light of day. Special thanks go to Theo Calderara and Alex Rouch, who helped move my manuscript through its various stages of review and into production; Hinduja Dhanasegaran, who, as project manager, oversaw the book's production; Tim Rutherford-Johnson, who copyedited the manuscript with great care; and Birgitte Necessary, who prepared the index. Finally, I want to thank my husband, William C. French, and my children, Molly and Noah French, who tolerated my absences several times a year for more than a decade while I traveled back and forth to Michigan to work on this project.

Portions of this book were or will be published in different form in six articles and book chapters. These are "From Local Goddess to Locale Goddess: Karumariamman as Divine Mother at a North American Hindu Temple" in *Inventing and Reinventing the Local Goddess: Contemporary Iterations of Hindu Deities on the Move*, edited by Sree Padma (Lanham, MD: Lexington Books, 2014), and "Shakti Garbha as Ark of the Covenant at an American Hindu Goddess Temple" in *Between Dharma and Halakha*, edited by Ithamar Theodor and Yudit Greenberg (Lanham, MD: Lexington Books, 2018), all rights reserved; "The Goddess's Shaligrams" in *Sacred Matters: Materiality in Indian Religions*, edited by Tracy Pintchman and Corinne Dempsey (New York: State University of New York Press, 2015), and "This is a Place Where *Shakti* Dances: Intensifying the Goddess's Power in Michigan," in *Sweetening and Intensification: Currents Shaping Hindu Practices*, edited by Amy L. Allocco and Xenia Zeiler (New York: State University of New York Press, forthcoming); "The Divine Mother Comes to Michigan," in *The Oxford History of Hinduism: The Goddess*, edited by Mandakranta Bose (Oxford: Oxford University Press, 2018), and "Rethinking *Diaspora* in the American Hindu Landscape: The Translocal Śaktiscape of the Hindu Goddess in Pontiac, Michigan," *Journal of the American Academy of Religion* 91, no. 1 (2023). I am deeply grateful to Fortress Press, State University of New York Press, and Oxford University Press for their permission to reuse material from these publications.

Note on Transliterations, Quotations, and Names

To make this book accessible to those who do not specialize in the study of Hinduism, I have minimized the use of diacritical marks. I do not use diacritics at all in the names of deities, places, or scriptures. When a Sanskrit word indicates either a common noun or a proper noun (e.g., Devī, "a goddess" or the Goddess), I supply the diacritical mark the first time I use the term and then drop it thereafter. I retain diacritical marks for common Hindu terms when first use the term and then drop them thereafter. In some places, where I offer a technical term only once or twice in a way that will be of interest only to specialists, I translate the term and offer the original, with diacritical marks, in parentheses. I have retained the original spelling and grammar of websites, conversations, and videos that I quote in this book, even if they contain mechanical errors, whenever I am quoting them verbatim. In a few instances, which I note, I have lightly edited these when needed to correct grammar or spelling that might otherwise be confusing. Readers will also encounter variation in the spellings of some Sanskrit terms: e.g., *shakthi* along with *shakti*, *bhakthi* along with *bhakti*, *vibhudhi* along with *vibhuti*, and so forth. These are variant spellings of Sanskrit words transliterated from South Indian languages, especially Tamil.

I have changed the names of devotees wherever possible. I have retained the names and titles of gurus and public figures, including Dr. G. Krishna Kumar, Vernon ("Ven") Johnson, Dr. V. V. Svarnavenkatesha Dikshitar, Dr. P. Pandian (a.k.a. Kaviyogi Bacon), ANK Swamy, Shrivatsa Goswami, Swami Divya Cetananda, and Guruji Shridhar.

Introduction

Callings

I was on hold on the telephone in my office in Chicago sometime in the summer of 2006 when I first happened upon the website of the Parashakthi Temple, a Hindu goddess temple that had been consecrated seven years earlier in Pontiac, Michigan, a small city about thirty miles Northwest of Detroit. I had been surfing the web aimlessly for a few months searching terms that intersected with my research interests. Earlier that year, I had completed and sent to press a book on Hindu women's religious practices and was ready to start a new project that would require me to return to India for several months of field research. I always imagined myself to be the kind of person who would take to the field no matter what, but in 2006, I had a six-year-old daughter getting ready to start first grade and a four-year-old son in preschool. Returning to India would mean leaving them and my husband for several months, and I kept putting it off. I knew other scholars who had left families or spouses behind to conduct research or brought infants and children to their field sites: so, I wondered, what was wrong with me that I felt completely paralyzed with guilt and anxiety at the thought of doing so?[1]

I cannot recall what internet search I had undertaken to arrive at the website of the Parashakthi Temple, but I do remember I was intrigued when I found it. The website described the temple as a place of many miracles; indeed, I would learn later, the occurrence of miracles at the temple is very much part of its identity, proclaimed on its website and described in its newsletters. I also noted that, at the time, ten out of the sixteen members of the temple board listed on the temple's website at the time were Euro-American, with only six listed board members being clearly of Indian heritage. This seemed to me to be unusual since Hindu temples in the United States are generally built by and for the

Goddess Beyond Boundaries. Tracy Pintchman, Oxford University Press. © Oxford University Press 2024.
DOI: 10.1093/oso/9780190673017.003.0001

American Hindu community of South Asian heritage. I bookmarked the site.

During the summer of 2007, I found out I would be traveling to Michigan in the fall of that year to attend a conference at Albion College sponsored by my friend and colleague, Dr. Selva J. Raj. I checked a map and saw that Pontiac was not too far from Albion, so I decided to visit the Parashakthi Temple in the days following the conference. I returned to the bookmarked site and studied it. The webpage noted that Dr. G. Krishna Kumar, a Tamil American gastroenterologist on staff at William Beaumont Hospital, was the founder and spiritual director of the Parashakthi Temple. I called the temple and left several phone messages asking for Dr. Kumar's contact information, all to no avail. Finally, I sent a letter expressing my interest, along with several of my publications, to Kumar at the temple's address. A couple of weeks later, a temple devotee called and left a message on my voicemail at work asking me to get in touch with Kumar at his medical office. He was busy with patients when I finally reached him but asked me to call one of the devotees most involved with the temple at that time, a professional woman whom I shall call Asha, to arrange a visit. Asha was welcoming on the phone when I called her and told me to drive to her place after leaving Albion and stay the night with her so I could spend time at the temple and meet Kumar.

As soon as the conference in Albion ended, I changed out of my professional clothes into a salwar-kameez, a traditional Indian outfit consisting of drawstring pants covered by a long, loose tunic. I got in my car and headed to Asha's house. I was not at all sure what, exactly, I was going to say to her or Kumar or even why I was going to Pontiac; I just knew I wanted to see the temple and talk to people involved with it.

Asha greeted me at the door of her spacious, modern town home dressed in an elegant black pantsuit. I felt utterly ridiculous in my salwar-kameez. But she was welcoming and kind and immediately put me at ease. We sat in her living room and talked over tea for perhaps an hour. She asked me about my interest in the temple; I asked her about her involvement with the Goddess; we discovered we both had fathers who had passed away earlier that year. Around sunset, we got into Asha's car and drove to Kumar's medical office, where I met him for the first time. He greeted us at the door of his office, still dressed in a smart grey suit, bubbling with energy and enthusiasm despite having just put in a full day of work. He offered us soft drinks and invited us to sit all together in the chairs in his narrow waiting room and talk. I was struck immediately by his charisma and intelligence. When Kumar spoke to me that night about the temple, his words spilled out excitedly; he left sentences unfinished as he rushed to get to the next thought and went back and forth with Asha in answering my questions. Hours went by. By the time we left Kumar's office, it was late, and the temple had closed, so I returned directly to Asha's house with a visit to the temple promised for the next morning. I went to the guest room that Asha had prepared for me and at once wrote out an outline for this book. Although my thoughts about the temple have changed a great deal over the years, I find it is surprising how closely the structure of the book as I have written it resembles the outline I wrote that night, pulled out of what seemed at the time to be thin air.

It is clear to me now, many years later, that the story of how I came to do research on the temple and write this monograph conforms per-fectly to the temple's larger narrative about the Goddess as a crosser of boundaries, ethnic and other, who orchestrates events according to her will. Dear Selva would be dead within six months of my first visit to Pontiac, passing away suddenly in the night of a heart attack only days before he was to come give a guest lecture on my campus, leaving a trail of grief and mourning in his wake. He never had the chance to accompany me to the temple, although he said he wanted to do so. Yet Selva—a former Catholic priest of Tamil, South Indian descent—was instrumental in bringing me to Pontiac in the first place. If I had not been unable to fathom returning to India for an extended period of fieldwork while my children were young, I might not have been in the United States in fall of 2007 to go to the conference in Albion and might have never pursued my interest in the Parashakthi Temple. Temple discourse maintains that no one can come there unless the Goddess calls them. Hence, some temple devotees have told me they are very sure that the 2006 phone call that started me down the path to write this book was in fact a different kind of call: it was the Goddess calling me to do her work.

The Hindu Goddess in Scripture, in the World, and in Pontiac

Goddesses and goddess devotion, called Shaktism (*śāktism*), form a vital part of Hindu religious life. Hindu texts, institutions, and communities acknowledge the existence of multiple individual goddesses, but they also tend to speak of "the Goddess," Devi (Devī), or "the Great Goddess," Mahadevi (Mahādevī), as a single, transcendent being who generates all that exists. John S. Hawley notes that many Hindus hold the Goddess to be both singular and multiple without any sense of contradiction; since the Goddess is beyond all limitation, she can assume an infinite number of forms (Hawley 1996, 8).

The Hindu Goddess also embodies certain principles or forces that permeate the cosmos: these are the principles *shakti (śakti), prakriti (prakṛti)*, and *maya (māyā)*. The identification of the Goddess with these principles forms over many centuries and has roots in even the earliest Hindu scriptures (Pintchman 1994, 2018c). Shakti, which means "power" or "energy," is a universal, divine potency that both causes the created world to come into being and sustains that world through time. Shakti is sometimes used as the Goddess's name since the Goddess is the power that she wields. The term *prakriti*, "matter" or "materiality," refers to the manifest, embodied, material universe. In some contexts, such as in the Hindu philosophical school called Samkhya, *prakriti* is contrasted with *purusha (puruṣa)*, a principle of pure consciousness that is separate from the material world. The term *maya* designates creative divine power or the material form that results from the activity of such power. *Maya* is sometimes portrayed as a force that can delude humans and prevent from experiencing fully Brahman, the divine power that creates and sustains all that exists, but goddess-centered materials tend to portray *maya* in a positive light and equate it with either *shakti* or *prakriti*.[2] David Kinsley describes the Goddess in her capacity as *shakti, prakriti*, and *maya* as "an overwhelming presence that overflows itself, spilling forth into the creation, suffusing the world with vitality, energy, and power;" she assumes forms that can be benign and loving or fierce and destructive as well as everything in between (Kinsley 1986, 136, 144).

As Hindus have emigrated from India to all parts of the world especially in modern times, they have brought the Hindu Goddess with them and have established her presence in temples all over the world. Joanne Waghorne observes that while temples might seem to be "the least likely aspect of Hinduism to be portable," in fact they are among the first indicators of "resettlement in an urban environment—be it hundreds or thousands of miles away from the homeland" (Waghorne 2004, 37). The building of temples is a "significant measure" of the life of Hindu immigrant Hindu communities since, for Hindu immigrants, the process of building a temple is "simultaneously the process of building a community" of devotees with common devotional interests (Eck 2000, 221, 223). In Hindu goddess temples in the United States, the goddesses revered tend to be the "highly spiritualized and universalized forms of the great Goddess of India" (Waghorne 2004, 175). However, the South Indian village goddess Mariamman (also spelled Mariyamman), "Mother Mari," in her many forms also takes on special importance among Hindus living outside of India. Mariamman temples have moved well beyond India's borders and have been at the center of Hindu religious life for decades in places like Singapore, Malaysia, the Caribbean, Guyana, and South Africa, where South Indian migrants came as indentured laborers (Harman 2004, 3; Waghorne 2004, 173–174). In parts of Europe and North America, where many members of the immigrant Hindu community have tended to come more often from the well-off professional classes, South Indian village goddess temples have arrived more recently. But they have arrived.

Karumariamman, the main deity of the Parashakthi Temple, is a form of Mariamman and a South Indian village goddess, called *amma* or "mother," in her original historical context. Many temple devotees refer to her simply as "Amma." But she is also elevated to the status of Great Goddess, the "Eternal Mother" or "Divine Mother" of all that exists and the ultimate source of creation. She is Parashakthi (in Tamil) or Parashakti (in Sanskrit) meaning "Supreme Shakti." Thomas Coburn notes that divinity is a relational quality that communities or texts assign to a particular deity (Coburn 2001), so different goddesses may assume the status of supreme Goddess depending on the context. The form that Karumariamman assumes in Pontiac is also greatly influenced by Hindu tantra, a specific type of orientation or emphasis within Hinduism and other South Asian religions. Tantra embraces ritual practices that enable humans to access and appropriate divine power for purposes of achieving both worldly enjoyment (*bhoga*) and spiritual liberation, *moksha* (*mokṣa*), a blissful state of awareness in which one perceives everything that exists as the Divine and in which one experiences freedom from all mundane attachments and cravings. I will say more about the tantric dimensions of the Parashakthi Temple in the chapters that follow.

Why This Book?

This book presents a case study of a single North American Hindu Goddess temple and its devotional community over the span of fifteen years, from 2007–2022. In making a "case for case studies," Joyce Flueckiger observes that case studies are important because they provide "a window into the ways individuals interact with, and their experiences feed back into" dominant ideologies (Flueckiger 2006, 24). Flueckiger makes note of Lila Abu-Lughod's observations (Abu-Lughod 1993, 32) that the "typical" or "normative" often exists "more in the imagination and scholarship" of the academic researcher than it does "in practice" (Flueckiger 2006, 24), where diversity and change are more often the norm. Catherine Bell argues, similarly, that analyzing specific instances of religion, such as one does in a case study, foregrounds individual agency, enabling us to "observe the ways individuals manipulate and negotiate with tradition to create meaning of their own circumstances, and understand culture-making as a dynamic process" (Bell 1998, 209; cited in Flueckiger 2006, 25). In examining closely this one temple and its community, I hope to demonstrate the creativity and dynamism in which both temple officials and devotees engage in embracing traditional Hindu practices, ideas, and deities but then adapting them to their lives in the United States. It is my contention that any impulse to refer to the Parashakthi Temple as simply a "diaspora" Hindu temple does it a disservice. We need more richly textured discourses when exploring forms of Hinduism that exist outside of India to acknowledge and honor the creativity that individual human agents bring to their religious worlds. I will return to this point in the postscript.

This book also calls for attention to the importance of place, and the specificity of place, when and where it matters in the study of Hindu institutions and communities outside of India. Writing two decades ago, Arturo Escobar argued that the importance of place had "dropped out of sight" in a lot of academic discourse about globalization and lamented that such an erasure of place in the study of cultural processes needed to be addressed or even reversed (Escobar 2001, 141). He asks, "Can the world be reconceived and reconstructed from the perspective of the multiplicity of place-based practices of culture, nature, and economy?" (Escobar 2001, 170). Escobar calls for elevating "place-based imaginaries" and wonders, "To what extent can we reinvent both thought and the world according to the logic of a multiplicity of place-based culture?" (Escobar 2001, 142). He acknowledges that individuals are not only local and place-based but are also "indissolubly linked to both local and extralocal places" through various networks (Escobar 2001, 143). Escobar is not interested in his work in religion per se or Hindu American institutions, yet his observations about the importance of place, and the way in which people and places are dynamically networked with other people and places provided inspiration for the approach I have taken here in my examination of the Parashakthi Temple in Pontiac.

Finally, this book attempts in a modest way to grapple with recent theoretical challenges to the way we do "business as usual" in the academy. José Cabezon has noted that the demographic and ideological hegemony of Christianity in the academic study of religion has led to a sense that religions other than Christianity continue to occupy for European and American academics "a preeminent position in the hierarchy of otherness" (Cabezon 2006, 27). He is especially interested in taking into consideration the larger theoretical, framing issues that are "operative in the religions we study" and in seeking to engage such religions at that level instead of just "grinding the data that is the Other through the mill of our own theoretical apparatuses." The goal, says Cabezon, is to challenge what he considers to be a kind of "theoretical parochialism" in the academy (Cabezon 2006, 30). Cabezon cites in his article Bernard Faure's proposition that Buddhism, which Faure studies, is something that academics should not only think *of*, but also think *with*" (Faure 2004, cited in Cabezon 2006, 31). Similarly, Walter Mignolo emphasizes as an option in academic writing the practice of "epistemic disobedience" in the pursuit of theoretical decoloniality, by which he means "affirming the epistemic rights of the racially devalued" (Mignolo 2009, 4). Mignolo and Madina V. Tlostanova together describe this pursuit in terms of "border thinking," to which, they argue, immigration to "the imperial sites of Europe and the United States" heavily contributes (Mignolo and Tlostanova 2006, 205). Borders are not only geographic and political but also epistemic and have to do with diverse ways of knowing; in this regard, Mignolo and Tlastanova describe border thinking as thinking that "brings to the foreground different kinds of theoretical actors and principles of knowledge that displace European modernity" (Mignolo and Tlastanova 2006, 206–207).

The study of Hinduism in the Western academy is dominated by Western frames of analysis, many of which I find helpful and engage in this book. But the interpretive assumptions I and others in the Western academy bring to the study of Hindu institutions, religious experiences, and practices often differ vastly from those that shape the experiences and perspectives of devotees. Hence, I have arranged the chapters in a way that attempts to acknowledge what Mignolo and Tlstanova call the "pluriversal" worlds of epistemology in which non-Western theoretical frames might fruitfully coexist with those that the Western academy has to offer (Mignolo and Tlastanova 2006, 216). The problem that Mignolo and Tlastanova present is one of how we in the academy might "think from the borders themselves" (Mignolo and Tlastanova 2006, 214) in ways that enrich our work.

The Arrangement of Chapters

The book begins with materials I collected during the first several years of my involvement with the temple and ends with interviews I conducted during my most recent research visit in August 2022. But the book is not arranged chronologically. I have instead constructed the chapters around two themes: themes of "crossing" and themes of "gross elements." I borrow the theme of "crossings" in part from Thomas Tweed's *Crossing and Dwelling: A Theory of Religion* (2006), a book that has influenced my own thinking about religion and one with which I engage at some length in the first two chapters of this book. "Crossing" also adumbrates the kind of theoretical openness necessary to engage in "border thinking," which implies crossing epistemological boundaries to think from the "other side" of them. Furthermore, the Hindu Goddess is, by nature, a boundary crosser who traverses worlds, bodies, places, and minds to make herself known and accessible to her devotees. It makes sense to me to consider these crossings as a defining element of her nature. Like the Goddess, Hindu migrants, too, cross geographical boundaries in moving their bodies and lives to the United States, bringing their religions with them, and creating these religions anew once they arrive and settle into their new homes. Boundary crossings bring change as religious practices, ideas, and institutions as well as deities and people adapt to their new context and invent new ways of being as they come to dwell in new places.

I also adopt an additional Hindu framing for the chapters, considering each "from the border" by correlating every chapter with one of the five traditional Hindu gross elements, or *mahabhutas* (*mahābhūtas*), enumerated in Hindu devotional and philosophical texts. Many Hindu scriptures maintain that twenty-three principles flow forth at the beginning of creation from *prakriti* when it interacts with *purusha*. The twenty-three principles plus *prakriti* and *purusha* all together constitute twenty-five *tattvas*, entities from which the entire manifest universe is formed. The last entities to emerge from *prakriti* are the five gross elements that constitute the material realm: space, air or wind, fire, water, and earth.[3] Like other Hindu texts, institutions, and traditions, the Parashakthi Temple presents the existing universe as evolving progressively from the subtlest gross element, space, to the densest, earth. Each of the five elements also correlates with a "sheath" or *kosha* (*kośa*) of the human body.[4] As one progresses on a spiritual path, one's awareness begins to evolve away from identifying with the most material "sheath" or layer of body—the *annamaya kosha*, which is correlated with the element of earth—through the other layers of body until finally one identifies with the most subtle sheath, the *anandmaya* or "blissful" *kosha*, correlated with the element of space.

This experience brings about a state of pure spiritual bliss in which one apprehends and comes to identify with the eternal, divine presence that permeates creation and transcends all form.

The Parashakthi Temple promotes and claims to facilitate this type of spiritual journey, symbolically reversing the evolutionary process and promoting movement of an adept's consciousness through the various layers of elements and body layers from the densest to the subtlest level, where all duality ceases to exist and one experiences everything, including oneself, as the Divine. The chapters of the book are arranged to imitate that journey, moving from preoccupation with the establishment of the physical temple itself to, finally, consideration of the nature of the Goddess as existing beyond all form and beyond all bounds. The book, therefore, moves mimetically through the elements—from earth to water, fire, air or wind, and space, in that order—progressing from the most materially substantial elements and layers/sheaths of body to the most subtle. This framing is meant to be evocative, not literal, and to honor the temple's own theoretical framing of the Goddess and her manifestation in the universe. Each chapter, however, like each of the gross elements and bodily sheaths, implies and is intertwined with the others. Hence, for example, there is a subtheme of "watery" flow in the first chapter, a subtheme of "fire," in the second, and so on.

The arrangement of chapters also imitates the structuring typical of a Hindu mandala (*maṇḍala*), also sometimes referred to by the terms *cakra* or *yantra*. David White describes mandalas as geometric forms that mediate between the macrocosm and the individual as microcosm (White 2000, 9). The Divine, the source of creation and ground of the mandala itself, resides at the center and apex of the mandala, which embodies the "hierarchized cosmos." All entities residing below the apex are situated at lower levels of being (White 2000, 10). The spiritual adept projects themself into the mandala to effect "a gradual return to the source of one's being;" at each level, the practitioner engaging the mandala in meditative practice is transformed into a "higher, more divine, more enlightened being" until they become one with the transcendent divine from which all things emanate (White 2000, 11). By moving from the establishment of the earthly temple in Michigan to the abstract, unbounded nature of the Goddess, the order of the chapters replicates mimetically the layers of a mandala or yantra. It is a book written in yantric form.

Chapter 1, "Geographical Crossings/Earth," highlights the Goddess Karumariamman's persona in South India and her crossing from India to the United States in the 1990s to be established on the earthly plane in a new form in her new, Michigan home. I investigate here the role that a variety of human agents, especially Kumar, played in helping effect that crossing as well as the methods in which the Goddess called these individuals to her service. Tantric ideas and practices shaped the temple from even before its founding, so I also explore how they have shaped the vision of the temple and its goddess. The second chapter, "Devotional Crossings/Water," focuses on the stories of six individuals, including three Euro-American temple board members and founders as well as three Indian nationals, who came to be devotees of the Goddess and helped Kumar create the temple. They continue to be involved in maintaining the temple to greater or lesser degrees. The chapter examines the watery, flowing presence of the Goddess as she moves across and through oceans, political and geographic borders, bodies, and minds to call to her service the human agents she needs to carry out her work. Chapter 3, "Material Crossings/Fire" explores the role of objects and structures in promoting spiritual transformation. Such transformation is often represented in Hindu traditions by invoking fire or flame as symbolic of the energy that transmutes earthly, gross-body desires and impulses into those that engage increasingly subtle realms. Temple objects and structures bridge the gap between mundane and divine worlds by capturing divine power and channeling it in constructive ways.

Chapter 4, "Ritual Crossings/Wind" explores the role of temple rites, pilgrimage, and other forms of religious performance in maintaining and growing the temple's spiritual potency. This chapter also investigates at some length the fire that destroyed the original temple in 2018 and the 2022 *kumbhabhishekam* (*kumbhabhiṣekam*), or rite of temple consecration, of the new, grander temple that took its place. The element of "wind" in this context indicates the subtle, ever moving, and transformative energy or power that gives the temple its spiritual potency. The fifth chapter, "Divine Crossings/Space," examines the nature of the Goddess herself at the Parashakthi Temple, from the highest, most abstract levels of creation—as vibration, light, sound, and space—to the most mundane, where she helps her devotees in their everyday lives get jobs, heal from illnesses, or overcome their shyness about talking to me, the academic researcher who kept showing up and asking a lot of questions. The postscript returns to issues pertaining to the use of the term "diaspora" in describing Hindu American institutions like the Parashakthi Temple and advocates for more theoretical nuance in thinking about such institutions.

1

Geographic Crossings/Earth

Beginnings

The Parashakthi Temple in Pontiac, Michigan, also called the Eternal Mother Temple, sits down a nondescript road off a bleak stretch of highway, past the Dixieland Flea Market and down the street from an abandoned strip mall. Once a center of automobile production, Pontiac has fallen upon hard times, as have many other parts of Michigan in and near metro Detroit, so it might seem hardly the kind of place that a Hindu goddess might choose for her home. Yet here, reportedly at the Goddess's behest, the temple was first built in 1999 on sixteen acres of wooded land—or, rather, the first formation of the temple was built in that year as the temple was later greatly expanded from its original form and then replaced, following a 2018 fire, by a new, much larger temple in 2022. In all its incarnations, the temple has given pride of place to an elaborately carved, lavishly adorned granite image, or *murti* (*mūrti*), of the goddess as the eternal, supreme, divine mother of the universe. Both iconic and non-iconic images of deities are common in Hindu temples. After the temple's founding in 1999, many additional deities were installed, resulting in the need to add an addition just a few years after the initial construction. After the temple was completely rebuilt following the fire, it was consecrated anew in 2022 with a plan in place to eventually install a total of thirty-three *murtis* embodying some deities that are common to North American Hindu temples and many that are not (see, for example, "Dr Krishnakumar's Speech on New Year 2021," 2021).

The goddess who calls this temple home is nominally the South Indian Tamil goddess Karumariamman, "Black Mariamman," who, the Parashakthi Temple website asserts, has manifested herself both in a temple situated in the village of Thiruverkadu, a suburb on the outskirts of Chennai in Tamil Nadu, a state in South India, and at

Goddess Beyond Boundaries. Tracy Pintchman, Oxford University Press. © Oxford University Press 2024.
DOI: 10.1093/oso/9780190673017.003.0002

the Parashakthi Temple in Pontiac, Michigan (Parashakthi Temple, "Shakthi Worship"). Karumariamman is a Tamil village goddess and a form of the goddess Mariamman, "Mother Mari," in her original South Indian context. Vineeta Sinha has noted that the forays of Mariamman far beyond her local, rural, South Indian grounding have been well documented (Sinha 2014, 78). Yet the goddess's appearance as Karumariamman in an American Hindu temple as the main object of reverence is, as far as I can tell, new. Parashakthi Temple discourse asserts that she has come to reside in her temple in Michigan, as Parashakthi, the Eternal, Divine Mother, to benefit all beings. The Parashakthi Temple website announces that Karumariamman wished to have a house of worship built in the United States so she could give her "eternal grace to all her devotees and protect them from harm and [any] tragedies that may befall" the world at large (Parashakthi Temple, "Mahadevi Parashakthi Sannidhi").

In this chapter, I examine the nature of Karumariamman in India as well as in her temple in Michigan. I delineate her roots in Tamil culture and the transformations she has undergone in India in recent decades. And I explore ways the leadership of the Michigan temple, following instructions understood to have come directly from the Goddess herself, came to build it, breathing life into a form of religiosity rooted in Indian Hindu vernacular goddess traditions but transformed and revitalized in dynamic conversation with other Hindu traditions and the temple's American context. Karumariamman's road to America is paved by visions, dreams, embodied manifestations, and miraculous interventions that herald, even preordain, her passage from India to Michigan. In Pontiac, the Goddess and her temple emplace themselves firmly in the American landscape while simultaneously participating in a transcultural, transhistorical, and translocal economy of divine power.

Mariamman and Karumariamman in India

Mariamman is revered in South India and is widely, although not always accurately, associated with illness. She is most known as the goddess of smallpox, but the list of illnesses with which she is

associated includes at least sixteen different varieties of poxes and mea-
sles (Srinivasan 2009, 4). As a goddess of disease, Mariamman has the
power both to afflict humans with illness and to remove illness. Elaine
Craddock notes that she is often depicted "as a fierce, angry goddess
with a voracious appetite for blood sacrifice and a capricious character,
a vivid manifestation of ambivalent power" (Craddock 2001, 146).

Mariamman is, however, much more than a deity of diseases. Like
all goddesses, Mariamman is also understood by her devotees to be
a mother goddess and the embodiment of *shakti* (Craddock 2001).
Since the worldwide eradication of smallpox, Mariamman's specific
association with pox illnesses has receded,[1] but her nature as a mother
goddess who can both punish and reward her human worshipers has
remained a central characteristic of her personality. She is known especially for possessing devotees both with and without their assent.

Mariamman is also a goddess of fertility, rain or water, and general
wellbeing. She is associated with snakes and anthills, both of which are
emblematic of fertility and abundance, and she can assume the form of
both. Perundevi Srinivasan observes that the "image of an anthill with
holes and serpents strikes an obvious sympathetic correspondence
with a body having *ammai* in the form of pustules" (Srinivasan 2009,
146; see also Irwin 1982). Anthills are also linked symbolically to Vedic
sacrifice, as Craddock has noted (Craddock 2001, 160–161). Craddock
refers to Jan Heesterman's observation that "standard elements and
acts of the ritual are referred to as the head of the sacrifice, their installation or performance signifying the severing and/or restoration of the
head" (Craddock 2001, 160, citing Heesterman 1967, 23). Reference to
the severing of heads also recalls real battles in which an enemy's head
was severed in battle. Hence Craddock notes that in the Black Yajur
Veda, an anthill containing seven holes replaces the head of an enemy
killed in battle (Craddock 2001, 161).

Anthills and snakes form part of a symbolic nexus of sacrifice, fertility, and rebirth, processes that Tamils associate with Mariamman
(Craddock 2001, 159; see also Srinivasan 2009). These symbolic
associations reveal themselves also in a well-known narrative re-
corded in the Mahabharata (3.116.1–18) and retold countless times,
in numerous versions, concerning Mariamman's origins from the
woman Renuka. In brief, Renuka is a virtuous, high-caste wife whose

firm vow of chastity gives her the power to carry water without a pot. One day, she sees in a river the reflection of a *gandharva*, a celestial being, and she admires his beauty, which causes her to lose her special powers. Her husband, Jamadagni, enraged that she has lost the powers conferred upon her by her chastity, orders their son, Parashurama, to kill Renuka, granting him a boon if he will do so. Parashurama chases his mother with an ax, catching up with her in the home of an untouchable woman, where Renuka has gone to hide. Parashurama kills both women by chopping off their heads. But he then asks as his boon that his mother be brought back to life. He attaches the women's heads back to the bodies and sprinkles them with water, rejuvenating both, but he accidentally mixes them up, attaching his mother's head to the untouchable woman's body and vice versa. Renuka in this hybrid form becomes the goddess Bavaniyamman, another form of Mariamman. Craddock's notes of this narrative:

> Renuka is like a sacrificial victim; her violent death catalyzes her regeneration in a more powerful form, as the Goddess. . . . The fierce power that Renuka gains through her suffering is transformed when Renuka becomes Bavaniyamman, whose fierce power is viewed by her worshipers as a protective potency that demonstrates a mother's supreme love. (Craddock 2001, 150)

This story also reveals Mariamman's association with transformation and the crossing of boundaries, processes that are embodied in her corporeal reconstruction as half untouchable, half high-caste goddess. In this regard, William Harman notes that while the term "Mari" can refer to disease or rain, it can also mean "change" (Harman 2010, 285). And indeed, Mariamman is a goddess capable of profound change across various boundaries and divides, moving in the past several decades out of villages and away from her very humble roots to capture new, middle-class, and high-caste devotees. Craddock notes that although Mariamman is "originally a low-caste goddess, emerging from the agricultural milieu in which the majority of Indians still live, she now draws devotees from urban as well as rural areas and across caste lines" (Craddock 2001, 147). Harman (2004) traces such transformations in South India, contrasting the goddess's traditional representation at her temple in Samayapuram, a well-known Mariamman temple in Tamil Nadu, with her incarnation in Melmeruvathur, a Tamil Nadu temple where the goddess manifests as Bangaru Atigalar, the male spiritual leader of the Adhiparasakthi Movement. Waghorne, too, observes that "Mariamman's mercurial rise in popularity over the last decade and the growing wealth and importance of her temples speak of her popularity among urban people. She and other Tamil *ammans* are fomenting a new solidarity that *somehow* cuts across caste lines, crosses class distinctions, and bridges the urban-rural divide—all under the banner of new middle-class respectability" (Waghorne 2004, 133-34). Waghorne refers to this process in India as the "bourgeoisification" of the goddess.

Karumariamman and Her Temple in Thiruverkadu

As a form of Mariamman, Karumariamman, the goddess of the Thiruverkadu temple, embodies many of Mariamman's traits. For example, in Tamil Nadu, Karumariamman is associated with pox illnesses, rain, processes of change, and general fertility. She is said to reside inside an anthill although she also appears to her devotees in the form of a cobra (Srinivasan 2009, 159). Srinivasan recounts a story that one of the priests of the temple in Thiruverkadu recounted to her about Karumariamman:

> The goddess was first born as the daughter of the Pandiyan king of Madurai: she was Minakshi. In the next *yuga*, she was born to *Dakshan*: hence she was called Dakshayani or Parvati. In this Kaliyuga, she is born not from a fetus (*karu*) but she has assumed a changed (*mari*) form which is that of a snake in the anthill. (Srinivasan 2009, 159–160)

Hence, Karumariamman is equated with both Shiva's wife Parvati and the South Indian goddess Minakshi, who presides over a famous temple complex in the city of Madurai in Tamil Nadu. She is also serpentine, and temple officials in Thiruverkadu told me when I visited in 2009 that snakes would not bite anyone who sets foot on temple grounds for this reason.

Many Tamil Hindu temples and shrines have a *sthalapurana* (*sthalapurāṇa*), a story of the temple's founding (Shulman, 1980). While the term *purana* (*purāṇa*) refers to a Sanskrit textual genre, in fact many *sthalapuranas* of temples are written in vernacular languages or kept orally. One version of the *sthalapurana* of the Karumariamman temple that I heard in Thiruverkadu is that the sage Agastya (a.k.a. Agasthiar or Agastiar), considered to be a Vedic seer or *rishi* (*ṛṣi*), worshipped Karumariamman at the spot where the temple would later be built. The goddess was pleased with Agastya's devotion and appeared to him holding a trident and drum. Fixing her trident into the ground, she told Agastya to build her a temple at that spot so she could perform miracles for her devotees. Another story I heard, which is told of other Tamil temples as well, is that at the time of Shiva's marriage to Parvati, all the deities went to the Himalayas to witness the wedding, creating an imbalance between north and south. Shiva sent to the south Agastya, who was small but powerful, to restore balance. There Shiva gave Agastya vision or *darshan* (*darśan*) of the wedding ceremony. Another description of Agastya's involvement in creating the temple in Thiruverkadu is posted on the website of the Parashakthi Temple in Michigan:

> This ancient temple in Chennai was built by Sage Agastiar during Vedic times and has been rebuilt many times since then. Here Agastiar visualized Divine Mother as supreme divine consciousness, which manifested in the material universe as mother-creator of everything in the material and the spiritual universe. Various gods are Her manifestations as realized by created beings. (Parashakthi Temple, "Mahadevi Parashakthi Sannidhi")

Today the Karumariamman temple in Thiruverkadu (see Figure 1.1) is under government administration, with ritual worship performed by formally trained, high-caste officiants (*pūjāris*).

Yet the temple has Paraiyar ("Untouchable" or "Scheduled Caste") roots. According to one of the main priests at the temple, Ganesha Gurukkal, who claimed to have served there for twenty-eight years when I interviewed him in January of 2009, the change in the temple from Paraiyar control to state control occurred in the 1960s, when the

Figure 1.1 Entrance to the Parashakthi Temple in Thiruverkadu in 2009

temple was taken over by the Tamil Nadu government. One elderly temple devotee listening in on our interview noted that the temple was at that time extremely popular and brought in a lot of money in donations, a factor that undoubtedly contributed to state interest in the temple. Before the 1960s, the goddess was represented in the temple by an icon of only her head, as is true also of other village goddess temples in Tamil Nadu. Srinivasan reports that the main priest of the Thiruverkadu Temple, Nagaraja Gurukkal, told her that until the change occurred, an earthen pot filled with water and adorned with turmeric paste and Margosa leaves was kept upon an anthill and was the major object of regular worship (Srinivasan 2009, 215). In South India, village goddesses often take the form of an anthill and may be worshipped in that form (Irwin 1982, 340). Today the temple houses a full *murti* of the goddess and a *murti* of just her head, a symbolic substitute for an anthill. The inclusion of this latter *murti* in temple space suggests an acknowledgement of Karumariamman's village roots. Yet the full form of the Goddess claims pride of place and functions as the main temple *murti*. Here the Goddess has been, to use Waghorne's term, "bourgeoisified." Yet her Paraiyar roots are clearly evident.

When I was in Thiruverkadu in 2009, at least two members of the Paraiyar family that had run the main Karumariamman temple there until the government takeover still lived in Thiruverkadu and continued to run their own, albeit smaller and less visited, Karumariamman temples where the goddess would possess them to prophesize and to perform healings. The granddaughter of the main Karumariamman temple's last Paraiyar officiant, a woman named Mariammal Sami, ran a small temple within walking distance of the main temple in Thiruverkadu. While in Tamil Nadu in 2009, I went with my Tamil research associate, Thavamani, to seek her out and interview her and members of her family. We sat with her one afternoon under the shade of a large tree that dominated the courtyard outside her home. Mariammal affirmed that the change in temple administration took place in the early 1960s. She told us that her great-great-grandfather had founded the main Thiruverkadu Karumariamman temple. Following his death, her grandfather and then her father presided over the main temple until the Tamil Nadu government wrested control away from the family. According to Mariammal, prior to the takeover, the temple had been a site of prophecy (*kurimedai*), miracles, and healing, and the goddess had accepted animal sacrifices. Ganesha Gurukkal, the priest I interviewed at the main Karumariamman temple told me, however, that there is no longer any prophesying done at the temple, and animal sacrifice has been banned. Mariammal also told me that the goddess used to "come into," or possess, the male head of the family in each generation, and these men then served her as diviners. The goddess later began "coming into" Mariammal as well. She claimed at the time I interviewed her that the goddess had been coming into her for forty-three years.

In 2009, several people living in Thiruverkadu reported to me that Mariammal's brother, Madurai Muthu, also continued to prophesize and perform healings in his own small temple in the village. I was unable to meet with him or interview him when I was in Thiruverkadu in 2009 because he was out of town.[2] I heard from people living in Thiruverkadu, however, that he was in the process of establishing a new, satellite Karumariamman temple in a forested area in the village of Thiruvadisoolam, about fifty kilometers away from Thiruverkadu. The goddess herself reportedly came to Madurai Muthu in a dream and told him to establish the new temple ("Tamil Nadu Tourism"). There seemed to be some family tension contributing to this move, but no one seemed eager to share those details with me.

Goddess on the Move: The Tamil Karumariamman Beyond Thiruverkadu

Thavamani and I drove out to see Madurai Muthu's temple in Thiruvadisoolam (a.k.a. Thiruvadisulam) in January of 2009 when it was still under construction even though we knew we would not be able to meet with Madurai Muthu. At that time, an enormous *murti* of the goddess was nearing completion. The temple has since been finished; it now has its own Twitter (@aathithiruvadi) and Instagram (@thiruvadisoolam) accounts, Facebook page (Thiruvadisoolam), and a set of short devotional videos on YouTube ("Thiruvadisoolam – VISWAROOPA DARSHAN"). The first of the English language videos on YouTube claims that the goddess revealed herself to Madurai Muthu in a dream and then led him to the very spot where she was already residing in a self-born (*svayambhū*) form twenty-two feet beneath the earth. The video claims that the name of the temple site is derived from two nouns, *thiruvadi*, meaning "feet," and *sulam*, meaning "trident," because the Goddess planted both her feet and her trident at that very spot. She took the form of a snake to show Madurai Muthu the location of her manifestation, disappearing there into a snake pit. Clearly, the *sthalapurana* of the temple in Thiruvadisoolam mimics that of the temple in Thiruverkadu and hence claims the same legitimacy. A website devoted to tourism in Tamil Nadu makes note of the unique, fifty-one-foot-high seated image, noting that Madurai Muthu is the descendent of Sri Thambu Swamy, the founder of the Karumariamman temple in Thiruverkadu ("Tamil Nadu Tourism," 2016).

The gigantic goddess *murti* housed at the temple in Thiruvadisoolam stands fifty-one feet high and towers over the surrounding countryside. It embodies the fifty-one *shakti pithas* (*pīṭhas*), or "seats" of the goddess, enumerated in Sanskrit texts. *Pithas* are popular pilgrimage sites as they are places where the Goddess has come to "sit" in the world and make herself and her power available on the material plane. The story of the *pithas* is recounted in several Sanskrit sources, including several of the Puranas, and has become well known in contemporary lived Hinduism. Upon learning of his spouse Sati's death, the god Shiva becomes distraught, and he wanders about in grief carrying Sati's corpse. To lift Shiva out of his misery, Vishnu or another divine agent intervenes to cause portions of Sati's body to fall to various spots on the earth. Each of these spots then becomes a *pitha*. Today, numerous spots claim *pitha* status, and many *pithas* endure as important pilgrimage places that honor a variety of goddesses. Yet by some accounts a standard list of fifty-one has emerged. Diana Eck notes that in some versions of the story, it is clear that Sati is a sacrificial victim who comes to be dismembered and then reconstituted as the land of India, a land constituted not by political borders but by portions of the goddess's body; this imagery creates for many Hindus a sense of unity that binds together a vast number of place-specific goddesses (Eck 2012, 287–297; see also Sircar 1973, 5–7).

The temple at Thiruvadisoolam, like the current Karumarimman temple in Thiruverkadu, presents a "bourgeoisified" version of

Karumariamman as Mahadevi or Mahashakti, the universal deity who creates and sustains all things. The goddess appears here as the transcendent, omnipotent godhead who assumes the functions and forms that are in other contexts attributed to Vishnu and Shiva. It is hard not to notice the many ways the image of the Goddess at Thiruvadisoolam subsumes Shaiva and Vaishnava iconography. The text accompanying the visual footage on one of the YouTube sites is as follows:

> The Mother, here, as Mahashakthi, the *devata* [deity] of dharma, places her holy feet on a golden lotus. Her face is glittering as though thousands of suns [are] put together, the crescent moon in her flowing tresses, with moon in the left eye, sun in the right eye and the fire as the third eye in the forehead. It looks as though she is calling us all, like children, with a flashing smile on her face and telling us that she is the omnipotent. . . . The Mother directs the world by performing her five activities of creating, blessing, protecting, concealing, and destructing [*sic*] with her weapons . . . in her ten hands. The representing principles of protecting the world by Mahavishnu and Mahalakshmi [are] presented here. . . . She is the source of all, including Brahman. ("Thiruvadisoolam - VISWAROOPA DARSHAN - English - Video 14," 2017)[3]

The text here describes the Goddess's face as "glittering as though thousands of suns [are] put together," recalling, for example, the universal form of Krishna revealed in the eleventh chapter of the Bhagavad Gita. Yet, like Shiva, the Goddess holds a crescent moon in the tresses of her hair and holds between her brows a third eye, widely associated with Shiva and symbolizing, among other things, spiritual insight. She performs the five functions that the theology of Shaiva Siddhanta, a South Indian school of devotion centered on the worship of the god Shiva, attributes to Shiva. She is higher even than the formless Brahman.

The temple in Thiruverkadu has been the source of inspiration for other Karumariamman temples scattered around the Chennai region as well, some of which have also been thoroughly "bourgeosified" and some of which, like Mariyammal's small temple in Thiruverkadu, hew more closely to their Paraiyar roots and are known as places of prophecy, healing, and miracles. Thavamani told me he had heard from a neighbor about a tiny Karumariamman temple in Shastri Nagar, a residential area in the southern part of Chennai. He and I drove out there to visit on a Tuesday, the day that the Paraiyar devotee, Srithar, who established and oversees the running of the temple, reportedly underwent possession and offered prophecies to those in attendance. We arrived around noon and seated ourselves with a handful of devotees in the small temple. Srithar was sitting on the floor across from an elderly woman who was telling him her troubles, and two drummers were seated with their backs against the walls, drums at hand. He sat and listened patiently, talking to her gently. Others also came up to talk to him. Meanwhile, another woman was busy creating a beautiful *kolam*, a sacred diagram drawn on the floor with rice flour and other substances. By the time she finished, the *kolam* had taken the shape of a lotus with a six-pointed star in the center and a pile of *sindhur*, red powder, at the center of the star.

Srithar left the temple at around 1 p.m. Suddenly, the drummers started playing their instruments and singing *bhajans*, devotional songs. After about thirty minutes, Srithar returned. He went to the front of the shrine room and performed a short *puja* (*pūjā*), or devotional rite, before changing into a sari, which he tied around his waist. He turned to face the *murti* of the goddess and waived a plate with burning camphor in front of the *murti* for several minutes. Abruptly, he stiffened and started to fall backwards; the goddess had come into him. One of the drummers jumped up and took the plate of camphor from him. Srithar's arms and upper body began to shake. Devotees rushed over and began to adorn his body: someone tied a ring of bells onto his ankles, while others placed garlands around his neck and smeared ash and turmeric on his arms, back, and chest. A woman grabbed a chair and brought it to him. He sat down and slumped forward. After some minutes, Srithar got up and began to dance rhythmically to the sound of the drum. A devotee came forward and handed him a piece of burning camphor, which he placed on his tongue for about half a minute before taking it in his hand and crushing it. He did this twice more, dancing the whole time on the *kolam*. A devotee then placed camphor on the floor in the center of the *kolam* and lit it; Srithar danced through the fire and, after about five minutes, stomped it out with his feet. Smoke filled the tiny room, which had grown extremely hot. After several more minutes, the drumming came to a stop.

We watched quietly as a line of both male and female devotees formed to approach Srithar, who had now become a living embodiment of the goddess Karumariamman, to ask for help with money problems, family conflicts, trouble getting pregnant, illnesses, and other difficulties. One woman began to weep when she came before the Goddess; another became possessed and started dancing, and people had to catch her to stop her from falling down the stairs. A third entered a trance. As each devotee approached, the Goddess, who had taken over Srithar's body, would stomp her feet back and forth to make the ankle bells jingle, as if grounding herself more firmly in Srithar's corporal form and the temple arena. She gave advice to every petitioner who appeared before her, speaking through the voice of Srithar who, with his eyes closed and seemingly in a state of trance, spoke words of guidance to everyone who approached. One couple seeking a child was instructed to take fruit and offer it to the Goddess; a frail, elderly woman fearing death was comforted and assured that the Goddess would look after her family once she was gone. When there were no more petitioners, the drumming picked up a steady rhythm again, and Srithar's body began to sway until the Goddess left and he slumped forward. After a few minutes of silent sitting, he stood, gathered fruit from a tray at the back of the temple, and performed a final *puja* to Karumariamman. He then exited the temple. We, along with all the devotees who had remained in the temple, followed behind him until we came to a large trident, a symbol of Shiva, standing in the courtyard. With a final *puja* to the trident, Srithar brought the ritual to an end.

Srithar's natal home is near Shastri Nagar, but he claims he established his small temple at the Goddess's behest. When I interviewed him during our visit to Shastri Nagar in January of 2009 (see Figure 1.2), he told us that in 1991, when he was in seventh grade, some friends invited him to visit the Karumariamman temple in Thiruverkadu, which he had never seen before. His family was strict and would not allow him to roam about with friends, so he went without letting his parents know where he was going. When he entered the temple in Thiruverkadu, he says, it felt to him that he was in heaven and he

Figure 1.2 Srithar with his Karumariamman murti in 2009

refused to leave. The boys he was with returned home but did not tell anyone where Srithar had gone for fear of getting into trouble. After a few days, a shopkeeper with a stall next to the temple began to take care of him. Shrithar said:

> I was in the temple. The shop owner asked me for my address, but I didn't give it to him. Only after four months, when he asked me for the address, I gave it to him. Then they went to my house and told my parents I was staying at the temple. My family put advertisements in all the media, but they could not find me. Only after four months they came to me since the shopkeeper went and told them where I was.

Srithar claims that his parents came to the temple to get him, but he refused to go home for fear that his father and older brother would beat him as punishment. He ran away for a night before returning to the temple. The shopkeeper agreed to continue caring for Srithar, who took to visiting his family every couple of months but had no desire to stay with them. He was not close to his father or siblings but loved his mother dearly and missed her.

One day, while he was attending a function in a nearby temple to Angalamman, another Tamil goddess, Karumariamman, possessed him. He reports that he was fourteen years old at that time, but the goddess, speaking through him, told the devotees who witnessed the possession that she had in fact been "coming into" him since he had been in his mother's womb. After that episode, the goddess would possess him only occasionally. After some time, she came to him in a dream and told him to build her a temple in Shastri Nagar, so he moved there and had a small, thatched hut built. He made the temple *murti* himself using concrete and shaping it with a ladle and spoon. At first, he made ends meet through donations, but he soon found another calling:

> In the beginning, I gave prophecy on Tuesdays, Fridays, and Sundays. But nowadays people call me from other temples to decorate *murtis* for functions and festivals. I am good at that. In August (Aadi), people will take me to decorate *murtis* for processions and such. I can make a goddess (*amman*) *murti* in one hour. I can make this goddess image in half an hour with mud. It is not our family

trade, but I have become very skilled at this work by doing it. It is a training. I am often not here, but I have kept Tuesdays for Mother.

Several other temples to Karumariamman have also sprung up in Tamil Nadu, and a quick internet search turned up one also in Calgary, Canada. Further research might reveal which of these temples present the more bourgeoisified versions of Karumariamman that now characterize the main Thiruverkadu temple and the Karumariamman temple in Thiruvadisoolam and which do not. It is clear, however, that Karumariamman has become more popular in the last decades and is moving around the globe with her devotees. Ganesha Gurukkal, the priest at the Thiruverkadu temple, recounted to me that the person most responsible for helping popularize the worship of Karumariamman in the region since the 1960s was a temple priest named Ramdass, who may have originally served as assistant to Mariammal's father. Both Ganesha Gurukkal and others referred to Ramdass as a yogi and diviner who was regularly possessed by the Goddess. Ramdass was no longer alive when I was in Thiruverkadu in 2009. But he helped launch the Parashakthi Temple.

Crossings: A Passage to Michigan

While the Parashakthi Temple does not have a formal, written *sthalapurana*, many of the individuals most involved with the temple's founding share a set of stories about how it came about. I would argue that these stories, which I have gathered here from both written sources and interviews conducted over the course of several years, constitute the temple's *sthalapurana* and are instrumental in shaping the temple's vision of the Goddess.

Like the Rajarajeshvari Pitham in upstate New York that Dempsey has written about, the Parashakthi Temple, too, diverges in significant ways from patterns that tend to characterize Hindu temples in the United States.[4] It is the only American Hindu temple of which I am aware, for example, where many members of the governing board have over the years been not of Indian descent but have instead been Euro-Americans. Although the temple is nominally *shakta*, focusing on

Karumariamman as Divine Mother, numerous other deities have also been installed; however, their presence in the temple is a result not of committee discussion (Narayanan 1992, 175) but of direct command from the Goddess. Finally, unlike in many American Hindu temples, the religious life of the Parashakthi Temple is shaped directly by one individual in particular, Kumar (see Figure 1.3). Kumar frequently claims he is simply a "caretaker" or a "mailman" whom the Goddess has elected to deliver directives and truths that she communicates to him directly through a series of ongoing revelations. He acknowledges, however, that his "payment" for this service is that he is allowed to read "the mail" before he delivers it to the congregation (see, for example, "Dr Krishnakumar's Speech on New Year 2021"). The temple community considers Kumar the principal founder of the temple, but Kumar often insists that the Goddess is the actual founder. Many other individuals were active in establishing the temple, and many in the initial group of devotees continue to support the temple financially and remain engaged in temple activities. However, no one else plays the kind of leading role that Kumar does in guiding the temple's ongoing religious life (see also Pintchman 2014, 2015, 2018a, and 2018b).

The story of the founding of the Parashakthi Temple is a story replete with miracles. Here I draw upon Richard Davis's understanding of miracles as "actions or events that so differ from the expected course of things that they evoke astonishment and wonder" (Davis 1998, 4). The "expected course of things" I understand as that which refers to the "orderly . . . and empirically intelligible" realm of the natural world (Davis 1998, 5). Miracles figure prominently in the *sthalapurana*s of many temples in South India, and the significant role given to the miraculous in the establishment of the Parashakthi Temple is certainly not unique. In the sacred history of the Parashakthi Temple, however, miracles that the Goddess is seen as perpetuating at this location do something that they do not necessarily do at other places: they emplace this Goddess and her temple firmly in the American landscape, helping define both Goddess and temple as embodied entities that are rooted in and spring forth from both Indian and American soil. Just as those most intimately involved in founding the temple understand the Goddess herself to be both local (as Karumariamman) and universal (as Parashakthi, "Shakti of All"), South Indian and American, Hindu

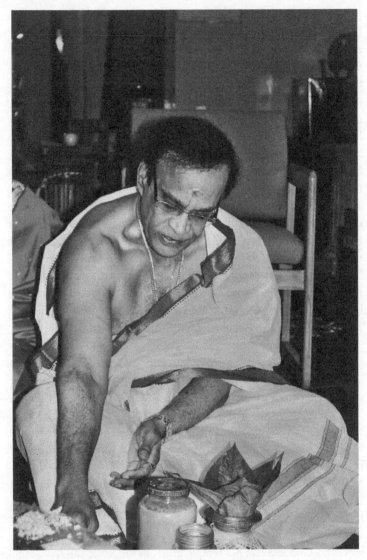

Figure 1.3 Kumar at the Parashakthi Temple in 2009

and pan-religious, the miracles that enabled the temple to be built in the first place similarly cross these borders, reflecting the boundary-transgressing nature of the Goddess herself.

Especially helpful in making sense of the dynamics surrounding the establishment of this temple is Thomas Tweed's emphasis on the spatial tropes of dwelling and crossing in interpreting religion (2006). Tweed claims that religion concerns in an essential way *dwelling*, that is, finding a sense of home for oneself, and *crossing*, that is, moving across space and time. Here Tweed is drawing on the work of James Clifford, who emphasizes not only dwelling, but also movement, travel, and border crossing as both metaphors for ethnography as a practice and the character of the fields academics study in fieldwork practices (Clifford 1997). Religions, says Tweed, are about home-making, coming to dwell comfortably in places; but they also entail traversing natural, corporeal, social, and temporal boundaries. Religions are intertwined with geographical crossings, corporeal crossings, and cosmic crossings pertaining to the ultimate "horizon of human life" (Tweed 2006, 123). Here Tweed continues to draw on imagery of movement and travel as he notes:

> We can understand religions as always contested and ever-changing maps that orient devotees as they move spatially and temporally. Religions are partial, tentative, and continually redrawn sketches of where we are, where we've been, and where we're going. . . . They situate the devout in the body, the home, the homeland, and the cosmos. (Tweed 2006, 74)

Tweed draws also on the aquatic tropes of confluences and flows in his discussion of how religions become grounded. Observing that religions are complex processes, not things, he argues that they necessarily involve confluences and flows "traversing multiple fields," with some forms of religion, functioning as "transverse confluences" that create "new spiritual streams" (Tweed 2006, 59–60). These processes involve the movement of individuals and groups. Tweed defines religions, somewhat infelicitously, as "confluences of organic-cultural flows that intensify joy and confront suffering by drawing on human and suprahuman forces to make homes and cross boundaries" (Tweed

2006, 54). Human neural, physiological, emotional, and cognitive pathways, along with the shifting cultural currents in which humans operate, all help shape the forms that religion takes in any given context (Tweed 2006, 62–69).

The spatial tropes of dwelling and crossing along with the aquatic tropes of confluence and flow are helpful in thinking about the nature of the Goddess and the religiosity she inspires at the Parashakthi Temple. The stories I tell here, and the stories devotees at the Parashakthi Temple have told and continue to tell about the Goddess and her temple, are, on the one hand, narratives of dwelling: they tell of ways the Goddess comes to abide in South Indian and American geographies, human bodies, visions, and dreams, where she gestates, metamorphoses, and finally emerges in a new form in her new abode in Michigan. They are, furthermore, narratives of crossing: they tell of human crossings between India and America, ethnic and religious crossings that signal the Goddess's call to devotees to enter into her service, and divine crossings into minds, bodies, and places.

Kumar reports that he came from India to the United States from Tamil Nadu in the mid-1960s to do his medical internship. During his first decade in the United States, he says he was not particularly religious but was instead absorbed in developing his career. He married a Euro-American woman, Margaret, and they had a daughter. Sometime in the early 1970s, he began to feel as if something important were missing from his life. A friend of his offered to take him to an astrologer in Tamil Nadu, and Kumar agreed. This astrologer, A. N. K. Swamy—to whom most people at the temple refer by the initialism "ANK," with each letter pronounced separately—was a reader of Bhrigu Nadi (*nāḍi*), a form of predictive astrology practiced in Tamil Nadu. It relies on a set of texts written in ancient Tamil and attributed to Agastya. Readers of Bhrigu Nadi claim that they can use astrological charts to conduct readings that will predict future events. I will address the story ANK told me about his life and involvement with the Parashakthi Temple at greater length in Chapter 2. Kumar told me that ANK revealed to him at their first meeting that Kumar would eventually be called upon to build a temple for the Goddess. Here is how Kumar described the reading to me in a conversation we had in October of 2008:

K: That was Minakshi, Mother Minakshi ... (She said) you will not call me Minakshi because [as such] I am a ritualistic form. But you will build [a temple] in another country, so I will come as Parashakthi Karumariamman ... where I am not ritualistic but will accept anybody, whether they eat meat or do not eat meat, are ritualistic or have no religious life. I'll accept everyone.... So, you will build the temple for me, but you won't call me Minakshi.

Here, as in the story Srinivasan reports from Thiruverkadu, we see a connection between Minakshi and Karumariamman. Kumar often describes Sanskritic, Brahmanical deities—those sanctioned by the dominant elite forms of Hinduism—as "ritualistic" forms of the Goddess, contrasting these forms with vernacular forms, like Karumariamman, which he describes as "non-ritualistic." Ritualistic deities, in his parlance, care about things like caste status and rules surrounding purity and impurity, while non-ritualistic deities do not care about those things at all but instead want to "reach everybody."

After this event, Kumar says he became increasingly interested in religion, taking up meditation and researching a wide range of religious topics. He reports he returned to India often during the 1970s and 80s, frequently meeting with ANK and having astrological chart readings done on his own behalf and on behalf of others. During this period Kumar also began to develop an important spiritual relationship with a Euro-American female colleague of his, whom I shall call Jane. I will recount Jane's story more fully in Chapter 2. Kumar claims, and Jane confirms, that one day, when passing him in the hall, Jane greeted him and teased him that he rarely stopped to say hello to her in the material world. However, she told him, he was coming to her frequently in dreams and offering her religious teachings. Kumar says he was surprised to hear this and didn't believe her. But when he next returned to India, sometime in the late 1980s, he brought Jane's biodata with him and had an astrological reading done for her. ANK confirmed that Kumar had been going to Jane and offering her spiritual instruction in her sleep. After that, the two developed a friendship and a close spiritual relationship. Jane and her husband, who have both also played a key role in creating and sustaining the temple, had several Euro-American friends who were spiritual seekers, and Kumar became friendly with them as well.

The formative moment for Kumar and the temple came in 1994 when, Kumar recounts, the Goddess as Divine Mother first appeared directly to him in a vision while he was in a deep meditative state. Kumar described the event in an interview I conducted with him in 2009:

KUMAR: From '72 to the eighties I was studying these mystical things . . . but I really did not communicate (with Divine Mother). In '94, when Mother appeared, at first I didn't know who she was. I was just meditating, and this form came (and said), "Build a house for me, because the world is going to go through major turmoil beginning 2000. So, install me, build the house for me, and I'll protect the earth."

TRACY: Had you had visions like that before?

KUMAR: I had visions, but not as specific as that. I had it twenty-seven times, same thing. Then I knew it was something genuine.

The number twenty-seven is significant in this context. Hindu astrology recognizes twenty-seven fixed minor constellations or nakshatras (nakṣatras), also called "asterisms" or "lunar mansions." These nakshatras occupy fixed positions in the sky, and altogether they complete the entire 360 degrees of the zodiac. As the earth rotates, the moon seems to move over time to a different portion of the sky and hence appears to move through all the different nakshatras over the course of the year. When a person is born, their astrological energy is governed by the nakshatras that appear in conjunction with the moon at the time of their birth. Every nakshatra is also linked to a particular deity. Hence the number twenty-seven indicates the totality of all people, all deities, and all entities in the entire universe. Kumar's claim that the vision occurred to him twenty-seven times points to the Goddess's desire to bring the totality of the universe into her protection with the energy that would emanate from the construction of her new, American house. Following these initial visions, Kumar reports that the Goddess has continued to appear to him and communicate with him regularly.

After experiencing the visions, Kumar conferred with ANK, who then confirmed that the Goddess in her form as Karumariamman was calling Kumar to her service. ANK sent Kumar a picture of Karumariamman's *murti* in the Thiruverkadu temple. Kumar maintains he was not at all familiar with this form of the Goddess until she appeared to him in the vision. Around this time, too, Jane told Kumar that some goddess had been appearing to her and insisting that Jane and Kumar build a temple for her. When Jane came to Kumar's office one day, Kumar showed her the photo of Karumariamman that ANK had sent him from India. Jane confirmed that it was indeed the same goddess who had also been appearing to her. Hence, Kumar reports, they both knew they had to build this temple. Prema Kurien notes that in many cases, the impetus for the building of a Hindu temple, whether in India or abroad, is often an injunction sent by a deity in a dream or vision demanding a home (Kurien 2007, 88). In this case, the injunction came independently to two different actors who perceived the Goddess's direct appearance to them in a form with which neither of them was familiar as a clear sign that they now had no choice but to do her bidding.

When I interviewed him in October 2008, Kumar told me the following about what happened. He reports that when he went to India and visited the Karumariamman temple in Thiruverkadu for the first time in the mid-1990s, he met Ramdass—the priest who, Ganesha Gurukkal claimed when I spoke with him in 2009, was of great importance in spreading the popularity of the Karumariamman temple in Thiruverkadu. Kumar refers to Ramdass as a yogi and guru of the Thiruverkadu temple, whom the Goddess had been "coming into" since childhood. Kumar reports he was walking in the temple when someone came out from a temple board meeting and told him that Ramdass, whom he had not met before, wanted to talk to him. When Kumar went to meet Ramdass, Ramdass told him that the Goddess wanted Kumar to pay for her chariot. As Kumar tells the story, Karumariamman had revealed to Ramdass in a vision that she wanted a temple chariot to be built to process her icon outside of the temple on festival days. Although many devotees offered to pay for it, the Goddess would not allow anyone to have it constructed for her until Kumar came to Thiruverkadu. She then revealed to Ramdass that Kumar was the person she had chosen to sponsor the chariot. Kumar says he agreed to fund it. When he was meditating that night after returning from the temple, Kumar recounts, the Goddess came to him again to reveal that the chariot had larger significance: it was symbolic of Karumariamman's desire to be transported out of the Thiruverkadu temple, taken to Michigan, and installed in a temple there. Kumar says the Goddess told him, "You are going to take me, and build a house, and establish me so I can give grace to the world. Symbolically, I am giving you the privilege of taking me out of my temple." Kumar told me:

> [Ramdass] called to me and said, "I must tell you something. Last night Mother came and told me that She is going to be more with you in your place of worship (in Michigan) than here." Then I said, "Swami, this temple was from Agasthiar [Agastya], (built) five or six thousand years ago." It was rebuilt many times after. . . . I told him, "You since childhood are a yogi, and Mother comes through you and talks to people. . . . I am a doctor." He said, "Doctor, I am not happy to tell you this. I am very hurt that Mother would leave me and go to you. I am telling you because she told me that. You've come to me, and I wanted you to know." I said, "No, don't say things like that. Mother would never leave you." He said, "No, she'll be here. But she'll be more intensely present (in Michigan) because the world needs her. That is the place she wants to be to protect the world." This country [the United States] should be protected. He was so sad when he told me this. [I told Ramdass,] "Maybe she knows I need her more than you do. Here she is already established [in the temple], and she is already with you. You are a guru. Maybe she meant it that way."

The Goddess's alleged miraculous appearances in dreams and visions in the 1990s crossed ethnic, religious, and gender boundaries. She appeared to both Kumar and Jane, enjoining them both to build a "house" for her, as well as Ramdass, enjoining him to play his part in allowing the Goddess to cross over the ocean out of India and be established in Pontiac. These communications to her human agents, furthermore, took place across time and space, spanning decades and the distance between India and the United States. The Goddess revealed her will through the 1972 astrological reading in India and the 1994 visions occurring in Michigan, both of which came to be filtered through ANK's interpretations and Ramdass's visions.

Kumar writes in the first Parashakthi Temple newsletter, *Om Shakthi* (2001), that the way the land was obtained was the result of a miracle (Kumar 2001, 4). ANK described to Kumar the land on which the temple would be built when he performed Kumar's first Bhrigu Nadi reading in 1972. After Kumar's vision in 1994, he began to search for this land. He reports that he was at the gym one day when he ran into a Bengali American acquaintance, a real estate broker whom he had not seen in a long while. This man had lost a great deal of weight and was suffering badly from diabetic neuropathy. Kumar had read this man's astrological chart several years earlier and told me he knew the man was going through a challenging time because of the presence of Rahu, a malevolent planet, in one of his astrological houses. Kumar told me this in October 2008:

> Suddenly it hit me—you see when you go through Rahu and it's not positive to you, you get a neurological problem. I knew that. I just felt it, instinctively. Now Rahu is controlled by the Goddess; only Parashakthi can control it, not any other deity. So, I said, "You know, I'm really looking into what to do about this temple.... you're a real estate man. Find me a place. If you do that and She [the Goddess] is appeased, that will help you, because she controls Rahu."

Kumar reports that after a week, the broker called Kumar and told him he had come across a plot of sixteen acres of undeveloped land in the middle of Pontiac that was for sale. Kumar says he knew this was the land the Goddess wanted. He then brought to the land the other people involved in the temple's founding, and they all also approved of it as the place the Goddess wanted for her house. The owner of the land is reported to have been an elderly Euro-American man who had moved to Florida, and when Kumar expressed interest in buying it, the owner insisted that Kumar come to Florida to discuss the matter. As Kumar recounts the story, it was January, and the weather was miserable in Michigan, but Kumar says he was busy with patients and could not leave the state. Inexplicably, according to Kumar, the owner agreed to come to Michigan and ended up selling the land to Kumar even though the owner had bigger offers on the table. Here is how Kumar explained it to me in October 2008:

> He didn't want to come here. He wanted me to go to Florida. At that time, I was working very hard. I was putting in eighty-hour weeks. I was getting panicky [about paying for the building of the temple]. I was thinking, "If mother wants it, he will come. Just tell him I am working, so I cannot go [to Florida]." . . . So, he had a [real estate] broker, and his broker called me and told me, "Doctor, he is very upset," because he didn't want to come [back to Michigan]. But then he just came. I met him in his office in Rochester Hills (Michigan). I was nervous he was going to be mad at me because here I was offering much less money [than he was asking].

When the seller learned that the land was to be used for a charitable organization and not to be developed into condominiums, for which the city had approved the land, he allegedly agreed to take the low offer from Kumar although he claimed to have several higher offers on the table. Kumar continued:

> He told me, "This land has been with me for thirty years. So many times, people would come and ask to buy it from me, and something would tell me, "No." It must be the right person. I told him, "You must be a spiritual soul, a blessed soul. That temple we are going to build is going to wake up the souls of many, many people, and you will be part of that, because you kept it [the land] for the temple."

The land on which the Parashakthi Temple now stands is in many ways topographically similar to the site of the Minakshi Temple in Madurai, a factor that is significant to devotees. When I interviewed him in Chennai in January 2009, ANK made note of the similarity between the name "Pontiac," the town in Michigan, and the name "Pandya," the imperial dynasty that ruled parts of South India until the fifteenth century and was responsible for constructing the Minakshi Temple, claiming that Pontiac is the New World recreation of the Pandyan

Empire. Temple discourse continues to describe the land on which the temple was built as land that was chosen and readied over the course of many centuries by Divine Mother herself, imbued uniquely with her concentrated energy. When the construction for the temple began, according to temple oral history, it was discovered that the land was built over a subterranean river that runs down about fifteen feet under the surface, so the original plans had to be modified to drive the pilings much deeper than had originally been anticipated. Kumar has asserted numerous times over the years that the Goddess chose this locale in part because of the subterranean river which, he says, draws to the temple all manner of spiritual beings (see, for example, "Mystical nature of temple land: Parashakthi Temple," 2022).

In the 1972 Bhrigu Nadi reading, Kumar claims it was predicted that the land on which the temple would eventually be built would have been occupied previously by priests of another religion. Kumar and others intimately involved in establishing the Parashkthi Temple maintain that the temple grounds had previously been considered sacred by Native Americans in the area and had been a site of powerful shamanic activity. Kumar reports that the presence of Native American shamanic spirits was revealed to him one day when he was deep in meditation, well after he had purchased the land. One Euro-American devotee told me that she and her daughter, who is also Euro-American but not a goddess devotee and not involved at all with the temple, were walking on the land one day before the temple had been built, and her daughter went into the woods. The daughter came out a few minutes later visibly frightened because she heard drumming in a particular pattern and voices singing in a language she had never heard before. The devotee understood the sounds to be the music and voices of Native American spirits still inhabiting the area (interview, October 2008).

Kumar recounts that the land is uniquely powerful because the Goddess had been present in it for millennia before he purchased it. She established there 300 shamanic spirits that continue to inhabit temple lands. He and others say they have seen on temple grounds huge, large-antlered deer that are invisible to most humans but are the spirits of the deceased shamans. The land's connection to its reported Native American past has become well-established as part of public narratives about the temple. For example, devotee Pamela Costa wrote in the temple's first newsletter about the temple's "mystical origins" claiming that "Local Native American Indians were drawn to the power of the land and selected it for their sacred worship site. Several devotees have commented on feeling the presence of these ancient spirits" (Costa 2001, 12). She writes further that "it is apparent to many that a vortex of energy exists at the site. We, at the Eternal Mother Temple, believe the Holy Land is aligned with the various planetary and star systems in such a way so as to heighten the energies at the present-day site" (Costa 2001, 4). I have also heard temple spokespersons describe the temple to large audiences in public temple events as a uniquely powerful place where communication with the Goddess functions via a "faster cable" than at other places.

Vasudha Narayanan makes note of a temple dedicated to Shiva Vishvanath in Hawai'i, where Hindus have come to view a sacred stone that was recognized as a deity in indigenous Hawaiian religion as a form of Shiva (Narayanan 1992, 2006). In Pontiac, however, devotees tend to view the reported Native American shamanic presence in the land as the Goddess's way of helping prepare it for her emergence there at the dawn of the twenty-first century. This discourse is one of indigenization; it turns the Goddess from a uniquely Indian Hindu Goddess into one who is also indigenous to Michigan and has always been dwelling there in that patch of land, simply waiting for the right time to make herself manifest.

Kumar reports that the Goddess told him in the 1994 Bhrigu Nadi reading that he should seek spiritual guidance and help from Dr. V. V. Svarnavenkatesha Dikshitar, one of the main priests of the Shaiva Chidambaram Temple, another well-known temple, also in Tamil Nadu.[5] At that time, Kumar had never met Dikshitar, but while he was still in South India that year he asked ANK to arrange a meeting. Kumar explained to Dikshitar that the Goddess had sent him to ask for a tantric mantra. Kumar claims the Goddess had revealed to him that Dikshitar was a master of tantric practice.

Tantra is, as Hugh Urban notes, "an extremely messy and ambiguous term" used to refer to a wide variety of texts and traditions (Urban 2010, 400). David Gordon White describes tantra as an Asian body of beliefs and practices based on the assumption that the universe as we experience it is "nothing other than the concrete manifestation" of the power of Brahman, the godhead (White 2000, 9). While popular discourse both in India and in the United States tends to emphasize tantra's connections to transgressive practices, sex, and the cultivation of dangerous magical powers, several contemporary scholars have attempted to put sensationalist portrayals of tantra in context and demonstrate the pervasive influence of tantra in shaping modern mainstream Hindu practices (e.g., Urban 2010; Burchett 2019). Tantric texts and traditions tend to be monistic, viewing the created universe as the transformation of a single, divine power that transcends all form but permeates the created world at all levels. Tantric practices, broadly speaking, are those that aim to harness that divine power for either worldly or spiritual advancement. Gaining access to that power requires divine grace (*anugraha*) (Brooks 1992, 84; Padoux 2017, 129–132). Urban observes that tantra "is best seen not as a coherent, unified tradition, but as a fluid and shifting collection of particular texts, practices, and traditions, woven and rewoven with a variety of other traditions" (Urban 2003, 43). I will not attempt to summarize here the nature and history of tantra or the robust body of academic work devoted to the study of tantra as doing so would be a fool's errand and, besides, is beyond the purview of this book. But I think it is fair to say that there can be no tantra without mantra. Patton E. Burchett has described mantras, which tantric traditions generally understand to be the powerful sound form of deities, as the "bread and butter of tantric practice" (Burchett 2019, 32, 264). Tantric mantras are often *bija*, or "seed," mantras, religiously powerful utterances consisting of one syllable that embodies a deity in sound form.

Kumar told me in October 2008 that Dikshitar reacted very angrily when Kumar asked him for a mantra and denied that he, Dikshitar, had any connection at all to tantra. However, Kumar reports that the Goddess had given him secret information about a yantra in Dikshitar's possession, information that he revealed to Dikshitar on a return visit about three months later. Yantras are often geometrical designs inscribed in metal that embody the power of a particular deity, as this one was. Dikshitar told Kumar to leave and return the next day. When he returned, Kumar reports, Dikshitar accepted the meeting, explaining that the deity Ganesha, the elephant-headed deity of boundaries and obstacles, had come to him and told Dikshitar that Kumar was worthy of his attention.

According to Kumar, Dikshitar was a master yantra maker and powerful tantric practitioner. Kumar also told me that while Dikshitar was heavily influenced by Shri Vidya, a South Indian *shakta* Tantric school, he forged his own, individual tantric path (interview, July 2012). The tantric foundations of the temple that Kumar traces back to his relationship with Dikshitar are integral to the ongoing life of the temple, which blends Tamil vernacular goddess traditions with Brahmanical devotional practices (*bhakti*) and *shakta* Tantric traditions. Kumar claims that Dikshitar eventually gave him the yantra he sought, and Kumar attributes his ability to "do Mother's work" to the spiritual power and insight he derives from that yantra. Kumar insists further that Dikshitar got the yantra from his guru, who got it from his guru before him, and so on, and "so that is the lineage." In Hindu traditions generally, those on a tantric spiritual path can take *diksha* (*dīkṣā*), "initiation," from a guru, and become that guru's disciple. Tantric *diksha* may involve the passing from guru to disciple of a powerful mantra or object that cements their relationship and passes spiritual power onto the disciple. Kumar claims that when Dikshitar gave him the mantra and yantra, he initiated Kumar as a disciple and passed to Kumar the responsibility of continuing Dikshitar's spiritual lineage. They developed a close relationship until the time of Dikshitar's death. A photo of Dikshitar hangs in the temple, and Kumar continues to refer to Dikshitar as his guru.

Kumar still keeps that yantra in a condominium that he says he allows almost no one to enter (I have not ever been there). He claims that the yantra has a special spiritual charge—one that is "more actively invoking energies" than other yantras—that could stimulate demonic (*asuric*) drives in a person or disturb them if they were to gaze upon it. As he put it to me in a conversation we had in October 2019, "You must be careful, because if you invoke those energies, sometimes negative energies also come there. And you don't know [if that will happen]. So, it is not a safe place for others." Yet, Kumar claims, he uses it every day in his meditation practice for the benefit of the temple congregation and anyone else he feels "can benefit from the yantra."

Kumar and others recount there were two major obstacles to building the temple once the purchase of the land went through, drawings had been completed, and the building had begun. The first was money. Kumar mortgaged the cost of the land but had not raised enough money to build the temple on it by the late 1990s. He told me he had sold many of his own assets to fund the temple's construction but was still short of cash. The rest of the money would come through loans and donations from the other individuals involved in building the temple. The second was paperwork: the architect and builder had failed to obtain all the proper building permits, and the city of Pontiac began threatening to demolish the portions of the temple that had been built and cease all construction until standard permitting procedure was followed. There was no guarantee, however, that the construction would then be allowed to go forward since there was some opposition to the temple in the surrounding community because of concerns about traffic. Three individuals actively involved in the founding of the temple told me that on the night of the hearing for the permit, the city council meeting where the temple's fate was to be decided ran unusually late. Kumar himself was not present at that meeting, but he found out later that the permit was finally approved, as he recalls, sometime around 1:00 AM. Kumar claims that more than a year later, an individual involved in the process told him a story about what happened that night.

Pontiac is a largely African American city, and this individual was a Christian African American man involved in the permitting process. I will call him Joe. According to Kumar and two other core devotees with whom I spoke in 2010, several years before the temple installation, Joe had been in New Orleans for work reasons and had gone to services at a Christian church where, once a month, the Holy Spirit would enter the body of the presiding minister, and the minister would make predictions—just as Karumariamman possesses the bodies of South Indian diviners for the same purpose. On that occasion, the Holy Spirit entered the minister, who approached Joe and told him to stand up. The Holy Spirit then declared to everyone present that in Joe's city, "a man from the East" would come and build a house of worship, "and I [the Holy Spirit] will be there; and as soon as it's done, your city [Pontiac] will grow luxuriously." Kumar reported to me in a 2008 interview that Joe told him he had been expecting a member of the sizeable Middle Eastern community nearby in Dearborn, Michigan to request a mosque, but when the permit for the Hindu temple was requested, he concluded this was the house of worship that the Holy Spirit had predicted would come. Joe allegedly worked behind the scenes before the meeting to convince all the council members involved in the process to grant the requisite permit post facto, making sure that everyone stayed that night until it was approved. Kumar claims he first met Joe and heard this story more than a year following the hearing, when Joe told him he had wanted to make sure the Parashakthi Temple got built because the presence of Jesus would be there, as predicted by the Holy Spirit speaking through the body of the Southern minister. I was able to interview Joe in May 2010. He confirmed that the minister in New Orleans "predicted a church would come to our city that would be a blessing to Pontiac." He also confirmed he wanted the temple to be built and believes Jesus is present in the temple.

One Euro-American devotee whom I shall call Barbara and who was very actively involved in temple life during the first two decades of its existence told me her own story of being called by the Goddess to help make sure the temple would be built (interview, September 2010). Barbara had been raised Baptist but converted to Catholicism in the 1970s, and her children had been raised Christian. She reports that she was only peripherally involved in the planning or building of the Parashakthi Temple until the construction started running into permitting and zoning constraints. She had an important personal connection to Kumar and other individuals involved in the initial temple construction. At that time, when construction was already underway, she offered her assistance with some of the planning. She maintains that one day, as she was leaving the temple, she got into her car and looked into the rear-view mirror. The Goddess was there:

BARBARA: It was the Divine as Goddess that I saw. . . . And she said to me, "I am She whom you call the Virgin Mary," but she was a combination—well . . . my third eye opened up. I heard electricity, heard something pop. It was just very strange, and I could see this blue light.

TRACY: And you looked in the rear-view mirror?

BARBARA: Yes . . . and I thought I'd look in a different direction and she'd go away, but no matter which way I turned, she was just still there. I thought, "Okay, either I'm crazy, or—this is just such a strange experience. So, I'll just sit here, and she'll go away." But she didn't go away. So, then I thought I would see what it is all about, because she was just so beautiful, like I said. In some of my meditation, I used to think that if I ever had a vision, how would I know the difference [whether the vision is divine or demonic]? And this little teacher voice that I have inside said, "If it's from God, you'll feel love. The devil cannot possibly make you feel love because he cannot experience love." And I thought, that's so simple, and yet so profound. I wouldn't have thought of something like that. But it's so logical. I don't know if it's the truth or not, but to me it's a logical thing. When I was looking at her, I felt love in a different form. . . . She was dressed in North Indian style, but she had no blouse. The sari came across and over her head. It appeared to be almost ancient Judaic, like the Virgin Mary might have dressed. So, she was a combination. . . . And she said, "I am she whom you call the Virgin Mary." And I just said, "What can I do for you?" And she said, "I have need of you at my temple."

In Barbara's vision, the Goddess appears miraculously in a hybrid form that is meaningful to her, forming a bridge between her Catholic background of Mary devotion and the Indian, Hindu Goddess tradition. After having this vision, Barbara became much more deeply involved in the life of the temple than she had been prior to the vision, and several devotees report that she was instrumental in solving the many regulatory problems that arose during the construction process. Similarly, Kumar reports that Frank D. Stella, the Italian American founder and former CEO of F. D. Stella products company, was from the beginning an important temple supporter and donor. I met him at the temple only once before he passed away in 2010 at the age of ninety-one. He was a practicing Catholic, but he understood the Goddess of the Parashakthi Temple to be a form of Mary, mother of Jesus, and hence worthy of his reverence. As of December 2023, Stella was still listed on the temple website as a member of the temple board.

At the Parashakthi Temple, the experience of the Goddess's desire and ability to communicate her will across religious, geographic, historical, and ethnic boundaries is sustained in miracle narratives that persist in nourishing the religious life of devotees who remain committed to her worship. Divine Mother, as temple devotees most often call her, communicates directly to those whom she "touches," as Kumar would put it. She does this frequently through miracles to make her will known and to impose it on human actors. These miracles in turn communicate the elasticity of ethnic, religious, and geographical boundaries to the Divine Mother, mirroring the elasticity of such boundaries in the lives of many of the temple's core devotees. The Goddess intervenes to direct the actions of not just Indians or Indian American Hindus, but also Euro-American and African American non-Hindus; they, too, are touched by Mother and called to her service in seeing that her temple gets built. The land chosen for the Goddess's house in the West, situated in a largely African American city, is declared to be infused with the religious power of the spirits of deceased Native American shamans and to mimic a South Indian Hindu landscape, specifically that of the Minakshi temple in Madurai. The Temple functions as a divine American power spot that transcends its Tamil and Hindu origins.

In the fall of 1999, as the date of the Goddess's ritual installation, or *prana-pratishtha* (*prāṇa-pratiṣṭhā,* "establishment of breath/life") approached, Dikshitar flew from India to Michigan to preside over the necessary rites, beginning with the installation of a yantra he had made specifically for this purpose. When *murtis* of deities are installed at Hindu temples, they are installed over an enlivening yantra. These yantras are inscribed onto metal sheets and are energized or "brought to life" through ritual means before the *murti* is installed over them. Without an underlying yantra that has been properly enlivened, temple *murtis* are just stone; with a properly installed and enlivened yantra underlying them, however, such *murtis* become embodied forms of deity and must be treated as such. At the Parashakthi Temple, Dikshitar himself enlivened the Goddess's yantra and prepared it for the installation of the Goddess's *murti*, which was set for 4 a.m. on October 19, 1999, as that had been discovered to be the most auspicious time for the installation. Flyers went out in the community announcing the installation, and laborers worked furiously to complete the shell of the temple and the pedestal on which the *murti* of the Goddess would rest. Kumar went to the temple early on the morning of October 19, and a devotee was sent to pick up Dikshitar and bring him to the temple to perform the ceremony. Here is how that devotee described to me in May of 2008 what happened that morning:

> So before 4:00 I picked up Dikshitar and Leena (a devotee of Dikshitar). . . . We were on a road where there was a train crossing. That train was the longest train, so we were a little delayed, and Guru-ji (Dikshitar) was a little upset—the timing had to be 4:00. That train was forever. . . . So, then we reached the temple, but there was no light in the building [the electricity was not yet up and running]. It was 4:00 in the morning and pretty dark in October. So, the day before they had cut a hole in the side of the wall to pour cement for the pedestal. So, through that hole—we left one car on to get light [from the headlights]. I still remember that light from the headlights coming through that little hole. . . . So 4:00 in the morning is when he (Kumar) and Guru-ji (Dikshitar) placed the first yantra, the yantra of the Mother.

That initial installation included four *murti*s of Karumariamman, Ganesha, the dancing form of Shiva (Shiva Nataraja), and Subramanya, also known as Murugan or Karttikeya, who is an important South Indian deity and Ganesha's brother. The Goddess's yantra was placed in a private ritual at 4 a.m., while the other installations occurred throughout the day. Present at the installation were the core group of devotees, including those of Indian heritage and Euro-Americans, as well as 150–200 interested members of the community.

The day the Goddess's image was first installed in 1999 was the day of Vijaya Dashami, "Victory Tenth," a religious festival that commemorates an important event described in the Devi-Mahatmya, "Glorification of the Goddess," which is an important Hindu text. While the Devi-Mahatmya stands on its own merits as an autonomous devotional work, it originates as a portion of the Markandeya Purana (fifth/sixth centuries CE). The Puranas are compendia compiled over long stretches of time between the third and sixteenth centuries

CE; they include a great deal of mythological material as well as ethical prescriptions and descriptions of temple rites, pilgrimage, and other religious practices. The Devi-Mahatmya consistently portrays the Goddess as the ultimate, highest reality and the supreme creator who wills creation and sends forth the cosmos. It also portrays the Goddess as a magnificent, powerful slayer of demons and divine protectress (Coburn 1991, 24–26). The Goddess battles and vanquishes her demonic rival, a buffalo demon named Mahisha, restoring moral order, *dharma*, to the world. The battle is commemorated every fall during the celebration of the festival of "nine nights," Navaratri, which culminates in the Goddess's victory on Vijaya Dashami. In this regard, the Goddess of the Parashakthi Temple assumes the protective and evil-destroying function often associated more traditionally with the Hindu goddess as she is portrayed in the Devi-Mahatmya. The temple was constructed at the time of transition between millennia to protect the Western world from danger during the first part of the twenty-first century (see Figure 1.4). This mission was modified about ten years after the temple's construction to include "sharing Divine Mother's grace with Humanity" and "experiencing and exploring the Divine" (Parashakthi Temple, "Temple History"). But the original and abiding mission is that of protection. Kumar has noted on several public occasions that the Goddess orchestrated the construction of the temple because the world would go through a catastrophic period during the first two decades of the twenty-first century, and the energy installed at the temple would offer protection from potential disaster.

At the temple, Kumar speaks frequently of demons (*asuras*) as active, malevolent forces that can be overcome with positive divine energy. He claims that when Dikshitar gave him the powerful mantra he received at initiation, it was to protect him from the demonic forces that would not want the temple to be built and hence would try to do him harm. Kumar alleges the Goddess told him, "When you bring me in this form, which has never happened before on this earth, all the *asuras* will attack you. They will not want me here" (interview, October 2008). As construction on the original temple continued and more zoning and building concerns arose, Kumar understood those to be the result of destructive *asura* forces. Conversely, the deities, or *devatas* (*devatā*), established at the Parashakthi Temple are described

Figure 1.4 Entrance to the Parashakthi Temple in 2009

as positive cosmic forces whose power comes to be embodied at the temple when their *murtis* are ritually enlivened.

The Parashakthi Temple is overtly Hindu and specifically South Indian in many ways, but it does not situate itself squarely within any individual religious lineage. The theological instruction promulgated at and through the temple, including the articulation of the nature and actions of the Divine, continues to unfold in a process of ongoing revelations that Kumar experiences as direct communications from the Goddess, revelations that he then transmits to the temple community. He refers to the way in which he receives these divine communications as the "ultimate form of wireless transmission." The temple's theology moves decidedly into the realm of vernacular South Indian village goddess traditions, Tantra, yoga, and even New Age discourse. And in this theology, the Goddess morphs from being a local goddess to being a goddess beyond boundaries, radiating *shakti* from her new American "house." Yet the Goddess cannot act alone; she requires human agents—for example, Kumar, ANK, Dikshitar, Jane, Joe, Barbara, and even me—whose interventions she orchestrates to make her emergence possible.

Dwellings: The Parashakthi Temple as Translocal Sacred Space

Waghorne notes that the globalization of local Hindu temple traditions has intensified as wandering devotees transport their originally local deities all over the world (Waghorne 2004, 146, 173). She describes this process as one that is generating a new type of transnational religion that serves as an alternative to "the ever-present neo-hinduisms and hindu-nationalisms" that are divorced from an emphasis on place and the emplacement of sacred power (Waghorne 2004, 173, 177). In this regard, Waghorne observes, both Murugan/Subramanya and Tamil goddesses act as predominant "icons of locality" even as they globalize (Waghorne 2004, 227). In the case of the Parashakthi Temple, however, it seems more accurate to view the type of "locality" at play less as something to which those most involved with the temple *return*, as Waghorne emphasizes, and more as something they *create* in conversation with the American landscape, American history, South Indian goddess and tantric traditions, and the place that the Goddess as Divine Mother Karumariamman has chosen for her Western manifestation.

In *Fluid Signs: Being a Person the Tamil Way*, E. Valentine Daniel notes that many Tamils experience personhood as intertwined with the soil of the territory they inhabit, referred to as their *ur* (*ūr*) (Daniel 1984, 63). He describes *ur* in his working definition of the term as "a named territory that is (1) inhabited by human beings who are believed to share in the substance of the soil of that territory, and (2) a territory to which a Tamil cognitively orients himself at any given time" (Daniel 1984, 63). The real *ur* is "the place whose soil is most compatible with oneself and one's ancestors," the place most suited to one's bodily substance (67). He notes further that Tamils also distinguish between the *ur* that "is merely one's current residence or home" and the *ur* that is their real home, "that is, the place whose soil is most compatible with oneself and one's ancestors" (Daniel 1984, 67). Hence the notion of "true home" or "*ur*" is defined, Daniel notes, "person-centrically, in terms of its relevance to a given ego" (Daniel 1984, 68). For Daniel, Hindu culture is broadly person-centric, so defining place as person-centric makes perfect sense. And, Daniel observes, Tamil beliefs about personhood include the belief that the earth essence, or what he calls soil substance, of a given *ur* is inextricably mixed with the bodily substance of its inhabitants (Daniel 1984, 79).

Daniel considers in his work the human-*ur* relationship. I wish to extend the image to include also divine persons, such as the Goddess. Daniel himself notes that the soil of an *ur* can be spoken of as a form of the local goddess who inhabits that soil (1984, 90). In Hindu traditions, *shakta* places of pilgrimage, which the Parashakthi Temple claims to be, are named as seats of the Goddess; the use of such language emphasizes the embodied, immanent nature of the goddess, indicating that the Goddess "takes a seat" in the world (e.g., Eck 2012, 268). The discourse of the Parashkthi Temple and its community narrates Pontiac as the Goddess's *ur*; it is both her current home and her real home. The soil of the American land on which the temple has been built has come to share in the Goddess's nature such that the

Goddess and the patch of earth she inhabits in Pontiac become one and the same.

In this regard, one might best understand this goddess and this temple as neither "transnational" nor "local" but instead "translocal." The terms "translocal" and "translocality" have come into use in the sciences and social sciences in the last few decades to denote "phenomena involving mobility, migration, circulation, and spatial interconnectedness" (Greiner and Sakdapolrak 2013, 373). The terms indicate especially notions of "mobility, connectedness, networks, place, locality and locals, flows, travel, transfer and circulatory knowledge" (Greiner and Sakdopolrak 2013, 375). Translocal spaces are spaces in which place and locality matter but may matter in ways that are fractured, permeable, or multiple. The term "transnational" implicates nation states as actors, whereas the term "translocal" may be invoked to include phenomena that occur below the surface of national and other elite discourses and phenomena, facilitating one's ability to interrogate what might otherwise be hidden from view. Translocality as both a concept and a methodological approach helps make visible local realities that participate in "relational dimensions of space created through mobility:"

> Such an approach overcomes the notion of container spaces and the dichotomy between "here" and "there." . . . Translocality thus refers to the emergence of multidirectional and overlapping networks that facilitate the circulation of people, resources, practices, and ideas. . . . Translocal networks are both structured by the actions of the people involved and at the same time provide a structure for these very actions. (Greiner and Sakdapolrak 2013, 375–376)

Translocality differs from globalization, although the two are sometimes conflated. Global phenomena are not necessarily rooted in specific locales and may even be completely divorced from the particularities of place. Translocal phenomena, on the other hand, are "material, spatial and embodied" (Brickell and Datta 2011, 13), although they are usually complexly so. Places are always connected to other places (Allen and Cochrane 2007, 1162). Charlotta Hedberg and

Renato Miguel do Carmo note that translocal actors "connect places through their mobility:"

> A translocal perspective of space brings the activities of mobile ac-
> tors, such as migrants, to the fore, not only through the activities
> that occur as they move but also through the consequences that are
> produced in space through this activity.... Consequently, a web of
> networks is established between places that is materialized through
> repeated communication, flows of knowledge and ideas, and po-
> litical, cultural, and economic activities. (Hedberg and do Carmo
> 2012, 3)

James Clifford emphasizes the nature of "translocal cultures" as entailing entanglements "at intersecting regional, national, and trans-national levels" (Clifford 1997, 7). He argues for thinking of locations more as "a series of encounters and translations" than as bounded sites (Clifford 1997, 11). Miriam Khan argues further that places them-selves are fertilized into being through a confluence of voices. Places are, she says, "complex constructions of social histories, personal and interpersonal experiences, and selective memory. . . . Places capture the complex emotional, behavioral, and moral relationships between people and their territory" (Khan 1996, 167–168). Massey, similarly, theorizes space in the postcolonial world in particular as "a product of interrelations" constituted through a process of interaction. For Massey, space is most adequately understood as "the sphere in which distinct narratives co-exist" or "the sphere of the possibility of the ex-istence of more than one voice" (Massey 1999, 279). Massey advocates imagining space "as disrupted and as a source of disruption. That is, even though it is constituted out of relations, spatiality/space is not a totally coherent and interrelated system of interconnections" (Massey 1999, 280). She further espouses a view of space as "the sphere of the meeting up (or not) of multiple trajectories, the sphere where they co-exist, affect each other, maybe come into conflict. It is the sphere both of their independence (*co*-existence) and of their interrelation" (Massey 1999, 283).

Translocal places may be imagined to þe, then, to use Massey's words, "particular articulations of social relations, including local relations 'within' the place and those many connections which stretch way beyond it" (Massey 1999, 22, quoted in Brickell and Datta 2011, 6). Taking a translocal perspective requires moving from a "place bound" perspective on place to one that is "place based" but acknowledges that as people become more mobile, locales also become multilayered (McKay 2006, 201; Castree 2004, 135; Brickell and Datta 2011, 6).

Narayanan notes there are many ways in which immigrant Hindus transform the American landscape into sacred liturgical space through ritual and argues that examining such rituals gives scholars an opportunity to "appreciate the ways in which individuals and institutions" that exist outside of India "co-opt the local landscape into a part of the Hindu world" (Narayanan 2005, 128). She details four such possible strategies, noting that her list is not exhaustive: (1) adapting Puranic cosmology by identifying the United States as a specific island (*dvīpa*) quoted in the texts; (2) composing prayers and devotional songs extolling the state in which the new temples are located; (3) physically consecrating the land with waters from sacred Indian rivers and American rivers; and (4) literally recreating the physical landscape of certain holy places in India (128). Hinduism in India, Narayanan observes, is "closely tied to land in the Indian subcontinent and is very territorial. . . . To transform and in some way acknowledge the American land . . . as sacred is a bold, innovative, and perhaps necessary act of being Hindu on foreign soil" (Narayanan 2006, 57). What is going on at the Parashakthi Temple, however, is different.

Scholars of cultural geography have employed the notion of "deterritorialization" to refer to the breaking of the bond between a group and its "territory," that is, a space with which that group has an established system of relationships. Némésis Srour observes that the term "deterritorialization" implies a lack, "a sense of deprivation" that in modern times many scholars link specifically to globalization (Srour 2015, 87). As groups scatter outside of their previously assigned territories, they may experience a sense of disconnection from the new places in which they settle. Marc Augé argues that an "anthropological place" is a space that can be linked to an identity, a relationship, or a history (Augé 2008, 43). A place that does not meet those criteria is, in his words, a "non-place." Augé argues that supermodernity tends to produce such non-places, which include supermarkets, highways, airport lounges, and other such spaces that are unmoored from any sense of place history (Augé 2008, 63–67). The other side of deterritorialization and the contemporary proliferation of non-places is often seen to be reterritorialization, the process of re-establishing or recreating homeland patterns in a new place in a way that bonds a group to its historical sense of identity.

I would argue here, however, that the process taking place at the Parashakthi Temple is more appropriately understood as a process of what I will call neoterritorialization, that is, the creation of a new "anthropological place" in a way that modernity—with its global patterns of communication, migration, and travel—makes possible. The impulse to root oneself somewhere, even in an era of intense global movement, extends to individuals, communities, and, apparently, even deities. Clifford Geertz notes:

> For all the uprooting, the homelessness, the migrations, forced and voluntary, the dislocations of traditional relationships, the struggles over homelands, borders, and rights of recognition, for all the destructions of familiar landscapes and the manufacturings of new ones, and for all the loss of local stabilities and local originalities, the sense of place, and of the specificities of place, seems, however tense and darkened, barely diminished in the modern world." (Geertz 1996, 261)

For the temple's devotional community, the Goddess remains "intensely present"—to use the words Kumar ascribed to Ramdass—in the patch of earth she has now claimed as her American domicile. According to temple discourse, the new land does not simply reproduce the Hindu landscape or "incarnate" it through imitation (Narayanan 2006, 149), however, but instead supersedes it, surpassing it in sacrality. In Pontiac, America is not "foreign soil" but rather is and always has been the site of a now-enlivened, earthly *pitha*, a "seat" of the Goddess, that is even more *shakti*-filled than many of its Indian antecedents.

2

Devotional Crossings/Water

Frictions and Flows

When I first brought my children to the Parashakthi Temple for an important religious event in 2013, my son Noah, who was eleven at the time, ended up spending most of our visit in the parking lot. He joined the group of children who, after sitting through hours of religious rites, made their way out to the pavement, away from the religious space of the temple, to entertain themselves by setting off firecrackers. It did not matter to Noah at all that he didn't know any of the other kids, and that didn't seem to matter to the other kids, either. They bonded over their shared love of setting stuff off and blowing things up.

This image of Noah in the Parashakthi Temple's parking lot came to mind as I sat down to write this chapter because it reminded me, albeit obliquely, of Anna Lowenhaupt Tsing's invocation in her book *Friction: An Ethnography of Global Connections* of "friction" as a metaphor for the sparks that sometimes fly because of global connection (Tsing 2005). Speaking broadly of culture and ethnography, Tsing notes that "cultures are continually co-produced in the interactions I call 'friction': the awkward, unequal, unstable, and creative qualities of interconnection across difference.... A wheel turns because of its encounter with the surface of the road; spinning in the air it goes nowhere" (Tsing 2005, 4–5). Tsing's preoccupations with global capitalism and its encounter with the rainforests of Kalimantan, as well as her efforts to complicate the story of neoliberal economic globalization's inevitability, are, however laudable, not the preoccupations I have here. Rather, I invoke the image of friction to emphasize its productive capacity and the energy that it generates.

Arjun Appadurai also writes of "friction" in his discussion of globalization, but in so doing he emphasizes the more negative connotations of the term, speaking of the "problems and frictions" that global flows

Goddess Beyond Boundaries. Tracy Pintchman, Oxford University Press. © Oxford University Press 2024.
DOI: 10.1093/oso/9780190673017.003.0003

may generate (Appadurai 2001, 6). Here, though, I think Tsing's acknowledgement of the potentially positive outcomes of friction is apposite. Friction, which generates energy and may cause flying sparks that can produce new "fires"—that is, new ideas, experiences, and relationships—strikes me as an apt metaphor also for the "awkward, unequal, unstable, and creative qualities of interconnection across difference" that happen when a parking lot yields its space to children coming together from diverse backgrounds to set things off and blow things up, or when devotees from diverging cultural and religious backgrounds come together to heed the Goddess's call.

Many of the individuals active in the founding of the Parashakthi Temple, including Euro-American devotees deeply committed to the Goddess and the temple community, have over the years moved back and forth, with varying degrees of comfort, between religious identities, cultural identities, and the terrains of India and the United States, engendering "friction" as they do so. Several individuals involved closely in the construction and maintenance of the temple and its community, including those not of Indian origin, have gone to India for healings, pilgrimages, and devotional visits. Others, residing in India, have been called to Pontiac or called to serve the Goddess in Pontiac even as they remain in India. Some have traversed far beyond familiar physical, emotional, and devotional boundaries and have returned to the temple in Pontiac renewed in their commitment to the Goddess. These encounters across various kinds of borders are not necessarily continuous or untroubled. Sometimes, they blow things up in such a way that people's lives are forever changed. Furthermore, as Tsing observes, global connections are often made in fragments (Tsing 2005, 271). Such connections depend on the circulation of people, ideas, practices, and things across national, conceptual, and religious borders, but that circulation is not always consistent or sustained. It happens in fits and starts, in bits and pieces. The Parashakthi Temple is the (metaphorical) point of contact where the core devotees who made the temple happen encounter ideas, objects, and other people in ways that spark miracles and facilitate the Goddess's intervention in their lives.

Appadurai (1990) has famously proposed as a framework for exploring the varied dimensions of global flows five distinct "scapes": ethnoscapes, mediascapes, technoscapes, financescapes, and ideoscapes. The first, ethnoscape, refers to "the landscape of persons who constitute the shifting world in which we live." Appadurai wants to bring into focus individuals and groups that move, including immigrants, refugees, guest workers, tourists, and others. He acknowledges the "warp" of stabilities that communities, institutions, and social networks provide, but he notes that these are "shot through with the woof of human motion" (Appadurai 1996, 33–34). He writes of objects in motion:

> The objects include ideas and ideologies, people and goods, images and messages, technologies and techniques. This is a world of flows.... It is also, of course, a world of structures, organizations, and other stable social forms. But the apparent stabilities that we see are, under close examination, usually our devices for handling objects characterized by motion. (Appadurai 2001, 5)

The lives of those who founded the Parashakthi Temple and keep it going participate in the ethnoscape that is the "woof" to the "warp" of the Parashakthi Temple. They are religious travelers who navigate the devotional, cultural, and physical terrain they inhabit in both Michigan and India. The scapes they cross tend to be not only physical but also spiritual and psychological, inner as well as outer.

Tweed adds to Appadurai's list a fifth "scape," namely, "sacroscape," which refers to religious flows (Tweed 2006, 61). The term, he suggests, "invites scholars to attend to the multiple ways that religious flows have left traces, transforming peoples and places, the social arena and the natural terrain" (Tweed 2006, 62). This book is, primarily, an attempt to explore and investigate the sacroscape of the Parashakthi Temple. But I want to take Tweed's observations one step further in considering the ways that the individuals most touched by the Goddess and called to her service experience the religious flows that have shaped the Parashakthi Temple, its community, and the inner spiritual terrain. Here I would like to introduce another possible "scape" that we can talk about in this context, namely, shaktiscape (*śaktiscape*). Rana B. Singh has used the term "shaktiscape" to describe the relationship between goddesses and spatial ordering in the north Indian city of Varanasi

(Singh 2009). I use the term here in a different way, however, to refer to the qualities of space that devotees at the Parashakthi Temple attribute to places both in India and outside of it that they consider to be especially "charged" with the Goddess's energy. The shaktiscape of the Parashakthi Temple comprises what devotees understand to be the ever-changing, mysterious, yet powerful flow of Divine Mother's power, her *shakti*, across and through regions, nationalities, ethnicities, bodies, and time periods. The Goddess's shaktiscape includes nonmaterial spaces as well, streaming from geographical into mental and emotional locations, penetrating people's dreams, visions, and feelings.

For those responsible for creating and maintaining the Parashakthi Temple, what has come to distinguish temple space more than anything else is its vital role in anchoring the Goddess's shaktiscape on both gross and subtle levels. It is the place where people encounter ideas, objects, and other people in ways that spark miracles and facilitate the Goddess's intervention in their lives. The temple and its devotees function collectively as a "dynamic point of confluence," a "node" or "hub" of the Goddess's perceived power and influence (Glei and Jaspert 2016, 3). The "woof" of the Goddess's shaktiscape flows through the "warp" of the temple building, land, and community, taking up residence in Pontiac and binding together in a new narrative the seemingly disparate places, objects, events, and people that devotees claim she engages to accomplish her plans.

In this chapter, I explore the devotional crossings that have occurred in the lives of some of the individuals other than Kumar without whom the temple would not exist. These individuals differ from most of the members of the temple congregation, some of whose experiences I will explore in Chapter 5, as they are among the small group of people responsible for the temple's founding and continued survival through their work, their money, and the time they have dedicated to making the temple succeed. I explore here the stories of several Euro-Americans who in some way heeded the Goddess's call to get involved in the building of her temple or financially securing its future and Indian nationals who, while residing far from the Goddess's Michigan home, nevertheless have been deeply involved in its maintenance. I narrate portions of the stories that these individuals were willing to share with me, including their descriptions of the Goddess's interventions in their lives.

Following Appadurai and Tweed, I indulge here in watery images of "streaming" and "confluence" in relation to the Parashakthi Temple community. Such language highlights the temple's positionality at the convergence of varied religious, cultural, material, and narrative flows. The stories I present here also reveal some of the confluences, disruptions, and interactions that arise as individuals experience the Goddess's *shakti* coursing through time and space and across the varied inner and outer landscapes that shape the experiences and commitments of devotional subjects. Stories that people narrate about themselves act as "windows on distinctive social worlds" and reveal ways that individuals' senses of identity and inner lives relate to these worlds (Gubrium and Holstein 2008, 244). We do not have access to experience directly; our access comes narratively (Gubrium and Holstein 2008, 246). The stories I tell here have a common theme: they are rooted in devotees' experiences of the Goddess in confluence and travel. As she traverses religious, cultural, and natural worlds, she flows into minds, bodies, and places across time, and she travels with her human agents as they navigate the diverse geographical, religious, and cultural worlds they come to inhabit.

The narratives presented here may be taken collectively as a way of framing translocal processes that offers an alternative to the ubiquitous economic paradigm that tends to inform discourse about globalization. This dominant paradigm frames global exchanges predominantly in financial terms as a flow of capitalist ventures in the neoliberal, global economy that ultimately function to serve primarily the interests of "the West" over "the rest." The accounts I offer in the rest of this chapter, instead, suggest a paradigm for understanding translocal flows in a way that grounds itself in individual experiences and perspectives, streams below the surface of elite discourses, and follows the path of a rationale rooted primarily not in economic values, but in religious, cultural, and personal ones. In this regard, they form an accounting of what Dietrich Reetz refers to as an "alternative globality" (Reetz 2010, 294) or what Appadurai calls "vernacular globalization" (Appadurai 1996, 10).

Jane and Family

I had met Jane at the Parashakthi Temple on numerous occasions by the time I interviewed her and her husband formally on March 21, 2010. Jane first met Kumar in the 1970s, when she was a medical student, and he was one of her instructors. They then became medical colleagues, and that was, for a long time, the extent of the relationship. Jane and her husband Sam were both involved in spiritual pursuits during the 1970s and 80s. They practiced yoga, for example, and Jane became a yoga teacher; Sam was a disciple of Master Kirpal Singh, an Indian spiritual teacher of the Sant Mat and elected president of the World Fellowship of Religions. They had been to India and had both also been involved in Native American religious practices and had a sweat lodge built on their land. Jane had an awareness of and reverence for the notion of a Divine Mother. They had like-minded friends with whom they undertook spiritual practices.

One day on hospital rounds sometime in the 1980s, Jane noticed a ring that Kumar was wearing and commented on it:

> He was sitting, writing charts at the hospital, and I was across sitting, and you know, this ring just kind of . . . I went, "Wow." You know, I mean, I didn't know anything about him other than he'd been my teacher and he's very well respected and so on, and I said, "That's really an unusual ring." And then he proceeded to tell me how a mystic made it.

Jane reports that she then realized that Kumar was, like her and her husband, a "spiritually alive person." Shortly after that encounter, Jane had a dream that she was in a cave, and the cave was filled with amethyst crystals telling her that Kumar and his wife were spiritual teachers, and that she was going to be connected to them. It was after Jane saw Kumar's ring, too, that the Goddess revealed herself to Jane in a vision. This was a powerful vision that Jane remembers vividly even over a decade later. Jane had not studied Hinduism and did not know what different deities ought to look like, but she notes, "I know what I saw. It was clear what I saw:"

It wasn't like, "You go build my temple right now." It was more fluid than that. . . . It was more like—the love for a place to be with Divine Mother becomes alive in you, and you fall in love with something that's inside of you. And you're not sure maybe at first what you should do, what it's going to be. But then you really feel . . . she needs to be here for other people. At the time it's like—this is a crazy idea, but it's really deep and meaningful, and I guess I'm going to have to figure out how to do this. She needs to come. She needs a place. She needs to be here. This is Divine Mother, and in a lot of the things I did, I was involved with Divine Mother for a decade before this even happened. . . . So, it's only natural that the people who love her with you, you're going to get them on board.

After she had the vision of the Goddess, Jane felt that she had to tell Kumar about it. This was also when she revealed to Kumar that he had been coming to her in her dreams. Kumar, Jane, Jane's husband Sam, and some friends of theirs all began to talk about building a goddess temple. Of the original group, only Kumar was of Indian origin; the rest of the group were all Euro-Americans, but they all report that they felt a deep love for and commitment to the Goddess. They began to meet once a week to plan for the temple, and they started to fundraise. Both Jane and Sam note that the original idea for the temple was that it would be devoted to "the feminine principle inside every religion" and would not be particular to the Hindu goddess. It quickly became apparent, however, that there was little community interest in such a place, but there was interest in building a house for Parashakthi.

During the 1980s and early 1990s, Jane made several devotional trips to India. Kumar had introduced Jane to ANK, and he accompanied her on at least some of these occasions, including one trip to the Minakshi Temple in Madurai. Although ANK didn't speak any English, and Jane did not speak any Tamil, they somehow managed. After the land for the Parashakthi Temple had been found, Jane and the other members of the original planning group went to see it:

The big thing I remember about that was the mosquitoes when we were out there in the woods. It was the summertime, and it had just rained. And I don't know if anyone else remembers them, but I think they took every ounce of blood out of me—which is sometimes important in ceremonies, that you must lose blood. Well, I did that day, so my blood is here in the mosquitoes of the land, but the other thing that I remember is—before the temple was, maybe when there was just a hole in the ground, I walked back and sat on the creek way in the back, and I did some Native American ceremonies back there, and the shamans of the land appeared to me. This was before anybody knew anything about that or had talked about it or anything. They appeared very strongly to me. They had been here, and they were blessing us and watching our project. They were holding a space in the land.

The theme of sacrifice, broadly construed, is foundational to devotional life at the temple as it embodies the notion that devotees must give something up to receive the Goddess's blessings. I will return to this theme in Chapter 4. Here Jane is commenting on the sacrifice of her blood that she gave, in addition to time, money, energy, and love, to ensure that the temple would be built. She also makes note of her experience of the presence of Native American shamanic spirits in the land, an experience that predates the claims that other devotees have made about their own encounters with these spirits. Jane does not remember if she even told anyone about that experience of Native American spirits, but she remembers it as feeling like "a completion of what I had learned and felt and studied. It was all here."

Jane continues to patronize the temple and experiences it as an especially powerful place spiritually. When I pressed her about this point and asked her to offer an example, she described what had taken place at a deity installation that took place in 2009. During this installation, Jane had an experience of being one with all that exists, an experience like the mystical experiences that the Upanishads are often understood to describe. She told me:

What happened to me that day is I became everything and everyone—I became every person in there, maybe even people I don't care for. I became everything. And it lasted for a long time. To have the knowledge that you really are everything—I mean, you can say it, you can think it, you can feel it. But to have it actually come upon you, and you take on that physical presence of somebody else and become them—it is a life-changing experience.

Jane and Sam have maintained a relationship with India as well. They returned to India to renew their wedding vows, for example, and sponsored a feast for 400 people. And when a relative was having a tough time, they followed ANK's instructions, obtained through a Bhrigu Nadi reading, to build a small temple in an Indian village. They traveled to India for the dedication when it was finished, and they believe that sponsoring that temple aided their relative. They also toured many important temples in South India with ANK and met the Shankaracarya of Kanchipuram, an important Hindu religious leader.

Jane and Sam, as well as other Euro-Americans who were part of the original group of temple founders and remain deeply invested and active in the ongoing life of the Parashakthi Temple, sometimes find it jarring that many Indian devotees they meet at the temple treat them as outsiders because they are not of Indian heritage. But they do not receive any such treatment from Kumar or the Goddess. As Jane told me:

> She just had to bring us all here and bring us in one spot together so we could be here and have this [temple] happen. It feels unlimited, that anybody can come here. They might not be drawn in, and they may not have a spiritual experience, but they are not going to be turned away. The energy is here if they're open to it, for them to receive it. It's not a sterile, static place.

Jane and Sam's daughter, Rachel, is also involved with the Parashkthi Temple. When I first interviewed her in 2009, she was in her mid-twenties; by the time I last encountered her in August 2022 for the temple rededication, she was married, settled, and the mother of two children. In our conversation in 2009, she noted that her parents provided a rich religious background when she was growing up. Her father Sam was born Jewish, and her mother Jane converted to Judaism, but Jane's mother was Christian. Rachel notes that she was also involved in the Native American ceremonies her parents conducted, often with others, in the sweat lodge they had built on their property. At first, she would just tag along with her parents to the Parashakthi Temple, but when she was in college, that changed. She was diagnosed with a serious illness and became depressed. At that point, when she was around eighteen or nineteen, ANK did an astrological reading for her when he was in Pontiac visiting the temple. It was then that she started to get interested in the temple on her own terms. She notes that it was around that time that she had an overwhelming experience in the temple sanctuary:

> I went into the main sanctuary, or sanctum, whatever you call it, and my body was completely taken over. I got numb. I don't remember the exact feeling, but I couldn't move, and I fell to the ground. I remember feeling complete, total bliss. I didn't notice anyone around me—I don't even know how long I was out.

She started then to really develop her own relationship with the Goddess through Kumar, who told Rachel that not only was Rachel's Kundalini awakened at birth, but she had awakened her mother Jane's Kundalini "at the same time when she was giving birth to me." She along with her parents continues to be closely involved with the Parashakthi Temple. The Goddess continues to be a presence in her life:

> Sometimes, you're just, you're on autopilot. And you are, I don't know, walking down the hallways at my work and everything is the same. You know, you were there that same time the morning before and the morning before and the morning before and the morning before. But some days it's like—I can feel that [presence] and I'm just so appreciative. I can feel Divine Mother's energy, and I feel that I look like I'm glowing, but I'm not. I'm like, "Wow, I would love to spread this to everyone else. I wish that everyone could feel this." And I just try to keep the smile on and spread it to everyone around me. It's kind of vague to speak about, but that's what it feels like.

Ven Johnson

Vernon "Ven" Johnson, is a tall, handsome, American lawyer with softly greying blond hair. After I began coming to the temple regularly starting in 2007, I noted his presence on several occasions and asked Kumar about him. Kumar chuckled. He told me I would love Ven's story and should talk to him about his experiences. Ven agreed to a lengthy interview in 2009.

In the late 1990s, Ven met Shalina Kumar, the daughter of Krishna and Margaret Kumar, at a courthouse near the Parashakthi Temple. Shalina, now a United States District Court Judge for the Eastern District of Michigan in Flint, was a young lawyer at the time. They started dating, and among the topics they discussed, according to Ven, was spirituality. Ven was intrigued by what Shalina told him about her father's idea at the time to build a temple to the Goddess. When he finally met Krishna Kumar, Ven says he was struck by how charismatic and energetic he seemed. Johnson had been raised Methodist and had been involved in the Methodist Church as a child but had grown away from it as an adult; he admits that he didn't like the "political aspects of organized religion, and the money, and all that." Ven and Shalina were married in 1999, the same year that the temple was consecrated. Although they divorced in 2004, Ven insists they remain good friends, and I had seen them both at the temple together on a few occasions by the time I interviewed Ven in 2009. Regarding the temple, Ven notes:

Doctor [Kumar] of course had the concept of the temple the entire time we were dating. I don't remember the groundbreaking per se, but I know this: I know I was in the temple when they put up the four walls, and there was barely even a roof on. I remember seeing the steel studs. There was no drywall yet. We were there from the very, very beginning.

Ven reports that his relationship with Shalina and her father began to awaken him spiritually as well, and he began to view the temple as not just theirs, but also his:

The more time I spent with them, the more I began to better understand spirituality. The best way for me to describe it is that it was awakened within me. I don't understand much of the Hindu religion, very candidly. I don't really have a burning desire to learn who all the gods are and all the right things to say. I just really enjoy it—there's

a feeling of home to me that's very difficult to describe. So, I know
I belong. I know that's where I come from. When I go to the temple,
I am going home.

A couple of years after Ven and Shalina were married, they and
Shalina's mother, Margaret, who has since passed away, flew to South
India to meet up with Kumar, who was already in Tamil Nadu at the
time. At that time, Ven went to the Chidambaram Shiva Temple and
met Dikshitar, whom he describes as "a very, very wonderful, warm
person." Ven, Shalina, and the older Kumars toured several temples,
and Ven observes that he "went through some religious experiences"
both at the Chidambaram Temple and at other temples as well. Back
in Michigan, Ven became increasingly involved in the workings of the
Parashakthi Temple and joined the temple board.

In his work life, Ven was also evolving during these years. In the
mid-90s, he moved from a law firm that he describes as "conservative,
representing companies that get sued" to a high-profile and controver-
sial personal injury law firm whose senior partner was Geoffrey Fieger.
Fieger is well known as a trial lawyer, especially for his legal defenses
of Dr. Jack Kevorkian, who achieved notoriety in the United States for
his role in helping terminally ill patients end their lives. Ven was not
directly involved in Kevorkian's defense, but he was busy handling
other personal injury cases for his new firm. Ven and Fieger were both
politically liberal. In 1998, Fieger ran as the Democratic candidate for
governor of Michigan against John Engler, the Republican candidate.
Fieger lost. Ven described to me his perception of what happened:

My partner ran for governor and lost in a very, very hotly contested,
name-calling, mud-slinging deal with John Engler, who was the stalwart of conservatism here. So that was a big deal, and it happened
while I was at the firm. Geoff is very, shall we say, outgoing and brash,
so he tends to just shoot off, you know, a shot across someone's bow if
he thinks that they're doing a crappy job running whatever program.

Although Fieger lost his bid for the governorship, he remained highly
active in Democratic politics and was a stalwart opponent of both
Engler and then President George W. Bush. Bush in fact blamed Fieger

when he lost the Michigan presidential primary to John McCain in 2000, a point of pride for Fieger (Lauerman 2000). As United States local and national politics shifted increasingly toward the right after 2000, Ven reports that Fieger continued to remain a political gadfly to many Republican politicians.

One night in the fall of 2005, Ven was out to dinner with a friend and, he told me, he got a call from Fieger, who told him the FBI was at Fieger's house and asking to be let in. Ven reports that Fieger told him the FBI was probably also raiding the firm and asked Ven to go to the law offices to check up on things. Ven did, and he discovered at his offices "dozens of FBI and IRS agents all over" the firm. They had a search warrant but would not tell Ven what they were seeking. Ven called his house:

They were at my home. And my son and the babysitter were there—I'm a single dad. And once I found out that they did not have a warrant to search my house, I had the babysitter kick them out, and I said, "Lock the door. Don't let them in unless they have a warrant to search the house." I had to stay at the firm. So, in any event, it was a long night. That was November 30th [2005] if I'm not mistaken.

The United States Department of Justice later indicted Ven and Geoffrey Fieger on charges that they "conspired to make more than $125,000 in illegal campaign contributions to the 2004 presidential campaign of U.S. Senator John Edwards" ("United States Department of Justice 2007"). Ven freely admits that the firm collected donations from employees to support Edwards's campaign but vigorously denies any wrongdoing. The case made both local and national headlines, with some commentators speculating that the charges were politically motivated. In an article published in *Harper's Magazine* in 2008, Scott Horton claimed:

Most observers who have taken a look at this case have come to the same conclusion that a Justice Department figure suggested to me: this is not a prosecution. It is a political vendetta. Its objective is not to enforce campaign finance rules, but rather to squelch fundraising by Democrats. It is an assault on the democratic process, driven by an abuse of the criminal justice system. (Horton 2008)

Both Ven and Geoff Fieger would go to trial in 2008 over the charges levied against them. In 2005, however, Ven was in the thick of the early investigation and was worried. About two weeks after the FBI called on his offices and home, Ven says, Kumar called him and asked Ven to come to his medical office to meet. Kumar gave Ven a ring that he said he had had made in India. He was wearing the ring when I interviewed him in 2009. Ven described what happened:

> It's red coral, and it's got the very stereotypical Indian gold ring around it, and it's Ganesha, and he [Kumar] explained what it was and how—you know, the red coral and the whole thing. Then he said, "The good news is this is my Christmas present to you." He normally doesn't give me Christmas presents, and then he said, "The bad news is you have to go to India with me by the end of February, or it won't work."

According to Ven, Kumar told Ven that there was a lot of evil swirling around him, and the only way to mitigate it was to go on a pilgrimage in India wearing that ring. In Hinduism, wearing gemstones on rings or pendants is a customary practice, as every gem is seen as having its own energy and healing properties. Astrologers may, for example, prescribe the wearing of a particular gemstone to clients who are facing a challenging planetary alignment or other negative force to help offset its ill effects. But this practice was new to Ven. Kumar told Ven to put the ring on the ring finger of his left hand. The only ring Ven had ever worn was his wedding ring, but since he and Shalina had gotten divorced, he no longer wore that one. Kumar told him to put it on because "this is [Divine] Mother, and now you're married to Mother."

In February of 2006, Ven reports that he flew to Mumbai, where he met Kumar at the airport. They drove from Mumbai to Chennai over forty-eight hours, stopping at numerous temples along the way. When they reached Mumbai at the beginning of the third day, they met up with ANK outside yet another temple. Kumar handed Ven a coconut and told him to break it in half as an offering.

> He [Kumar] showed me how he held it, and he threw it on the ground, and of course it split perfectly in two. And then ANK did

it, and it bounced. And he did it again. And it bounced. And I went, "Okay, now it's my turn, right?" I'm getting a little intimidated. So, I did it and split it in two the first time [I tried]. And it was just—I don't know how to describe that feeling, but it was like I knew something big was happening, and that I was there for a reason that I was probably not wholly, a hundred percent cognizant of at the time.

They then proceeded to another, smaller temple. This time Kumar had Ven dress in a traditional Indian garment, a lungi, and break another coconut. Finally, they pulled up to the third temple of the day. Ven observed that there were at least a couple hundred devotees gathered at this temple when he was there, but Kumar got him up to the head of the line to view the deity. And there he noticed a clock:

I thought that was strange. It was just a clock—a wall clock. Okay? Right next to the deity on the wall. I thought, "That's kind of weird." And I looked at it, and it said "Veni Kumar." Now what's funny about Veni Kumar, is—my name's Vernon, but I go by Ven, and one of my nicknames is Veni. And so, one of the little jokes that Shalina and I always had was, like, "If you think that I'm going to take your name"— because she didn't take my name—"then I'm going to give you mine. You can be Veni Kumar." And that was a "Ha" moment: Veni Kumar on this clock. So, I said to Doctor [Kumar], "What's going on here?" And he said, "You feel it, don't you?" And I said, "Yeah." There's something very ... I don't want to say strange because that's almost bad, but there's something strange going on here. And he said, "You were a king here. And these people all know it. And they all recognize you, and they all know who you are, and you came back to visit your kingdom, and they're excited to see you. So, they want you here, and they want you to lead the prayer, and they want you to be right here in front of the deity."

Ven admits that he has little time to read about Hinduism and understands little of what took place during his pilgrimage to India. He says that on the journey, Kumar gave Ven enough information to make sure that Ven was open to what was happening and would not make any significant errors in ritual conduct. Yet the feeling of transformation, he says, was unmistakable:

By that time at that on that date at that temple, there's no question, I am now as part of the prayer process getting into a very, very deep state of meditation. . . . I could feel that something was changing within me—literally, within those moments. . . . It's a feeling and a sense of home to me. I knew at the end of it (the trip)—the first time I went to India I think I pretty much felt it—but I knew by the end of that trip that I've been there before. There's no question I have. And I feel very, very comfortable there.

When Ven returned to the United States, he says he felt a renewed sense of love, a "warmth within my soul that it's going to be okay." Ven reports that Kumar told him to keep praying and meditating, to wear the ring, and to keep going to the Parashakthi Temple regularly. Ven did. He also continued to practice law during this time and racked up a string of judicial successes, winning in succession four judgments worth a total of twenty-four million dollars—an almost unheard-of feat, according to Ven. He describes these successes as miracles.

In August of 2007, Ven and Geoff Fieger were indicted. They were tried in April of the following year. During this period, Ven reports that he was in close contact with Kumar:

And he would say that everything's going to be okay. And not just okay, but it's going to be better than before. And I hear this thinking, how can you possibly say that? I mean, my name is being dragged through the mud. So, Doctor just kept saying, "You've got to understand. That's part of the plan. Very few people shine in moments like this, and that's going to happen to you. Just keep on believing and keep on praying and doing the right things."

One night, before the trial had begun, Ven says he was in the Parashakthi Temple praying. He reports that he closed his eyes and had a frightening vision of a serpentine monster. When he shared what had happened with Kumar, Kumar told him that it was a vision of the evil that was swirling all around him and that he would have to hold on.

Both Ven and Geoff Fieger were acquitted of all charges on June 2, 2008. Ven remains on the Parashakthi Temple board and is a major donor for temple activities. He attributes his exoneration and that of his partner to the Goddess's grace. He proclaimed toward the end of our interview:

> There are so many different things in my personal life that are obviously wrapped up and included in all this. It's been.... Doctor talks about miracles at the temple, right? And all that's happening, and I've given you a brief overview. That's a third of the miracles that have happened to me, you know?

Laura

I interviewed Laura in September 2010. Laura was part of the original group that founded the temple. She has become less involved over the years, but she served on the board in the 1990s and 2000s, when the temple was getting up and running. Laura graduated from high school in 1973 and attended a small liberal arts college in Michigan. She later completed a master's degree in social work and a doctorate in psychology. Laura is a Euro-American woman who got involved in the temple initially through Sam and Jane. She was raised Presbyterian and traces her family lineage back fourteen generations to the pilgrim settlers of New England and specifically to a minister who organized and brought over one of the groups of pilgrims who made the journey from England to the United States. She was proud to note to me that there is in her family "a long history of spiritual pursuit, questioning—you know, not necessarily buying the party line. And, certainly, being independent thinkers as well."

Laura told me that she started learning transcendental meditation when she was in high school, but it was not until her college years that she got serious about spirituality. One of her college majors was religious studies. She toyed with becoming a minister but decided instead that her calling was in psychology. She pursued her graduate studies throughout the 1980s, but she was still meditating daily. Around the time she completed her PhD, she was feeling keenly that she needed to be more connected to people "on the spiritual plane," as she put it to me. That was when she met Sam, Jane's husband, at a conference. Laura told me:

At that time (the early 1990s) Sam and Jane had just met a Native American traditional healer and were having solstice gatherings at their home.... They were very open and generous to people coming. Sam invited me to one, and we kind of just started pursuing it, the three of us. I met Jane, and we instantly connected, and so we worked with this healer in the Native American culture, which was wonderful. We still love him and care about him, but we don't see him very often because—we've just gone different ways, but we are still close. And I pursued that, I mean, you know, I did vision quests, and Sam and Jane each did a vision quest. And we built a private sweat lodge in their backyard and had our own ceremonies for quite a few years actually.

Like all the other members of the initial group that founded the temple, Laura asked ANK for an astrological reading. Jane and Bob introduced Laura to Kumar, and "that's when he started talking about his visions and his readings, his experiences, and he invited us to join him."

During this period, too, Laura had taken and failed—by a single point, she reports—her final licensing exam, and she was feeling devastated about the outcome. At that time, Laura told me, the exam was administered only once a year, so she would have to wait a full year to take it again. In the meantime, while she could practice as a psychologist, she would not be able to accept as many insurance policies as a fully licensed practitioner could, so not passing the licensing exam the first time had a tangible financial effect on her career. She reported to me that she talked about the issue with Sam and Jane, who recommended that she get ANK to do a reading for her. Laura herself did not travel to India for the reading but asked Kumar to have it done for her during one of his trips. Laura observed that "we all had readings, and it became pretty apparent to all of us that we were connected to Mother energy."

Laura reports that Kumar told her to undertake a period of daily spiritual practice that included mantra recitation, ritual bathing during the night, and so forth, and that she would then pass the exam after a period of five years. She told me:

I was doing this for about six months, you know, and I think I did my mantra like four times a day and getting up super early, and then I had to take this bath at like 3:00, and I'd have to go back to bed, and you know, I started to feel like, "I think I'm nuts for doing this. What am I doing?" And so, one night I had a dream. And in my—now at this point I had never seen a picture of Mother, I didn't, I just had my own images, I had never seen a picture. And I had this, anyway, I had a dream, and in my dream, I was crying and really upset. I just felt like such a failure. I was going to have to do all this and even though I knew I was going to grow from doing it, I just felt like, "Why is this happening to me and isn't there something I can do to make it go faster?" And in my dream—this is before we met to form the temple or anything—in my dream, Mother came to me and said, "Yes, you can do this faster." And I was like, "Well, how?" And I said, "Who are you?" And she told me who she was, and she said, "You can do this faster. You're just going to have to do the mantras, you're going to have to, instead of doing these four once a day, instead of doing it for five years, you have to figure out how to do it in two years and still say all the mantras." Which means hours of doing it [mantra recitation]. And she said, "And you can do that and you're capable of doing that. And you should do that."

Laura recounts that she had at this point never seen a picture of Karumariamman and did not know who she was. She told me, "For me, it was more just like a female deity, you know what I mean? It could have been Mary; it could have been Buffalo Woman." It was not until "a couple of years later" when she saw a picture of Karumariamman that she realized that was the Goddess who came to her in her dream. Laura says she talked over her dream with Jane, who advised her to start a period of more rigorous spiritual practice. And the next time Laura took her licensing exam, she passed it. She told me:

I think the fact that she came to me and said, "You can do this faster," was like a—just a strong loving and affirming energy that gave me the courage to really say, "Okay, I can do this. I'm going to do this. You know, Mother says I can do this, I'm going to try and give it my best shot."

In the mid-90s, Laura notes, the idea of a temple was "just a dream." Kumar, Jane, Sam, Laura, and a small group of other Euro-Americans involved in the initial planning formulated a plan to build a non-denominational temple for "the female divine:"

> So, the plan originally was that the Parashakthi Temple would be built and that would be our first project. But then from there, on the property, on our property, there would be, you know—it wasn't all planned out exactly where it was going to be or what it would look like—but there would be something for Mary. There would be something, you know, in different parts of the property so that it could really be more non-denominational and be for female deities. To balance, to help balance the planet.

When they located the land and put a bid on it, Jane asked Laura to go walk on it and see how she felt being there. Laura reports that she felt "very safe and energized" the first time she walked on the property and continues to feel "this fresh, almost revived feeling" whenever she drives into the parking lot.

After Kumar purchased the land and the initial, small structure went up, Kumar revealed to the group his vision of the Goddess telling him that the temple should be only to Parashakthi, and the plan changed. While Laura was not initially thrilled with the decision, she says, she has nevertheless stayed involved in temple life. However, the increasing Indianization of the temple has made her feel less connected than she was in the beginning.

A. N. K. Swamy and Dr. P. Pandian
(a.k.a. Kaviyogi Bacon)

Mr. Nalla Kurunthappa Swamigal, also known as ANK, was almost eighty years old when I interviewed him in Chennai in January 2009. Since he spoke only a little English and no Hindi, and I speak Hindi but no Tamil, but Thavamani and ANK's disciple, Kanchan, assisted me with the interview and with translating ANK's words into English. ANK is a crucial figure in the history of the

Parashakthi Temple since he first predicted in 1972 that Kumar would build it.

ANK was born in the village of Kadiyapatti, Tamil Nadu, in June of 1929 as the only son of his parents. When he was a child, he reported to me in our interview, his father used to take him to the Minakshi Temple in Madurai every full moon day, and he became an ardent Minakshi devotee. When he was about nine years old, he told me, he went to live at the home of two brothers, Mahalingam and Amirthalingam, to learn how to write astrological charts (*jathagam*) according to the traditional Hindu system. In India, traditional astrology is taken very seriously as an important field of study, and many Hindus call on trained astrologers frequently. ANK was apprenticed to two expert astrologers so they could pass their knowledge on to him.

One day when he was about eleven years old and was visiting the Minakshi Temple on the day of the full moon, he claims he was approached by an elderly sage who gave him a bundle of documents written on palm leaves and tied up in a cloth. ANK says he asked what the documents were, but the sage did not answer, saying only, "This is for you. You should keep it." ANK took the bundle home and opened the cloth, where he found several palm leaves with ancient Tamil writing on them. Not knowing what they were, he kept the bundle and included it in the array of sacred objects to which he performed daily *puja*.

Around the age of sixteen, when he had completed his initial training, he began writing up astrological charts for clients who came to him. He states that one such client took the chart ANK had done for him to a reader of Bhrigu Nadi, a Tamil Muslim named Wahab Sahud, for a reading. ANK recounts that when Wahab Sahud saw the chart ANK had made for the client, Sahud said, "Who has written this horoscope for you? That person is going to be very famous. I want to meet him." The client returned to ANK, narrated his encounter with Sahud, and after that, the two astrologers met. ANK discovered that the bundle of palm leaf texts he had in his possession were Bhrigu Nadi texts and matched the texts that Sahud was using in his Bhrigu Nadi practice. ANK then moved to Tiruvannamalai to apprentice himself to Sahud for a period of six years and learn how to do readings. Sahud, though a Muslim, acted as ANK's guru in matters concerning astrology.

Kumar came to ANK in 1972 because at that point ANK had already garnered a reputation as an expert reader of Bhrigu Nadi, and Kumar was feeling that he was at a crossroads in his life and wanted answers (see Figure 2.1) He brought his chart to ANK and asked him to do a reading. Kumar claims that when ANK told Kumar that he would build a temple, Kumar did not at first believe him. Here is how Kanchan translated to me what ANK said about that encounter:

> Dr. Kumar just laughed when he [ANK] first did the reading. He said, "What? I am a doctor. I am in no way connected to this spiritual stuff." He just laughed and said, "Where would I build a temple?" But ANK told him, "No, these are the things I see; they are written for you. In the end, you are going to build it."

ANK also told Kumar that the spot on which the temple would eventually stand would resemble the land that houses ANK's own chosen deity, or *ishtadevata* (*iṣṭhadevatā*): Minakshi of Madurai.

Over the next two decades, whenever Kumar would return to Tamil Nadu to visit family, he would call on ANK He also brought others to see ANK, including, eventually, the members of his family, and,

Figure 2.1 ANK Swamy doing a reading in 2009

as noted above, Jane and Sam, Ven, and other Euro-Americans who were or became under his influence goddess devotees. Kumar and ANK developed a close bond. ANK also introduced Kumar to many of his acquaintances and religious teachers in Tamil Nadu, including Dikshitar and a Tamil Kundalini Yoga teacher Dr. P. Pandian (a.k.a. Kaviyogi Bacon), to whom he introduced Kumar in 1980 and whom I also interviewed, in English, in 2009. Pandian was an officer in the Indian Administrative Service, but in 1960, he had a mystical experience when he was extremely ill and lying in a hospital bed in Chennai. His website states:

> The Cosmic Mother revealed Herself to him as the Ineffable OM (the Logos) and smokeless pure light as if a cloud burst of a million suns. Dr. P. Pandian was found cured of his ailment by the divine power as if descending from the Cosmos. He felt surcharged with divine vibrations activating his every cell in the body and he was floating on a sea of ambrosial bluish white efflorescence. (Kaviyogii Shop, n.d.)

After this experience, he reported to me, he became a goddess devotee. When I spoke with him in 2009, Pandian told me that he had initiated Kumar, Jane, and other Parashakthi Temple founders into the practice of Kundalini Yoga. He considers Kumar to be his disciple, but he also told me in 2009 that Kumar had surpassed him in spiritual understanding and ability. Several other individuals I met with and interviewed in Tamil Nadu during that visit echoed Pandian's assessment of Kumar's spiritual status as the student who has surpassed the master.

By the late 1990s, ANK had become an important figure in the life of Kumar and many of the devotees involved in founding the Parashakthi Temple. He had functioned as an intermediary, helping Kumar find Dikshitar, Pandian, and other gurus and spiritual guides; he helped Kumar locate the goddess calling on him to build the temple in Michigan; and he had helped several of Kumar's American associates connect with deities, temples, and spiritual teachers in Tamil Nadu. It is not surprising, therefore, that he came to Michigan in 1999 to participate in the installation of the original temple *murtis*. ANK stopped first to see his son, who was living at that time in Washington DC and then traveled on to Michigan to take part in the installation. He has also returned to the Parashakthi Temple in Michigan several times since it was first constructed.

When I asked ANK about the feeling he gets when he is at the Parashakthi Temple, he invoked the reported Native American shamanic past that other devotees also invoke, noting, "Three hundred people have done meditations and things like that on the land. So, the spiritual power is still there. That's why the temple has got a lot of *shakti*. It's because of those three hundred shamans." When I asked him how the *shakti* in Michigan compares to what he feels at the Minakshi Temple, this is what he said:

> The *shakti* is the same; it is one and the same. The names are different. But it [the Parashakthi Temple] has a lot of power because of the three hundred sages who are there. Because their power is in the soil, because of that, it is in the temple. The power is in that place, so that is why the temple came to that place. It was meant to be built right there. See, in Tamil Nadu, if you go and see all the important temples, there will be at least one sage who has attained a *siddhi* (supernormal power) there. The temple will have a big name only because of the power of the sage. It is like this there [in Michigan]. This temple [the Parashakthi Temple] will have a lot of power, and in the future, it is going to get even bigger.

What is remarkable here is how ANK's comments reinforce the discourse of indigenization to which I allude in the previous chapter. The *shakti* at the Parashkathi Temple in Michigan and the Minakshi Temple in Tamil Nadu is the same; the *shakti* that is produced by religious sages, whether Indian or Native American, is the same across time and space; only the names and locations are different. But place here still matters; the *shakti* that is clearly present in Michigan, at least to those able to perceive it, is in the soil on which the temple was built. The Minakshi Temple in South India and the Parashakthi Temple in Michigan are connected by the subtle tendrils of Divine Mother's *shakti*.

Ravi

Kumar was born and raised in Chennai and travels back there frequently, so he maintains a network of ongoing relationships. Some are familial or are grounded in longstanding friendships from the years before he emigrated to the United States. Others are based on his religious pursuits or the ongoing work he and other core devotees at the Parashakthi Temple oversee in India, such as the completion of yantras and *murtis* for the temple. For this purpose, Kumar maintains an office in Chennai that is run by a trusted employee, Ravi. Ravi is a lawyer by training, but by the time I met and interviewed him in 2009, he had already been working for Kumar for several years. He describes his role to be that of a "roaming man" who goes anywhere he is needed to get things done for the Parashakthi Temple. While his native language is Tamil, he also speaks English fluently.

Ravi told me he was not particularly religious before he met Kumar in 1988 but was caught up in the pursuit of wealth. He had a lucrative law practice that centered on defending gangsters and other lawbreakers. He says he made a lot of money but was not satisfied with his work. He knew Pandian's son since they had been schoolmates, and he met Kumar through Pandian. He says that the first time he met Kumar, they talked for an hour, and something in him changed:

Something passed through my mind. Earlier, I had the feeling that I had to go and work for some spiritual people. . . . When I met Dr. Kumar, I thought, "Maybe this is the man I have to work for."

Ravi says he asked Kumar for a job during that first meeting. He reports that Kumar did not give Ravi an answer right away but said he would think about it and let him know after he had returned to the USA. At this time, the temple was in the planning stage but had not yet been built. When Kumar was back in the United States and in a state of meditation, Ravi reported, Divine Mother told him that she had sent Ravi to him so he could work for the temple. When Kumar did offer Ravi a job managing the operations on the ground in Chennai, Ravi says he jumped at the chance to leave his legal practice behind even though it meant a huge decline in salary. He says he immediately quit being a lawyer.

Like others involved in helping found the Parashakthi Temple, Ravi claims to have experienced several miracles after he became a servant of the Goddess. There are two that stand out to him and that he narrated to me during our time together in Chennai. The first took place shortly after he began the new position. In 1998, about two months after he started working for Kumar, he told me he was in his *puja* room doing *puja*, when suddenly, his servant, a young boy, started pounding on the door to the *puja* room and shouting. The servant boy entered the *puja* room in a state of deity possession. Ravi claims that this servant had been possessed by Pandi, a male protector deity with a small temple in Madurai near the Minakshi temple. Pandi is also called Pandimuni, Pandi Munishwaran, *ayya* Pandimuni, and a number of similar names. He is one of several male guardian deities revered by Tamil Hindus in India and abroad. Sinha notes that throughout Tamil Nadu, goddesses are often held to be supreme, with male deities often acting as guardians and attendants. She argues, however, that in such cases, male deities are not less important than the goddesses they guard; rather, "they have a clearly defined role regarding the female deities, coupled with the idea that all need protection—including goddesses" (Sinha 2005, 87). In this case, Ravi claims, Pandi entered the body of Ravi's servant boy to deliver a message to Ravi. Pandi told Ravi that he, Ravi, was Pandi's son and therefore was also charged with protecting the Goddess:

> He was shouting, and he told me, "I am Pandi. You are my son." He says this to me. He's my servant, but he used very familiar language. So, he says, "Parashakthi asked me to send you to work for Dr. Kumar." And he [the servant] does not know who Dr. Kumar is; he doesn't know his name even. . . . [Pandi said,] "I am leaving you to work for Dr. Krishna Kumar. And once your job is over, you will die. . . . Parashakthi said to me, 'Send your son to work for Dr. Kumar because Dr. Kumar is working for me.'"

The second miraculous event that Ravi discussed with me had to do with a serious car accident he was in sometime after he began working for the Parashakthi Temple. He was not hurt, but other passengers involved in the accident were seriously injured. He told me that a boy who was in the car became possessed by the Goddess right after the accident and spoke to him, saying, "Your boss is constructing a temple for me, so I am letting you live. I am leaving you alive only for the sake of the work you must do for Dr. Kumar." Ravi feels very strongly that he owes his life to Divine Mother and the work he is doing for the Parashakthi Temple in Michigan.

Ravi handles the production and delivery of all the yantras, *murtis*, and other sacred objects that various agents create in India to be shipped over to Michigan and installed there in the temple. At times, the job is very wearing, according to Ravi, because of the politics involved: he must choose individuals to create the objects needed, negotiate the timetable and cost, and deal with the resentment of those not chosen for commissions. He chooses the individual he feels is right for the job, which means that some of the craftsmen he has chosen to make *murtis* and other temple objects are Muslim. He alleges, for example, that a Sufi Muslim craftsman created the *hundi*, or donation box, that sits in the Parashakthi Temple as well as some of the temple *murtis*. Ravi says that he has chosen that craftsman to create certain objects because he was "very mystical" and therefore appropriate. When I pushed him on this a little further, Ravi proclaimed that even before he met Kumar, he was attracted to Sufism and had visited many *dargahs*, tombs of Sufi saints, throughout India. He reported that Kumar had encouraged him to look beyond the Hindu/Muslim religious divide and choose craftsmen who are spiritually awakened regardless of religious background.

Ravi not only commissions the various yantras and *murtis* that Kumar asks him to have made; he also participates in their production. He helps pour the molten metal from which the yantras and some *murtis* are made, and he adds touches to the face, particularly the lips and eyes of the *murtis*, because, he says, "There should be a smile on the lips. There should be grace in the eyes." Although he has no formal training in the manufacture of religious objects or temple icons, he feels the Goddess has inspired him to make the appropriate small modifications that will bring life to them. He claims that because he feels and demonstrates tremendous devotion to the Goddess, the craftsmen he hires allow him to take part. Kumar allegedly has told Ravi that Ravi has a *yakshini* (*yakṣiṇī*), an auspicious spirit, in his body, which protects him from demonic energy and gives him special grace to complete the *murti*s. He recalled for me one particular *murti* of the goddess Lakshmi with sixteen hands that was installed in the Parashakthi Temple in Pontiac in 2004. At the time it was being made in India, Ravi was busy with other temple business and was not able to participate in the production process. He told me that the hands kept breaking when the craftsman making the *murti* tried to complete the very delicate work on the fingers. That night, Ravi claims, the Goddess came to the craftsman in his dreams and told him, "Call Ravi and ask him to do that." Ravi was able to complete the craftsmanship on the *murti*'s hands without any breakage.

Kumar introduced Ravi to the temple in Thiruverkadu, and Ravi continues to go there regularly for worship even when Kumar is not in India. But Ravi also became a devotee of the Parashakthi Temple in Michigan even though he has never been to the United States. He keeps photographs of all the *murti*s that sat in the original Parashakthi Temple in his *puja* room at home, and he does *puja* to them every night. Ravi also introduced to Kumar a wealthy and in-fluential Tamil businessperson, Krishnan, who has made pilgrimage to the Parashakthi Temple in Michigan numerous times. A friend of Ravi's asked him to set up an introduction for Krishnan soon after Ravi started working for the temple. Ravi reported to me that Krishnan fell to Kumar's feet the first time they met, held onto them, and prayed for ten minutes. Krishnan and Kumar have become close friends. I have also encountered Krishnan at several events at the Parashakthi Temple in Michigan over the years, most recently at the rededication of the temple in August of 2022. Krishnan claims that the temple in Pontiac is spiritually alive and full of positive energy in a way that many Indian temples are not.

Transcendent Lives and Translocal Shaktiscapes

Several themes emerge in these accounts that are common in Hindu narratives about being called to serve the Goddess. First, a person experiences some difficulty or suffering that the Goddess alleviates, resulting in them becoming a devotee. Hence Ven, for example, insists that the pilgrimage journey that he undertook at Kumar's behest, including the many acts of devotion that he performed at several temples, resulted directly in his acquittal at trial years later; and Pandian claims the Goddess cured him of a severe illness, resulting in his need to devote himself to her. Second, the Goddess reveals herself to devotees in subtle ways, through dreams, visions, possession, or inexplicable impulses. Hence, for example, Jane has a vision of the Goddess without even knowing who she is; ANK sees in Kumar's chart that Kumar will build a temple for Divine Mother; and Ravi has an urge to quit his job and work for Kumar when they first meet. Third, those called to her service must make sacrifices of blood, time, money, occupation, and such to fulfill the Goddess's demands. So, for example, Jane donates her blood by allowing mosquitos on the temple grounds to take it from her. Finally, devotees experience the Goddess's call as something so urgent that, to quote the Borg in *Star Trek*, resistance is futile. Yet she provides for them, in response, the temple, an abode of *shakti*, where they can experience, as Ven claims, a feeling of "home," or as Jane notes, a place where she can experience the life-changing experience of being the Divine.

All these accounts, too, portray the Goddess as intervening in people's lives directly and in tangible, often material ways, orchestrating events and transforming her devotees in the process. She creates friction, and she often blows things up, so to speak, catalyzing changes, both large and small, in people's lives. The Goddess is not distant; she actively calls individuals to her service and her temple, demanding things of them and intervening, in a miraculous way, on their behalf. Here we have confirmation of Waghorne's observation that Tamil goddesses often intrude directly into the lives of devotees as "living energy, the vibration of the universe and the pulse of the devotee" (Waghorne 2004, 227). The shaktiscape that these stories adumbrate is, however, not bound to the confines of *jambudvipa* (*jambudvīpa*), the historical homeland of Hinduism that comprises India. This shaktiscape crosses oceans. It is global, transtremporal, and transmaterial, flowing like water across the boundaries of space, time, ethnicity, religion, and national origin, streaming through minds and bodies through continual engagement in the material realm.

3

Material Crossings/Fire

Matter that Matters

Toward the end of June 2019, I was sitting at my desk at home when I received a phone call from one of the devotees actively involved with the Parashakthi Temple asking if I would be willing to speak with the temple's lawyers. The call took me completely by surprise. At that point, I had not been to the temple for over eighteen months since I turned my attention from gathering data to writing this book, so I did not know what was going on in Pontiac daily. The devotee who called me said that there had been a serious fire in the temple on April 21, 2018, during a *homa* rite. *Homa*, a modern form of fire sacrifice, is frequently performed to generate auspicious divine power. During a *homa*, food and other valued items, such as silk saris or shawls, are offered into the fire, often in honor of a specific deity. On this occasion, however, the vent above the *homa* pit had suffered a serious creosote buildup that caught fire during the *homa*, destroying the roof and damaging most of the existing temple structure. There was almost nothing salvageable.

Following the fire, the temple board consulted a Hindu architect in Tamil Nadu with knowledge of the rules of traditional Hindu architecture, *vastu* (*vāstu*) and design, *shilpa* (*śilpa*). This architect created a report based on verses he had compiled from the Shilparatna of Shrikumara, an authoritative text on craftsmanship in the South Indian Dravida or Maya school of architecture. The conclusion at the end of the report was clear. The fire had irreparably damaged the subtle energy present in the temple, so the structure would have to be completely rebuilt. Most of the *murti*s that had survived the fire materially would have to be replaced by new *murti*s created and installed by Indian craftsmen, or *shilpi*s (*śilpi*). The insurance company was balking at covering the cost of the temple's proposed plan to move forward. They wanted to know why the new *murti*s could not be

Goddess Beyond Boundaries. Tracy Pintchman, Oxford University Press. © Oxford University Press 2024.
DOI: 10.1093/oso/9780190673017.003.0004

constructed by US-based *shilpi*s, or why the current *murti*s could not just be cleansed ritually and reinstalled. Kumar was insistent not only that everything be replaced, but also that the work be entrusted only to *shilpi*s who were aware of the divine on an intuitive level and able to communicate directly with deities and receive divine energy—that is, those who were "thinned out," to use Kumar's phrasing. He declared that the Goddess had revealed to him the *shilpi*s she wanted him to appoint to do the work. The temple's lawyers called me to see if I could offer them any examples of similar situations in the United States, so I put out a call for assistance on my professional listserv. Nothing. But I knew even at the time that it might have proven difficult for me to draw direct parallels with other American Hindu temple situations anyway given the material theology that prevails at the Parashakthi Temple, a theology that shapes devotees' perceptions of and feelings toward the sacred objects and structures that the temple houses. Here, I understand "material theology" to encompass ways of thinking about and experiencing the places where matter and divinity merge in ways rendered possible by the networks of translocal relations that the temple both facilitates and exemplifies.

Parashakthi Temple discourse postulates that the Goddess uses material objects in deliberate ways for a variety of reasons, including to communicate her wishes to human devotees. Hence, for example, as I described in Chapter 1, Kumar claims that the Goddess communicated her desire that he establish a temple to her in the West by calling him to commission a chariot at the Karumariamman Temple in Thiruverkadu; the chariot was the primary channel of divine/human communication. Even more frequently, however, the Goddess is said to engage material objects and structures at the temple, including *murti*s, to channel and transmit not just her wishes, but also her power, especially her protective power. Hence, at the temple, objects matter not only for what they mean but mostly for what they do. As Flueckiger notes of Hindu religious objects, "Their performativity also *creates* identity, theology, transformation; they *do* something" (Flueckiger 2020, 25). Temple discourse portrays, and many devotees perceive, objects that are installed ritually at the temple as possessing unique potency because of their origins, the specific ways they came to be called to the temple and ritually installed there, the spiritual gifts of people who installed them, and the places at which they are installed. Their significance and power reside in the amalgamated effect of all the layers of their particularity.

Indian cultures are, as Flueckiger notes, "replete with examples of materials that are assumed to cause things to happen or to prevent them from happening, which both create and reflect an indigenous theory of the agency of materiality." She observes, for example, that gemstones might deflect the negative forces of specific planets; black kohl markings may deflect the evil eye; or rice-flour designs might invite the goddess Lakshmi into one's house (Flueckiger 2020, 18–19). Indian material traditions, says Flueckiger, emphasize the agency of material itself without dependence on human intervention in causing the assumed effects (Flueckiger 2020, 19). While these observations are often demonstrably true in Hindu traditions broadly speaking, they are often not true at the Parashakthi Temple. Instead, in Pontiac, specific material objects and structures usually must become, through ritual intervention, instruments of the Goddess and vehicles through which divine power is conveyed and wielded. They come to act not entirely on their own, but instead at Divine Mother's behest. Yet they act. Their power resides at the intersection of Divine, human, and material worlds.

Parashakthi Temple discourse maintains that the material realm has evolved directly from the Divine and contains the full potential of *shakti*, manifest as oscillating heat energy, within itself. Everything that exists has a spark of divine energy and has the potential to manifest that energy. But not all matter realizes that potential, for some material forms may be or may become more "charged" and active than other forms. Many of the temple's objects, including not only its *murtis* but other objects and structures as well, are so "charged." But bringing concentrated divine power to temple objects, and thereby extending the availability of that power to the temple community and the larger community beyond temple confines, requires the coordination of three kinds of agent: the Goddess; human brokers who, as beings embodied in the gross, material realm, can act in ways the Goddess cannot; and specific objects and structures well-suited to and carefully prepared for their intended tasks. The idea that spiritually qualified religious practitioners can infuse specific objects with divine power in a concentrated way through ritual action is also broadly tantric, demonstrating again the influence of tantra in the temple's self-understanding.

In this chapter, I focus on some of the objects and structures that came to reside at the temple from the time it was constructed until the time it was destroyed in 2018. I emphasize the significance these objects and structures assume in relationship to their embedded contexts. I return toward the end of the chapter to the *murtis* housed at the temple during the nineteen years of its initial existence before they came to be rendered unsuitable for temple use by the 2018 fire. Finally, I explore the implications of the temple's material theology for how we might rethink some of the larger categories often brought to bear on the kinds of phenomena that the Parashakthi Temple and its devotional community exemplify.

Arjun Appadurai's seminal edited volume, *The Social Life of Things: Commodities in Cultural Perspective* (1986), was one of the first academic works to take seriously the nature of "things" as highly significant, and often shifting or complex, loci of meaning, identity, agency, and culture. Objects cannot be reduced to any set of intentions or meanings because of the existence of "an indefinite number of qualities" in any given object (Keane 2008, 230). Things are therefore unstable because what they are, what they mean, and what kind of value people invest in them is context-dependent and ever-changing. As Igor Kopytoff famously noted in "The Cultural Biography of Things"—and as other scholars have since emphasized—objects have unique biographies (Kopytoff 1986; Davis 1997) and exploring an object's biography "can make salient what might otherwise remain obscure" (Kopytoff 1986, 67). Kopytoff observes:

In doing the biography of a thing, one would ask questions similar to those one asks about people: What, sociologically, are the biographical possibilities inherent in its "status" and in the period and culture, and how are these possibilities realized? Where does the thing come from and who made it? What has been its career so far and what do people consider to be an ideal career for such things? (Kopytoff 1986, 66–67)

Translocal objects have especially complex biographies that traverse time and space, even if people encountering those objects are not aware of those biographies. Such objects have histories that may be concealed (Morgan 2021, 183), and "as an object moves from one person to the next, from one social setting or one culture to the next, it acquires different values and associations" (Morgan 2008, 228). But materials come to rest in specific places. My approach to exploring materials at the Parashakthi Temple will be one that considers material agency on different scales, from the translocal to the local, but will focus especially on the place "where situatedness is experienced" (Brickell and Datta 2011, 5–6)—in this case, the temple complex itself. For at least some members of the Parashakthi Temple devotional community, the Goddess's new abode in Michigan has become more sacred than many of the temples in India at least in part through the ritual emplacement at the temple of objects and structures that have been rendered spiritually powerful through the merging of Divine command and human action.

*Murti*s (Temple Images) and Yantras

Sunday, June 22, 2008: Venkateshvara Installation

Venkateshvara was, it seemed, being a bit stubborn. The enormous, heavy *murti* had been lifted and gently lowered into its proper place, but it was not situated correctly on its pedestal. Several devotees, all adult males, had hauled it about twenty feet already using two long bars and ropes but had not succeeded in placing the *murti* squarely in its seat. We were all squeezed into a tight, hot space behind a curtain separating us from the audience of devotees sitting on the temple floor, and the men were sweating and tired from their labors. It had taken a great deal of effort to get the *murti* into location, and now it would have to be lifted again and repositioned. Tempers were running a bit short, and the men responsible for the move were arguing with each other about how best to proceed. After a brief rest, the men repositioned themselves along the bars and hauled the *murti* up again, shouting directions to each other as they moved it just enough to slide it squarely into the space that had been created to house its base. The relief was palpable. The cloth that had been placed around the *murti* for this transition was then removed, and the temple priests, who had been watching from the sidelines, moved in to ready the *murti* for the final steps of the consecration rites.

I had driven from my home in the Chicago suburbs over to Pontiac two days earlier to be present for the weekend's activities. This was the first complete deity installation I could attend at the temple, and I wanted to be present for all of it. I arrived mid-afternoon on Friday, later than I had hoped, because of traffic; Asha was getting ready to go to the temple when I arrived at her house, so I left after her, on my own. I made a wrong turn and was late getting to the temple. When I arrived, the chanting of *mantra*s had already begun, so I took my seat in the audience and joined in. There had been five hours of ritual preparation Friday night; then Saturday brought an all-day *homa*, starting at 8 a.m. and ending around 5 p.m., followed by chanting, a lecture, and more temple rites. Now it was approaching noon on Sunday, and we had all been there since 8 a.m.

I peeked out to the main hall to see what was going on there and then stepped out from behind the curtain for a moment to catch my breath. The temple was completely packed, with wall-to-wall people—devotees who had come to witness the deity consecration—filling every space and spilling out the doors. The crowd's density, combined with the warm day, turned the temple into an oven. I peered out over the audience. Guruji Shridhar, a visiting religious teacher who had flown from India to Pontiac to help with the installation, was chanting Sanskrit mantras with the help of his entourage of priests and devotees, unaware of the drama that had been unfolding behind the curtain. I looked out at the audience of devotees—some were listening intently to the *mantra*s, others were chanting along, some were looking around or chatting, and others were sitting with eyes closed, meditating or dozing.

I am still not sure how I suddenly was able to be behind the curtain for this important event. This was only my fifth visit to the temple. The night before, a member of the board handed me a camera and made me an apprentice photographer, admonishing me to keep an eye out for good angles and shots. At some point, one of the volunteers told me to move, so the board member handed me a "volunteer" badge, which gave me the authority to move around freely. I relished the position, moving in and out of the crowd, aiming my camera to catch critical moments in the consecration ritual, trying to capture the faces of devotees. I slipped back behind the curtain, aiming my camera at the action. The battery was not working correctly, so the camera was overheating and then stopping, but we managed to document a good portion of the *murti* installation. When Venkateshvara finally claimed his spot and was fully enlivened later that afternoon, everyone moved on to the installation of Garuda, the bird that operates as Venkateshvara's vehicle (*vāhana*). Venkateshvara, the "Lord of All" whom many consider to be an incarnation of the deity Vishnu, is quite popular among Hindus, including North American Hindus, as he is believed to grant prosperity and wealth (see Figure 3.1).

One of the characteristics of the Parashakthi Temple that I found most striking when I first started visiting was the continually growing and seemingly eclectic collection of *murtis* that the temple housed before the 2018 fire. At the Parashakthi Temple, the Goddess claims pride of place, of course, and the temple is named after and dedicated to her. However, numerous additional deity *murtis* came to be installed in the

Figure 3.1 Venkateshvara and his wives after installation in 2008

temple between the installation of the first four—Karumariamman, Ganesha, Subrahmanyam, and Shiva Nataraja—at the time of the temple's founding in 1999 and the fire in 2018, including both pan-Indian Hindu deities, such as Shiva, Durga, and Hanuman, and several South Indian deities, such as Ayyappan, Lakshmi Narasimha, Minakshi, and Chottanikkara Bhagavathy. Hindu temples are in general replete with sacred objects and deity images, and in that sense, the Parashakthi Temple is no different. But, as one of the Indian American board members said to me when I interviewed him in 2012, "This is the only temple that I know that will have all these deities in one place. . . . In other temples, there might be Guruvayurrappan, but there is not Chottanikkara Bhagavaty. There is no Kodungalloor Bhagavathy anywhere, to my knowledge, in North America. This is the only temple [with all these *murtis*]" (interview, November 12, 2009).

At Hindu temples, *murtis* function as embodiments of a deity and as human devotees' "point of access" to the divine (Davis 1997, 31). As Diana Eck notes, the entire process of fashioning a *murti* is governed by ritual prescriptions. Instructions and rites are established for selecting and extracting the substance, such as stone or wood, that will be used to make the *murti*; the *shilpi* is enjoined to approach the creation of the image as a religious discipline. When an image is completed and is to be installed in a temple, a temple priest will perform rites of purification and consecration, culminating in the rite of "establishing breath" (*prāṇa-pratiṣṭhā*) that brings the *murti* to life (Eck 1981, 52). *Murtis* are therefore not symbolic representations of divinity but living embodiments of the deities that inhabit them. Richard Davis describes what he calls the "devotional eye" with which devout Hindus may gaze upon temple images, an eye that perceives "the living presence of God" in the temple icon, perceiving therein the fullness of God's being and "the paradoxical quality of this transcendence within immanence" (Davis 1997, 43). While Davis's comments applied specifically to perspectives on temple images found in the poetry of medieval South Indian saints, his observations about the "devotional eye" are applicable more broadly to contemporary Hindu devotional perspectives on temple images.

In India, the *murtis* present in Hindu temples tend to reflect the sectarian emphasis of the temple: so, for example, Vaishnava temples will house primarily Vaishnava deities embodied in Vaishnava *murtis*, Shaiva temples will house primarily Shaiva *murtis*, and Shakta temples will highlight Shakta *murtis*. This pattern tends to continue in the United States, although many American Hindu temples emphasize deities who appeal to Hindus across sectarian boundaries, such as Venkateshvara or Ganesha, the elephant-headed deity of boundaries and obstacles. At the Parashakthi Temple, however, it is the Goddess herself who is said to choose which *murtis* are called to take up residence there. Furthermore, deity icons are described in temple discourse as the material manifestations of the Divine Mother's vibrations, so they are lesser portions of her *shakti*. On many occasions, Kumar has announced to the temple community that the Goddess had asked him to bring a particular deity to the temple because the vibration of the deity was needed at that specific point in time to offset the negative energies that would be coming soon and would affect the earth. In a conversation we had in July of 2012, Kumar told me that when the Goddess calls for a new *murti* to be installed at the temple, she reveals to Kumar the deity's pattern of vibratory energy, which he then uses to design the temple *murti* for that deity. While some of the temple's *murtis* are common and appear at the Parashakthi Temple in the same, standard form that they take in other Hindu temples, some do not. Kumar described the process by which he visualizes the form each *murti* will take:

> It has color. It has beautiful music. It has a vibratory pattern. And then I give the form. But the form comes from the vibration and from the music (*rāga*), the color—a combination of all of these. It is like a painting. I painted her the way I see her. And then we install [the deity] in that form. For some of them, I have seen them [already] in anthropomorphic form [in other temples]. But the others: did I create the form? Maybe. I don't know because no one has seen them [before]. The new ones [that I have not seen before], I don't know if they have appeared to others like that. But they are there in a highly vibratory form. You know a guitar string? You know, when you play the guitar, you can't see the strings anymore. They are there, playing music, but you don't see the strings anymore. This is the same thing but in reverse. (July 2012)

E. Allen Richardson argues that among Hindus in the United States, there has been a cultural trajectory away from perceiving *murti*s as actual embodiments of deity and toward an understanding of them as symbolic, aesthetic, or consumer objects, especially among second- and third-generation American Hindus (Richardson 2019). He notes, however, that first-generation Hindu immigrants, American Hindu temple priests and leaders, and gurus tend to continue to perceive deity images "through a traditional lens of embodiment" (Richardson 2019, 155). While I heard devotees at the Parashakthi Temple express both kinds of views, official temple discourse maintains that all the *murti*s it houses are in fact vibrant, living forms of divine energy that not only embody the manifold vibrations of the Goddess but also enhance her grace-giving and protective power. Kumar has on numerous occasions asserted that all the *murti*s emplaced at the temple embody specific divine energies that were already present in the land even before the temple was built, but their embodiment makes those energies more effectively available to human worshipers. Hence, the *murti*s are material vessels and transmitters of types of power that the Goddess wanted to embody in image form to both increase their potency and make them accessible. The energy that each *murti* embodies must be given form to be "activated" and, hence, to become "consumable," as Kumar puts it. Furthermore, Kumar maintains that the Goddess herself decides which *murti*s to bring to the temple by revealing those decisions to him during his meditations. The Goddess further guides Kumar to the specific *shilpi* selected to construct each *murti* and curates the form that each *murti* will take.

Kumar and others have told me that the Parashakthi Temple follows South Indian *shakta* prescriptions for the installation of *murti*s, including both the practices that the congregation witnesses as well as the numerous practices that occur outside of the public eye and often back in India before the *murti*s are completed and sent to the United States. There are, however, some public practices that are highlighted as especially suited to the temple's vision of the Goddess, including the idea that she is more egalitarian than she is understood to be elsewhere. For example, when *murti*s are installed in Hindu temples, both yantras and collections of nine-jewel packets, *navaratna*, are placed under the *murti* to bring it to life (see Figure 3.2). After yantras are given life through the recitation of mantras and placed under deity *murtis*, the nine small gemstones are placed on top of the yantra. Without the energized yantra and the nine jewels—which represent, among other things, the nine planets (the *navagraha*)—the *murti* remains lifeless. At the Parashakthi Temple, as at other Hindu temples in the United States, devotees can sponsor a yantra or packet of nine jewels and place them on the deity's pedestal themselves before the deity is installed so that the devotee will be eternally connected to the energy of that *murti*. At the Parashakthi Temple, several days are often given over to this process to make sure that all who wish to participate may do so. While sponsorship costs money, Kumar has noted on more than one occasion that for those who cannot afford the cost, sitting in the temple and thinking about the deity will offer those devotees the same spiritual merit.

Although Dikshitar placed yantras under the first few *murtis* installed in the temple in 1999, he passed away many years ago, which now leaves the work of making and installing temple yantras to others. Kumar argues that he chooses each yantra maker according to the Goddess's wishes. In a conversation we had in July of 2013, Kumar

Figure 3.2 Packets of *navaratna* placed in a pedestal awaiting a deity installation

declared that it is hard to find a good yantra maker because "not only do they have to know the various aspects of the yantra—square, triangle, lotus, whatever—but they have to instill the mantra into the lines [of the yantra]. It's like a CD. You see lines [in a CD], but they are not just lines. You see just a line, but there is music in that line." In a public talk that he gave in August 2022, Kumar claimed:

> The person who makes the yantras must know the deities personally, meaning he has communicated. The communication is real. When they (the deities) come into you, you are a different person because there are so many *nadis*, so many [bodily] channels [of energy]. When they wake up, our ability to know everything –the future, the past, the present—and many other mystical energies wake up. And then you realize you really have not used your potential. . . . The person who makes the yantra has to be spiritually evolved. And whatever information he gets from them[the deities], he puts it [into the yantra] as *nādabrahman* [the divine in sound form]. That is why you see the circles, the triangles, the squares; they are like computer software programs. Much information is there. . . . When you place them and do the proper dedication, with the proper *bijas* . . . the deity will come . . . When you place the yantra, the nine jewels, all the precious objects, and saying the mantra, then you become connected to the deity. You develop a relationship. ("Yantra sthapanam and kundalini ascension" 2022, lightly edited)

Here Kumar notes the connection between speech or sound (*nāda*) and objects in the material realm, reflecting tantric cosmologies where sound is the form of the godhead and unfolds into the material realm as power and then matter (e.g., Padoux 2017, 102–103). For devotees, yantras then function as a kind of spiritual anchor, binding them eternally to the deity whose yantra they have sponsored. But temple discourse has a more expansive understanding of yantra as well. In its general description of deity consecration rites, the temple website proclaims:

> A Yantra is the use of certain external objects, symbols or some mechanical means to worship the divine. The act of folding of hands in

front of the deity is but a kind of yantra only. The manner in which a fireplace is built for the performance of some vedic sacrifice, the method in which the place is prepared and the materials (sambhra) are assembled, the manner in which the oblations are poured into the fire, the way the priests sit around the altar, and in fact the very act of chanting of the mantras with mechanical precision form part of yantric worship. The very design of the temple as an outer symbol of the existence of the Divine on the material plane, the act of visiting the temple, circling around the temple, entering the temple, the lighting of the lamps in front of the divine, the decorations and the ornamentation so characteristic of Hindu temples and places of worship, the manner in which the images are built and installed, the lighting of the lamps, the offerings, the method of worship, the partaking of prasad, and in short any practice that is mechanical, symbolic and ritualistic to a degree, form part of this approach. (Parashakthi Temple, "Prana Pratishta," lightly edited)

Prasad (*prasāda*), mentioned here, refers to items that have been offered to a deity, blessed, and then returned to devotees for their consumption or use. In this text, yantra is described as any kind of material process or arrangement—of bodies or objects—that occurs at the temple in a manner that is worshipful.

Temple discourse maintains further that the *murtis* the temple houses, along with other powerful objects and structures located there, collectively establish and then intensify with each addition the totality of the Goddess's embodied energy present at the site and, consequently, the temple's evil-destroying potency. The Goddess functions at the Parashakthi Temple as divine vibration curator, carefully selecting the energies that will be most efficacious in bringing her power and grace to her devotees. The energies that the *murtis* embody are called into being as they are needed to respond to calamities and disasters, which are themselves in turn manifestations of *asuric*, or demonic, forces. As different demonic energies become active in the world, they necessitate the creation and installation in the temple of new *murtis* that embody the specific power needed to counter those demonic energies. Kumar insists that the energies embodied by *murtis* only become available when the *murtis* are installed at the temple so that devotees become aware of them. Each new *murti* also enhances the temple's ability to foster spiritual transformation in those who enter its doors. During a conversation we had in 2013, Kumar told me that the *murtis* "are there giving grace, actively, energetically. . . . They [also] enhance our receptivity because of our limitations, our sense-based limitations. They must give you supersensual ability, and these objects Mother has granted to us enhance our ability."

The Goddess's Shaligrams

On March 21, 2009, I was present at the temple, as I had been many times before, for a ritual occasion. In this case, I had come to Pontiac to attend a day of temple rites performed for several deities. The culminating event at 6:30 that evening was an *abhishekam* (*abhiṣekam*), a ritual in which liquid offerings are poured over a deity image or religiously significant object. This *abhishekam* was of two special stones that had been brought to the temple from India. These were shaligram (*śālagrāma*) stones that Kumar had brought back to Pontiac with him on two of the several trips he had made to India during the prior year. These large, round, black stones, covered with distinctive markings, had already played a role in several temple functions beginning in June 2008, although this evening of ritual was dedicated specifically to their worship. Dozens of devotees had gathered that night to see the Shaligrams, attend the *abhishekam*, and hear Kumar give a short lecture on the "Significance of Shaligram worship at the Parashakthi Temple." According to Kumar, these particular shaligram stones were extraordinary, mystical, powerful objects whose arrival at the temple had been orchestrated by the Goddess herself for a specific purpose.

Shaligram stones (see Figure 3.3) are forms of fossilized ammonite, a kind of mollusc, that developed in the Gandaki River in contemporary Nepal. They function in the Hindu tradition as natural, aniconic manifestations of the deity Vishnu that form only in the Gandaki River in Nepal. Shaligrams are black and round or oblong in shape, and they come in a variety of sizes. In his comprehensive study of shaligrams, Allen Aaron Shapiro notes that Indian Hindus

Figure 3.3 Shaligrams on a plate with flowers in 2009

tend to classify shaligrams as either perforated or nonperforated (Shapiro 1987, 5–6), with perforated shaligrams containing visible ammonite markings. Both types of shaligrams are worthy of worship, but those with perforations that resemble *cakras*, wheel-like images, are considered most meritorious. Many Hindus consider these *cakra*-like perforations to be the mark of Vishnu. Kirin Narayan notes that in Kangra, where she has done field research, most upper-caste households keep a shaligram stone in the home shrine, but married women are not supposed to touch it (Narayan 1997, 32). More widespread, however, is the belief that Vishnu makes himself available to all devotees in his shaligram form, and the Skanda Purana states that anyone initiated into shaligram worship, including women and Shudras, should worship shaligram stones (Shapiro 1987, 33). There is a long history in Hindu traditions of shaligrams being recognized as objects of reverence, going back to the Vedic or even pre-Vedic period (Shapiro, 44-52). In several the Puranas, they are proclaimed to be natural, aniconic forms of the deity Vishnu.

How Vishnu came to take the form of a shaligram stone is recounted in a well-known narrative told in a variety of versions, both textual and oral. The Devi-Bhagavata Purana (9.17–25) recounts one such version. Tulsi, a goddess who also takes form as the basil plant, marries a demon named Shankhacuda (or Jalandhara in other versions of the story). Tulsi here is described as a form of Lakshmi, and Shankhacuda is the incarnation of Krishna's dear childhood friend, Sudama. Both Tulsi and Sudama are said to have been compelled to take human births because of a curse visited upon them by Radha, Krishna's consort.

Shankhacuda soon gains more power. His ascendency culminates in a battle between divine and demonic forces. Because Tulsi is a devoted wife (*pativratā*), she can generate power that protects Shankhacuda, whom the gods are unable to defeat. Vishnu intervenes by going to Tulsi in the form of Shankhacuda and tricking her into having sex with him. Tulsi has now broken her wifely vow by having sex with a man other than her husband, thereby depriving Shankhacuda of the protective powers that resulted from Tulsi's spousal devotion and chastity. Shankhacuda is killed, whereupon he is reborn in Krishna's heaven as the loyal Sudama, with his bones becoming conch shells, which are used in Vaishnava worship. Tulsi curses Vishnu to become a stone, which results in his manifestation as the shaligram. Vishnu invites Tulsi to become his wife, proclaiming that her body will become the Gandaki River, the only river in which shaligram stones are said to naturally manifest.

In contemporary lived Hinduism, shaligrams are associated with both Shiva and Vishnu. But they are most consistently accepted as natural forms of Vishnu (Shapiro 1987, 12–14) and are kept in many Vaishnava temples. In contemporary Hinduism, shaligrams sometimes also have tantric associations and may be seen as having a special power that humans can access. Shapiro tells the following story about his encounter over shaligrams with the *pujari* of a South Indian Śiva temple:

This priest, whose name was Sivan, was very unimpressed with the salagrama stone given to me by the priest of the Muktinatha shrine, because it did not have any perforation, but decided to test it anyway. He placed it upon a small disk of copper and put another small piece of copper as a lid on top of the stone. We waited to see if the lid would

be turned by the power residing in the stone: my stone failed mis-
erably. However, he was more intrigued by another stone I have. . . .
I cannot say what the actual reason for Sivan's interest in the latter
stone was, for it, too, was unperforated. It was, however, adorned
with a pair of small eyes made of conch shell, applied with wax in
the manner typical of the Vrindaban area. He tried the same copper
plate test on the Govardhana stone, but it also proved powerless to
move the copper lid. (Shapiro 1987, 7–8)

The idea that shaligram stones are powerful religious objects is part of
contemporary Hindu thought. It is their association with supernatural
power, much more than their association with Vishnu or Shiva, that
characterized the two shaligrams that came to be consecrated with an
abhiṣekam in Michigan in March of 2009.

When Kumar went to India in early 2008, he did not set out to
bring shaligram stones back to Michigan. Rather, he was making
one of many trips he usually makes to India annually, often at the
Goddess's behest, to do her bidding for the temple and to visit his remaining family in Chennai. In 2008, he journeyed back to India four
times, with the first trip occurring in February of that year. During
that trip, Kumar called on ANK in Chennai, and ANK took Kumar
to meet a person residing about fifty miles outside of Chennai.
Kumar describes this individual as a *siddha*, an accomplished or
"perfected" yogi who has attained supernormal powers through
meditation, tantric practice, mantra recitation, asceticism, and/or
the performance of rites. Kumar usually translates the term *siddha*
simply as "mystic" in temple lectures and discussions. Siddhas are
often attributed supernatural powers due to the intensity of their
spiritual practice and the elevated level of spiritual attainment they
are said to have accomplished. The *siddha* or *siddhar* tradition is still
practiced in Tamil Nadu and has been picked up at the Parashakthi
Temple. In fact, some temple devotees consider Kumar himself to be
a *siddha*.

Kumar reports that the *siddha* to whom ANK introduced him
showed Kumar a very special shaligram stone and announced that
he was going to give it to Kumar. Kumar told me the following:

KUMAR: When I saw that, it had what is called—you know, Sudarshana is called Vishnu's *cakra*, Vishnu's emblem. Actually, it looks like a spiral galaxy. And there were thirteen of them [*cakra* markings].

TRACY: Okay.

KUMAR: I've seen one or two. I've never seen thirteen.

TRACY: So, there were thirteen *cakras*—

KUMAR: Sudarshana *cakras*.

TRACY: —on this shaligram?

KUMAR. On the shaligram. . . . And then he showed me—I shook it, and there was water in it, entrapped matter. . . . And this is a valuable fossil, 140 million years old. The continent shifted, and that's when the Himalayas formed. . . . That was not enough. Mother had told him, "You have to charge it before you give it. I want my place to be completely energized for the devotees."

Sudarshana (*sudarśana*) Cakra is the name given to the disk-like weapon that the Hindu deity Vishnu uses to protect the world and destroy evil or obstructing forces, both external and spiritual. The language of "energizing" or "charging" objects with sacred power is well-established at the Parashakthi Temple. While sacred objects and important temples can be found all over India, Kumar insists that most of them are "lifeless." Sacred objects and temples become powerful only when they have been properly infused with divine power, which can only be done by someone who is "thinned out." According to Kumar, most Hindu temple priests are not thinned out and hence are unable to really become in any authentic way vehicles of divine power. Kumar himself, as well as the "king of yogis," on the other hand, were immediately sensitive to the dynamics of divine energy surrounding the special shaligram stone. Kumar reports:

He said, "I have this for you. But I want to energize it for you so you can—" see, what he does is—when you have a shaligram, you have to do certain [things]. We call it feeding the cosmic forces. You've got to do that.

Kumar reports that he had to return to the *siddha*'s home two or three days later to participate in a big *homa* that he and the *siddha* conducted together before an audience of about forty to fifty invited participants. He was accompanied by ANK and ANK's daughter, but Kumar and the *siddha* had to work together to infuse the shaligram with the appropriate energy. Kumar describes this *homa* as "the longest *homa* I've ever been to there [in India]:"

> It took about four or five hours of intense, intense energy. And the herbs—we use some at the temple, maybe five, six seven—but, yeah, [there were] 153 [herbs used]. Highest I've ever seen. He must have spent years accumulating those herbs. . . . 153 of them he used, and each one used is one deity (*devatā*). I was sitting next to it. The energy was so intense that Swami [ANK] didn't even stay. He couldn't stand it; he walked away. Even the *siddha* walked away. And they're watching from outside about fifty feet away, and many people thought I was burnt because they said the flame engulfed me. . . . I felt like I was burnt. I felt like I was dying, but I didn't know it—I was not burnt. For them it looked like I was also part of the *homa*.

According to Kumar, everyone else at the *homa* experienced the introduction into the fire of each herb—with every herb corresponding to one deity—as suffocating energy, so they were unable to remain near the *homa* fire. Kumar told me that the Goddess wanted only Kumar to remain with the divine energies infusing the shaligram, so she made the air impossible for everyone else to breathe. Even Kumar felt almost overwhelmed:

> I felt that suffering. I felt that intense death-like thing, but I was not burnt. But they felt I was consumed by [the flames]. Some people were trying to get up and come and open the windows. The door was closed; through the window, they were watching me.

Kumar returned to Michigan with the newly charged shaligram. It was brought to the Parashakthi Temple and, on August 9, 2008, a special *abhishekam* of the shaligram was performed publicly.

Kumar told me that he returned to India in November of 2008 and met again with the same mystic, who gave him a second powerful shaligram at the behest of Divine Mother. The second shaligram had fourteen perforations on it. Kumar reports:

> When I saw that, he said, "She also wants you to have it." And I said, "You know, there must be a reason." I said, "If Mother says, I'll take it." That night, when I meditated, Mother said, "I want my devotees on earth to get all the energies from twenty-seven constellations. Each [*cakra* perforation] represents one constellation. So, I want twenty-seven." See, I didn't know that. When I got [the second shaligram], I didn't make the connection.... So, twenty-seven we will have. Ours will be the most energetic [shaligram].

Kumar's understanding of what Divine Mother has revealed to him is that each *cakra* on the two shaligrams he was given corresponds to a *nakshatra* as well as the presiding deity of that *nakshatra*; their divine energy is being captured and channeled through the shaligrams' *cakra* perforations in such a way that every devotee coming to the temple— since everyone is associated with one or another of the twenty-seven *nakshatras*—will receive the protection and divine grace being channeled through the shaligram stones. During the March 2009 function, Kumar again made a direct connection between the twenty-seven *cakra* perforations on the two shaligram stones, the twenty-seven *nakshatras*, and Divine Mother's protective energy, noting that the temple's shaligrams, taken together, would protect everyone in the world since the stones had been infused properly with the Goddess's energy. As I was following Kumar around the temple with my tape recorder before the shaligram *abhishekam*, he also stopped to shake the stones gently to allow me to hear the sound of the fluid trapped in them. Kumar insisted that spiritually sensitive individuals at the temple could hear music emanating from the shaligrams; both Kumar and two of the priests at the Parashakthi Temple told me they could hear the music clearly. Both Kumar and one of the temple priests, Swami Mama ("Uncle Swami"), insisted, too, that he distinctly heard the mantra "OM" coming from the shaligrams when they were shaken.

In his work on the material culture of enchantment, David Morgan observes that "human beings collectively construct material webs of relatedness that include themselves within all manner of agencies around them" and that "technologies and networks are what extend the body to spheres of power beyond its own" (Morgan 2018, 75). In the religious economy of the Parashakthi Temple, objects like the shaligrams function in just this way, extending the Goddess's powers of protection and grace to all the members of her devotional community and beyond.

The *Rajagopuram* and *Shakti Garbha*

In 2012, under Kumar's direction, the Parashakthi Temple started construction on a grand, seven-story *rajagopuram* (*rājagopuram* or *rājagopura*), "royal tower," that was completed and ritually consecrated on August 23, 2015. It now stands majestically at the front of the temple's entrance. Kumar gave a talk at the temple in 2012 announcing that the Goddess had appeared to him in his meditation and requested that it be built. Thereafter, the community devoted a great deal of money, time, and energy to realizing his vision. The occasion of the *rajagopuram*'s consecration in 2015 was noteworthy, with dignitaries and devotees coming from India and other parts of the United States to be in attendance. The consecration was reported on Indian TV news ("Parashakthi Temple Rajagopuram Opening on August 17th in USA," 2015) and in the *Detroit News*:

> Thousands of supporters from across Metro Detroit and around the world—including those who identify with other religions— flocked there this month to celebrate the official grand opening for an edifice they say transcends earthly boundaries. "The fact that this Rājagopuram is in America is a very special and auspicious thing," Ayesha Khan, a musician living in Texas, said while wearing all white nearby on a recent evening. "It shows this unification of all people, regardless of race, color, ethnicity. It's very exciting." (Hicks 2015)

The *rajagopuram* contains on its four faces 520 embedded stone images, called *vigrahas*, of Hindu deities. Kumar and the temple board oversaw the construction of the *rajagopuram* and the placement of each *vigrahas*, with an Indian *sthapati*, a traditional temple architect named Santhana Krishnan, and several *shilpi*s executing its production. Kumar insists, however, that the Goddess herself identified through direct revelation to him each *vigraha* that had to be installed. Kumar also insists the Goddess commanded that the *rajagopuram* be constructed according to her precise directions to intensify the channeling of her healing and protective energy more effectively to the Western world in keeping with the mission of the temple. For this to happen, Kumar has noted on several occasions, the Goddess demanded that Vishvakarma, a Hindu deity who functions as a divine architect, would himself have to do the construction as only Vishvakarma was qualified to lead it, although Kumar would be acting on the human level on the Goddess's behalf. Kumar noted in his talk on New Year's Day in 2021, for example:

> She said, "I need Vishvakarma to participate in what we are doing."
> How do you invoke Vishvakarma? He is a cosmic person. He is not a
> human. He is a divine being. She said, "I will make him come. Here
> is a mantra. You do a special *homa*. You invite the [earthly] architect
> [Santhana Krishnan] and do the *homa* exactly the way I want it, and
> there, you invoke Vishvakarma. . . . So, we had our *sthapati* [archi-
> tect] come here and do the *homa*. ("Dr. Krishnakumar's Speech on
> New Year 2021" 2021)

Kumar has declared on several occasions that while ordinarily humans build temples to reach the divine, in the case of the Parashakthi Temple—including its *rajagopuram*—the Divine has built structures to reach down to the human realm because "she knows the time is bad, and we need protection. This is a temple of protection."

In the earliest stages of construction, Kumar insists he did not know how many *vigrahas* would finally occupy the *rajagopuram*—at first he thought fifty, then 350, then 450—but in the end, he insists, the Goddess revealed to him the need to bring to the *rajagopuram* the energy of 520 deities, *devatas* (*devatās*), in order to properly channel her complete healing and protective energy to the earth. These 520 *devata*s, according to Kumar, represent the totality of all the divine energy in the universe. At the Parashakthi Temple, the *rajagopuram* functions the way several other sacred objects at the temple also

function to channel and transmit divine power, especially protective power. In a conversation I had with him in July 2015, Kumar also
noted that like other objects at the temple, the *rajagopuram* serves to
enhance the spiritual receptivity of all who set foot on temple-owned
land, serving as a kind of giant spiritual antenna that both draws divine energy to the temple and radiates it outward.

The *rajagopuram* is an architectural element most often associated with the grand temple complexes built by the South Indian royal
dynasties. George Michell notes that *gopuras*, "towered gateways,"
originated among the Pallavas (sixth–ninth centuries) in Tamil Nadu
and emerged as a dominant temple element by the time of the Pandyas
during the twelfth century (Michell 1977, 150). He observes further
that gopuras functioned as gateways to temple grounds and became
increasingly important as large temple complexes, with defensive
walls built around them, began to absorb more community functions
(Michell 1977, 151–155). A *rāja-* or "royal" *gopura* or *gopuram* is the
tallest among a temple's *gopuras* and marks the entrance to the temple
itself. While several art historians have discussed the *rajagopuram*
in the context of South Indian temple styles (e.g., Kramrisch 1976;
Michell 1977), little has been written about their religious significance.
Samuel K. Parker notes that at its simplest, the *rajagopuram* functions
as a sign indicating the location of the temple, "just like the sign that
you put in front of your house to let people know where you live"
(Parker 2009, 152). In an interview I conducted with Kumar in 2013,
he claimed the location of the Parashakthi Temple's *rajagopuram* just
outside the temple was in fact significant, but for a different reason. He
noted that the Goddess wants the energy embodied in the *rajagopuram*
to reach anyone who might come near to it or even look at it from a
distance—in Hindu terms, get *darshan* of the *rajagopuram*—even if
they are not Hindu or even religiously inclined. Kumar's remarks echo
in some ways Parker's observance in his discussion of the construction of new *gopuras* in South India that traditional temple architects
continue to construct new *gopuras* with reference to former caste
restrictions, where "people who are not allowed to have the lord's *darshan* ('sight') inside the temple can take *darshan* of his or her image
on the *gopuram*" (Parker 2009, 158). At the Parashakthi Temple, however, the limitation to be overcome is understood as one that is not

socially imposed but is instead related to spiritual development. The Goddess wants to reach outward to help and protect all humans and hence strives to overcome potential resistance or lack of religious interest by having this spiritually powerful structure built in a location where it can radiate energy even to those who do not actively seek it. One Euro-American man active in a Michigan-based environmental organization claimed when he attended the *ragagopuram* installation that he saw "a thousand arrows" coming out of the *rajagopuram* at the time it was ritually consecrated, noting that this was "Divine Mother's energy going out in all directions" (interview, August 2015).

There are many distinctive elements to this *rajagopuram*'s design. For example, the collection of 520 *vigrahas* that adorn the tower's four faces is, I have been told, unique to this location since each is said to have been chosen by the Goddess herself, revealed one by one over the course of almost three years. Kumar proclaims that the Goddess wanted these *vigrahas* to be placed on the *rajagopuram* so that the individual energy of each could be brought to the temple site. A booklet distributed at the *kumbhabhishekam* or "Grand Opening" celebration for the installation of the *rajagopuram* in August of 2015 claims:

> Periodically, the world goes through [a] major crisis, at which times, the Divine manifests in various forms and protects the world. The reason for the Rājagopuram, as foretold by the Divine Mother, is that the whole world is going to go through major turmoil in the current millennium, and She has manifested to protect the world and promote global love, peace and harmony at [the] Parashakthi Temple which is a vortex of energy. . . . Divine Mother revealed the need for her "Powerful Aspects" to be installed at the Temple. Since it would be physically impossible to build 520 Sannidhanams (Sanctums), she revealed the need to have them on the Rājagopuram. This makes the Gopuram unique. ("Rajagopuram Devi Parashakthi Temple" n.d., 12)

The booklet distributed around the time that the *rajagopuram* was ritually consecrated lists all 520 *vigrahas* and shows photos of each ("Rajagopuram Devi Parashakthi Temple" n.d., 27–34), noting that the list includes some that are "rare, unknown aspects of the Divine" (12).

There are other unique elements to the *rajagopuram*. For example, the entire structure is said to have been made of granite from a single mountain and a single quarry in India that Kumar insists the Goddess herself chose since it served as a repository of her dormant energy. Furthermore, the installation booklet declares that the granite was mostly chiseled out by hand instead of being blasted out—which, Kumar noted to me, added a great deal of time and expense to the project—because the Goddess wanted to minimize the chances of destructive energy making its way into the stone and hence demanded that it be removed to the extent possible without the use of any kind of explosive device ("Rajagopuram Devi Parashakthi Temple" n.d., 13, 15; conversation with Kumar, August 2015). Kumar told me that the Goddess demanded this because one of the deities to be installed on the *rajagopuram* is "pure love and compassion. She does not know violence. That act [of blasting out stone] is a violence to her because trillions of organisms will die if you use TNT . . . So, the poor *sthapati* has an extra fifty people carving out the granite by hand" (interview, July 2012).

The *rajagopuram* is fifty-four feet high and contains "nearly 3,000 stone carvings weighing 450 tons" ("Rajagopuram Devi Parashakthi Temple" n.d., 13; see Figure 3.4). A formal consecration rite was done for each of the 520 *vigrahas* placed on the *rajagopuram* so that each would be the living energy of the deity placed there and not just a stone image ("Significance of Devi Mahamariamman" 2022, 2:52). The booklet makes the claim that "a complete granite stone architecture both as a structural support and for deities has never been accomplished before," asserting that the stone out of which the *rajagopuram* was made enhances its spiritual efficacy:

> The natural stone on our Rajagopuram resonates with nature and the Panchabhootas- Five basic elements, i.e., Earth, Water, Fire, Air, and Akasha (Ether [or Space]) creating an antenna-like effect radiating the entire planet with powerful "ripples" of energy to activate Global peace, Harmony, and Protection. ("Rajagopuram Devi Parashakthi Temple" n.d., 13)

The base layer of the structure is a lotus representing the *muladhara* (*mūlādhāra*) *cakra*, the "root" *cakra* or center of energy described as

Figure 3.4 Devotees outside the *rajagopuram* in 2015

residing in the human at the base of the spine in kundalini (*kuṇḍalinī*) yoga traditions, with the structure itself imagined as a divine body. Here the influence of *shakta* tantra is again obvious. Gavin Flood observes that in tantra the body functions as a "root metaphor" serving as a vehicle for conceptualizing "tradition and cosmos" such that the structure of the cosmos replicates itself in the structure of the body (Flood 2006, 4–5). The body becomes, says Flood, a "cosmography" or a "writing of the cosmos" (28). In both Shri Vidya and Kashmir Shaivism in particular, the two tantric schools that have most heavily influenced Kumar and therefore shaped the theology promulgated in Parashakthi Temple discourse, the Divine is singular at the highest level but polarizes itself into male and female aspects; the created world results from the interaction between these two gendered polarities, which pervade creation at every level. In the human body, the Goddess dwells as a specific kind of *shakti*, the kundalini, envisioned as a coiled serpent residing at the base of the spine. The kundalini is both the Goddess and a psychospiritual energy that can move up and down various energy centers in the body, the *cakras*, uniting with the divine male energy that resides at the level of pure consciousness, *purusha*, often identified with Shiva (see also Flood 2006; Silburn 1988; White 2003). In a temple talk Kumar gave in July of 2021, he claimed:

> This temple is a kundalini temple. If your kundalini had not woken up, you would not be here. But you have to take it up and use it to activate your *nadis* (*nāḍis*) [bodily channels of spiritual energy]. You have to make the kundalini go up and down and experience the journey. . . . Ultimately, any knowledge is through kundalini. This place is full of kundalini deities (*devatas*). They are very active here.
> (Devi Parashakthi Temple Facebook video 1, July 7, 2021)

Kundalini yoga is, in essence, a spiritual reversal of the process of creation (Brown 2002, 10) that functions as a basic paradigm for the process of spiritual liberation; it is a return to a primordial unity that transcends all duality and all creation, embodied in the duality of male and female, god and goddess, pure consciousness—as the male *purusha*—and manifestations of the Goddess as *shakti*. As I note in the introduction, one of the main missions of the Parashakthi Temple is to facilitate this kind of spiritual journey by providing a space where devotees can access the *shakti* needed to instigate this kind of spiritual transformation.

At the Parashkathi Temple, deities are placed on the *rajagopuram* in an ascending spiritual order that is meant to denote the unfolding of consciousness during meditation until the achievement of "self-realization" or liberation, *moksha* ("Rajagopuram Devi Parashakthi Temple" n.d., 15). Hence, the *rajagopuram* embodies, in granite form, the spiritual journey that the temple encourages in all its devotees. The *rajagopuram* is also a "gross" or material manifestation of the Goddess herself. The installation booklet proclaims:

> This structure is called "Sthula Lingam" or gross energy form. Divine Mother Parashakthi our primary deity in the main sanctum will be 'Sukshma lingam' or subtle energy form. Rajagopuram (Sthula Lingam) is not a mere structure but a manifested form of unmanifested primary energy source, Divine Mother or Sukshma

Lingam, and an embodiment of primal energy of Devi Parashakthi. ("Rajagopuram Devi Parashakthi Temple" n.d., 14)

Each of the four sides of the structure is dedicated to a different form of divinity: the west contains forms of Vishnu; the north, Brahma; the south, Shiva; and the east, Parashakthi, with the totality of the structure embodying the five major divine roles of creation, maintenance, dissolution, concealment, and revelation ("Rajagopuram Devi Parashakthi Temple" n.d., 14).

In a talk that Kumar gave at the temple when the *rajagopuram* was consecrated on August 23, 2015, he claimed that the tower's energy was such that it would enable humankind to achieve a higher level of consciousness by "taking human evolution to the next level." He compared the contemporary world to a "dirty pond" and the *rajagopuram* to a lotus as represented by its base, claiming that it would function to elevate humankind out of the "dirty pond:"

> The *rajagopuram* is for the world. She [Divine Mother] said, "Bring me the way I want to be brought. I will touch my devotees all over the world. And I will make them grow to the next level of consciousness." . . . The *rajagopuram* will help us because it will bring the *devatas* to our level of consciousness and bless us—bless the world— so that we can evolve intellectually and spiritually—go to the next level of consciousness.

At the bottom of one of the slides that Kumar presented during this talk, he noted, "Gopura darisanam koti punyam"—that is, "*darshan* of the *rajagopuram* will give you ten million times of spiritual merit." He explained to the audience of devotees that if they look upon the *rajagopuram* with faith and understanding, knowing what it means, they will receive the amount of spiritual benefit that would normally take many lifetimes to achieve.

The *rajagopuram* is adorned with nine slightly different versions of the Shri Cakra (*śrīcakra*), also called Shri Yantra (*śrīyantra*), the quintessential Hindu representation of *shakti* in *mandala* form (see Figure 3.5).

Figure 3.5 One of the Shri Cakras on the *rajagopuram*

In the Shri Vidya tradition, the Shri Cakra is recognized as a geometrically embodied form of the Goddess Lalita Tripurasundari ("Beautiful Goddess of the Three Worlds") and a cosmogram, a map of the created universe from the moment of its emanation from a single, unformed dot to its current state. The Shri Cakra consists of nine essential layers: there is a central triangle with a dot, or *bindhu*, in the middle followed by four concentric series of triangles, two layers of lotus petals, and three layers of circles, all set in a square base. The Shri Cakra therefore has nine "enclosures" or "levels," called *avaranas* (*āvaraṇas*), encoded in its design, with deities who constitute the goddess's retinue inhabiting all nine levels. In Shri Vidya theology, the five downward-facing triangles of the Shri Cakra represent the Goddess, while the four upward-facing triangles represent her male aspect as Shiva (Brooks 1990, 107). The Parashakthi Temple's website, however, describes the downward-facing triangles on the *rajagopuram's* Shri Cakras as representing "overflowing divine grace" and the upward-facing triangles as embodying "the urge of the soul to reach Her." It further claims that the unique stone design on the *rajagopuram* "envisioned by Dr. G Krishna Kumar under the guidance of Divine Mother" is the only location in the world that has come to contain, through proper ritual installation, all nine different *avaranas* (levels) in one location. Hence, worshipping the Goddess at the Parashakthi Temple through means of the Shri Cakra "channels energy of our soul or self towards Cosmic union with 'Her.'" Normally, invoking the energy inherent in a Shri Cakra to access its power and receive its blessings would require the performance of the Shri Cakra *puja* or, at minimum, the recitation of specific mantras. Because all the deities of the nine *avaranas* of the Shri Cakra are already actively present on the *rajagopuram*, however, the temple's website maintains that simply having *darshan* of the *rajagopuram* is sufficient to obtain the Shri Cakra's religious gifts—but only if the devotee is spiritually receptive and ready to receive them (Parashakthi Temple: "Sri Chakra Nava Avarana representation on our Rajagopuram").

Kumar has said in several public talks during the years since the *rajagopuram* installation that neither he nor anyone else involved in the consecration of the *rajagopuram* can recall any of the mantras that he used to enliven the structure. Hence, while the physical structure can be reproduced, the power now inherent in it can never be reproduced. In his 2021 New Year's Day talk, Kumar noted:

> Strange thing: it's a very beautiful mantra she gave [me] to invoke [Vishvakarma]. I cannot even remember one *bija* (syllable). Usually, you remember one or two *bijas* sometimes in a mantra. It is gone completely, strangely—because I know so many mantras. How could I not even remember a couple of *bijas*? No. It's gone forever ... That means, this (*rajagopuram*) cannot be rebuilt. ("Dr Krishnakumar's Speech on New Year 2021" 2021)

Both Kumar and the *rajagopuram* architect, Santhana Krishnan, have said in public presentations at the temple that devotees from Tamil Nadu who came to the Parashakthi Temple in Michigan wanted to reproduce it in Mumbai, so they asked Santhana Krishnan if he could do it. Krishnan allegedly told them he could rebuild the structure, but without the *mantra* he could not recreate the *rajagopuram* with its power since any reproduction would lack the involvement of Vishvakarma. Hence, any reproduction would be lifeless as the Goddess had erased from human memory the mantra needed to imbue it with *shakti*. Santhana Krishnan told me in an interview I conducted with him in August 2022 that while most of the temples he constructs are for their sponsoring communities, this one was constructed by and for the Goddess. He asserted: "Mother told Vishvakarma, and only then Vishvakarma created this *rajagopuram*." In a talk now on YouTube that Kumar gave at the temple in June of 2021, he elaborated on this point:

> There is a man in Bombay [Mumbai] who saw the *rajagopuram* and wanted it built in Bombay, and our *sthapati* told him he cannot do it. So naturally, he got upset, so the *sthapathi* he called me ... I told the *sthapati*, "You have to tell him everything." He said, "What is everything?" I told him, "Before you start building the temple, you have to have a special *homa*. That *homa* has to be done in the presence of Vishvakarma. So, she [the Goddess] gave a mantra of Vishvakarma. Do you know I do not remember even one *bija* of that. . . . You need Vishvakarma, the heavenly architect. Who can hire him? He's a

cosmic person. Here [at the Parashakthi Temple], she [the Goddess] made him come and do this. So, this is very unique.... So, I told [the *sthapati*], call him and explain this to him, at least he will have peace, why do you refuse to do that? Not out of malice. You *cannot* do that. You can if you can hire Vishvakarma. But who can hire Vishvakarma? She [the Goddess] did. Only she can do it. ("Importance of Gouri Kund and Its Relevance to Creation" 2021)

It is notable that several pages (2–10) toward the front of the installation booklet reproduce letters of enthusiasm and support sent to the temple by US local, state, and national elected officials serving at that time, including the Oakland county treasurer (Andy Meisner), the mayor of Pontiac (Deirdre Waterman), the governor of Michigan at (Rick Snyder), both US Senators from Michigan (Debbie Stabenow and Gary C. Peters), and four congressional members of the US House of Representatives, including Tulsi Gabbard, the only Hindu member of congress at the time. The placement of these supportive letters at the front of the booklet suggests that the Goddess and her power, as manifest in the *rajagopuram*, have received an official welcome onto US soil at local, state, and federal levels.

Perhaps the most distinctive aspect of this *rajagopuram* is the golden box that is now buried in the southeast corner, the corner of Agni, deity of fire, who is associated with both transformation and communication. In Vedic sacrificial traditions and ongoing Hindu temple *homa* practices, Agni is considered a divine messenger who transforms sacrificial offerings into smoke to nourish the gods and carries human prayers to them. The box buried in Agni's corner is an object called *shakti garbha* or *shakthi garbha*, "the womb of Shakti," that mimics the Israelite Ark of the Covenant. In 2013, Kumar brought this object back from India allegedly at the Goddess's behest. Kumar claims that the Goddess had revealed to him back in 2012 the need for a box-like object that would function to energize the *rajagopuram* and make it effective. Kumar claims that she also revealed to him what it would look like and commanded him to get it made according to her instruction.

On one of the many trips he took to India, Kumar recounted to me in a conversation we had in August of 2013, that he met a *siddha* near Rishikesh who said he could get such an object for Kumar through a contact he had in South India. Santana Krishnan, the *sthapati* hired to oversee construction of the *rajagopuram*, coordinated the making of the *shakti garbha* according to the instructions that Kumar passed on. Kumar says he does not know who made it and notes that he did have to pay for it, but when I pressed him on this point, he noted only that he did not pay very much. Kumar reported, too, in a temple talk he gave in August 2012 that the *shakti garbha* would have to be filled with sixty substances that he would have to collect. In our August 2013 conversation, Kumar told me that among the items were several herbs and roots that had to be obtained from the Kolli Hills in Tamil Nadu. Kumar claims that Krishnan coordinated the collection of items, which also included Vaishnava, Shaiva, and Shakta symbols—that is, symbolic elements associated with Vishnu, Shiva, and the Goddess, the three most widely revered deities in Hinduism. These objects included, for example, a small trident, a miniature version of an object that Shiva carries; a conch shell, which is used in Vishnu worship; soil from various natural bodies (like ant hills, lakes, mountains, and oceans); gems and metals; eight types of aromatic herbs; eight types of medicinal herbs; and other sacred objects, some of which are considered secret and are not to be revealed to the public. These sixty items were ritually consecrated in the *shakti garbha* in July of 2015. Kumar claims that these sixty substances all together contain all the seeds of creation and hence are all that would be needed to recreate the universe if it were to be destroyed. The *shakti garbha* itself contains twenty-five chambers representing the twenty-five elements, the *tattva*s that constitute the created universe (see Figure 3.6).

The temple has promulgated through Kumar's public talks, temple literature, and the temple's main website the equation of the *shakti garbha* with the "Ark of the Covenant" described first in the Hebrew Bible and elaborated in later Jewish and Christian sources. When Kumar first made this equation, he told me he was not completely satisfied with it, although it is by now an established, official part of temple discourse. He reported to me in our August 2013 conversation that after the *shakti garbha* was made according to his instructions, Krishnan—the *sthapati* he had hired to make the *rajagopuram* and coordinate the creation of the *shakti garbha* according to Kumar's instructions—immediately exclaimed that the object looked like

Figure 3.6 The top and bottom of the *shakthi garbha* with a temple priest placing items in the base

the Ark of the Covenant, at least according to artists' renditions of it. Kumar thought the parallel was meaningful, but he was unhappy with what he saw as the word's implication that punishment would be involved for those who choose to break the covenant, as detailed in the Hebrew Bible. For Kumar, Divine Mother is never punishing. When Kumar first spoke about the *shakti garbha* both publicly, in the 2012 temple talk, and in the conversation I had with him about it in 2013, he noted that nevertheless he then continued to use the word "covenant" because, he said, "In a historical way, the only thing I can connect and compare that would be the Ark of Covenant, the Ark of Covenant that was given to Moses."

In the book of Exodus (25:10–22) in the Hebrew Bible, God is said to reveal to Moses instructions for making a receptacle to contain the stone tablets on which were to be inscribed (and later reinscribed after the original tablets were destroyed) the Ten Commandments proclaimed at Mt. Sinai. This became widely known as the "Ark of the Covenant," with the term "ark" here indicating a "chest" or receptacle. Exodus 25:10 describes the ark as two and a half cubits long, one and a half cubits high, and one and a half cubits wide (approximately 45 x 27 x 27 inches, assuming a biblical cubit is about 18 inches). It was to be made of acacia wood but covered in gold both inside and out, with gold rings at each of its four feet for poles to be attached so that it could be carried (Exodus 25:11–12). God commands that his "testimony," the Ten Commandments, be placed inside the ark, which is to be covered with a cover or lid made of pure gold (Exodus 25:16). Two cherubim, angelic beings, are to be fashioned on each end of the lid and placed facing each other, spreading their wings upward, and looking down to the lid (Exodus 25:20–21). The cherubim function both to guard the ark and to form a throne for God's presence to dwell above the lid, with the tablets containing the Ten Commandments at God's feet. God announces he will come to dwell there in that place just above the ark and between the cherubim and from there will communicate with Moses and the rest of the Israelites (Exodus 25:22). The ark is thus described as the earthly embodiment of God's concentrated presence, moral instruction, and divine power, bridging the divide between God and human devotees.

Numbers 10:33–36 claims that the Israelites carried the ark with them when they left Sinai; God also journeyed alongside the ark and the Israelites in the form of a cloud. Hence we also find "accounts of the miracles that occurred alongside the ark—the drying up of the waters of the Jordan when the ark preceded the people (Josh. 3–4) and the fall of the walls of Jericho after the ark encircled them seven times (Josh. 6)" (Grintz and Freedman 2007, 467). The ark is associated with military victory and conquest, as its presence in the Israelite camp is viewed as ensuring God's help in battle. The ark eventually came to rest in the first temple in Jerusalem, although the fate of the ark after the first temple's destruction is not known. When it came to reside in the Jerusalem temple, "there were apparently no cherubim on the ark cover, but two, ten cubits in height and made of olive wood overlaid with gold, stood on the floor in front of the ark" (Grintz and Freedman, 466).

God's divine presence, his Shekhinah, is also said to come to dwell at the first temple. The Ark's associations with divine power, especially military might, and its mysterious disappearance after the destruction of the first temple served as inspiration for the 1981 hit film *Raiders of the Lost Ark*, in which the fictional character Indiana Jones heads up a US Government attempt to locate and take possession of the Ark of the Covenant before the Nazis are able to find it and thereby access its incredible power, which might enable them to succeed in taking over the world. Christian traditions later equated Mary, the mother of Jesus, with the Ark of the Covenant; just as the original Ark had been a unique vessel blessed with the ability to contain God's power and moral teaching, so Mary was the "new" Ark of the Covenant, able to contain divinity and the new covenant (embodied as Jesus) within her body (Livius 1893, 76, 77).

The *shakti garbha* installed at the Parashakthi Temple is gilded, as the Ark of the Covenant is said to have been; on the top, instead of cherubim, sit two lions, representing, as one devotee wrote to me in an email, "The beast qualities of a human being and how the Divine Mother will help us conquer that beast and use it for the welfare of society" (private email, October 28, 2015). Like the Ark of the Covenant, the *shakti garbha* has rings around the edge for staves to be inserted so it can be carried. When the Ark was installed in the first temple in Jerusalem, it is said to have been given a special place in the Holy of Holies, the inner sanctum, where it resided "at the exact center of the whole world;" in front of it stood the "foundation stone" that was described later in Rabbinic commentary as "the starting point of the creation of the world" (Grintz and Freedman 2007, 468). Similarly, at the Parashakthi Temple, the installed *shakti garbha* represents the new world center, the womb that contains creation in microcosmic form. One devotee actively involved in the temple even described Kumar as the new Moses, founding a new religious movement that would now grow following the installation of the *shakti garbha* and *rajagopuram*. The *rajagopuram* consecration booklet describes the *shakti garbha* as the "universal ark of covenant" whose mission is "BUILDING and BRIDGING peace BETWEEN NATIONS and Individual spirit covenant with the Divine." The goal of this new, "Cosmic Covenant" is the "illumination of mind and spirit, leading to connection with supreme spirit" ("Rajagopuram Devi Parashakthi Temple" n.d., 44). On a web page that no longer exists, the Parashakthi Temple website noted:

> Similar to the ark in the ancient Jewish tradition, the sacred garbha box containing 60 materials will be made with gold, silver, brass, along with other mystical materials with cosmic energies will be placed in the holiest of places in the stone engraving of the Rājagopuram as instructed by Divine Mother Parashakthi. The garbha, in which are preserved the germs of all things necessary to repopulate the earth, including many mystically energized herbs and metals, representing the survival of life, and the supremacy of spirit over matter. Prophet Moses received the instructions for making the Ark of Covenant by God and Solomon's Temple, also known as the First Temple, was the main temple in ancient Jerusalem that housed the Ark of Covenant. The chest was said to be a source of miraculous power. . . . At our temple as designed by Divine Mother, the Shakthi Garbha which is the source of all energies will have miraculous powers that will bring immense spiritual and material benefits to Devotees and make the *rājagopuram* at Parashakthi Temple one of the holiest places in the world. (Parashakthi Temple, "Shakthi Garbha or Ark of the Covenant")

The *shakti garbha*, like the Ark of the Covenant, also embodies an ethical agreement between Goddess and devotees such that "Human Beings will follow Satya ('Truthfulness') and Dharma ('Righteousness')" ("Rajagopuram Devi Parashakthi Temple" n.d., 44). It represents a new moral contract that will enable humankind to navigate the murky, dangerous waters of modern times.

Material Theology at the Parashakthi Temple

Many scholars of material culture have noted that what objects, including religious objects, "mean" often cannot be separated from the specific relational, historical, and material contexts in which they come to be embedded. In her study of material Christianity, Colleen Mcdannell observes that people "need objects to help establish and maintain relationships" not only with other people—friends and family, for example—but also with supernatural characters (e.g., Mcdannell 1995, 272). At the Parashakthi Temple, the Goddess, too, needs objects to "help establish and maintain relationships" between herself and her human devotional community. Through objects and structures, the Goddess establishes her power in the manifest world and makes it available to her creation. She cannot do this, however, without the intervention of the humans she chooses to bring her power down to earth through ritual action. The divine, the human, and the material realms are implicated in an indissoluble web of performative relationships that allow divine power to become manifest differentially in specific, divinely chosen substances, structures, and locales and to take up residence at the temple and its grounds.

Flueckiger emphasizes what she calls the "agency of context" (2020, 210) pertaining to materials by drawing on A. K. Ramanujan's well-known description of Indian culture as tending to be "context-sensitive" more than "context-free" (Ramanujan 1989). Ramanujan observes that some grammatical formulations are free of contextual rules (e.g., sentences always have a subject and predicate), but others are dependent on context (e.g., how to indicate a plural depends on the term: "cat" becomes "cats," but "child" becomes "children"). He applies such grammar rules analogously to cultural phenomena, concluding that Indian culture tends to be shaped by rules that are more context-dependent than context-free (Ramanujan 1989, 47). Flueckiger articulates a vision of material agency that is similarly "context-dependent," noting, for example, that "the materiality of a sari will create differently if it is worn on a male or a female body, or if it is worn by a woman working in the fields or a woman at an upper-class wedding" (2020, 209). Such agency of context is abundantly on display at the Parashakthi Temple. Every object, every *murti*, and every structure at the temple that is imbued with divine power is so imbued only insofar as it has been ritually prepared for, installed, and consecrated in temple space.

Morgan observes that the agency of religious objects is not encased in the things themselves but is instead "made to happen by a variety of enabling circumstances—an encompassing ecology. . . . The shape of materiality is webs. Objects, spaces, and people are nodes within these webs that mediate the relations among individuals, groups, and entire networks:"

> The agency of things in religious experience is perhaps most apparent in the way they engage human beings. Objects, spaces, and places invite, threaten, scare, comfort, and inspire people interacting with them. And for this reason, people form relationships with such things that endure over time and shape personal and social life. (Morgan 2021, 22)

A religiously meaningful thing, therefore, is actually "a network or assemblage, a gathering of many human and nonhuman actors" that cannot be reduced to the physicality of the thing itself and that is "always more than humans can perceive or control" (Morgan 2021, 183). Religious objects can function as what Morgan calls focal objects, "places where a number of strands fuse, enabling access to the broader network" (Morgan 2021, 184). Altars, devotional images, wands, talismans, and other objects may function this way in various religious contexts. People imbue focal objects with the power to function as one aspect of that network and to serve as the part "through which they address the whole" (Morgan 2021, 185–186).

At the Parashakthi Temple, the Goddess, the objects she chooses to transmit her *shakti*, and the humans she calls to her service all function to anchor her in the material realm and spread forth her demon-destroying, grace-giving potency. The Goddess, her faithful "mailman" Kumar, the chosen architects and craftsmen, and temple devotees all function, to use Morgan's term, as human "nodes" in the "encompassing ecology" of divine power that takes up residence in Pontiac. Once established, temple objects become themselves agents wielding divine power. The temple's objects and structures become focal vectors of *shakti* forged from the network of relationships that exist between the gross and subtle realms and extend across the globe.

4

Ritual Crossings/Wind

Performing Religion

I arrived at the temple later than I had hoped to arrive in late August of 2022, right in the middle of the week-long celebrations taking place for the temple's grand reopening. I had not been to Pontiac in person for about two years at that point and was a bit nervous about what I would find and how I would fit into the community. The temple fire and the COVID-19 pandemic had interrupted my research and writing plans, and heavy traffic and highway construction en route that day had delayed my arrival. When I pulled into the parking lot, there was a small crowd gathered at the front steps performing a *homa* in front of the temple entrance. As soon as I arrived, several devotees that I knew from previous years came up to greet me and welcome me back to the Goddess's abode. Although driving through the gates to the parking lot felt like coming home in a lot of ways, I drove up to a vastly different, much larger, grander temple structure than the one I had begun visiting and studying in 2007.

Over the fifteen years I spent studying this temple, I noticed an increasing South Indianization and tantricization of both its community of devotees and its religious practices. By 2022, the same core devotional group was still, for the most part, deeply involved in temple life, although some individuals who had been dedicated temple volunteers were no longer engaged, and new individuals had joined the temple board and executive committee. Several of the North Indian devotees I had met on earlier visits had dropped away, and on this visit, almost everyone I met who was of South Asian heritage hailed originally from one of the South Indian states. Many were first-generation professionals who had traveled from various parts of the United States—including California, Florida, and a variety of Midwestern states—to attend the new temple's grand opening, the

Goddess Beyond Boundaries. Tracy Pintchman, Oxford University Press. © Oxford University Press 2024.
DOI: 10.1093/oso/9780190673017.003.0005

kumbhabhishekam; some had even flown in from India as news of the temple's reopening had spread in Tamil Nadu, Karnataka, Telangana, and Andhra Pradesh. I began to settle in for what turned out to be five days of almost non-stop ritual performance lasting from early morning until almost midnight.

Indian Hindu temples, especially South Indian or South Indian-inspired temples, are, in general, places that abound in religious activity, and the Parashakthi Temple is no exception. Ronald Grimes, one of the foremost scholars of ritual theory, has argued that the term "ritual" refers to the "general idea" of which rites are specific instances: "ritual" is, says Grimes, a scholarly concept, what one refers to in formal definitions, while "rites are what people enact." Hence, he argues, ritual itself does not exist except as an idea that scholars formulate (Grimes 1990, 9–11). Following Grimes, I will use the term "rite" to refer to the formal, public practices that occur at the temple on a regular basis. I retain the word "ritual" in the title of this chapter, however, because it addresses the "general idea" of religious practice, only one example of which is specific temple rites. Furthermore, at the Parashakthi Temple, devotees seem thoroughly undisturbed by academic machinations surrounding ritual terminology and use the term "ritual" frequently to describe their own religious activities and all the formal practice that priests and other religious functionaries perform on site. Hence, for many of the Goddess devotees with whom I spoke, the distinction between "rite" and "ritual" is meaningless.

Kumar has noted in temple lectures he has delivered that the gap between humans and the divine realm is immense, but the Goddess wants us to reach her despite the enormous gap that exists between her realm and the embodied, mortal realm. Temple rites and other forms of religious activity are the vehicle for bridging that gap. As I have already noted, Hindu tantric traditions emphasize the use of rites to access and harness *shakti* for spiritual as well as worldly benefit, and that emphasis is evident here. Kumar proclaimed in a temple talk posted to YouTube in 2022, for example:

We have to go through the rituals because the separation is too intense. We are sense-based organisms. And with senses you really cannot connect –all these supersensual beings, how do you break through and meet them? So, you need intense energy to take us through that journey so we go to higher levels of consciousness, supersensual consciousness. ("Significance of Devi Mahamariamman" 2022, 5:30)

Kumar sometimes uses financial imagery to speak about the spiritual progress needed to overcome this gap. In lectures he gave during 2021 and 2022, for example, he noted that one's physical body is merely what he called a "short-term rental," given we are all mortal and will have to leave the embodied realm behind when we die. Therefore, he encouraged devotees to make a "long-term investment" in a relationship with the temple and the Goddess to make the most effective use of one's "short-term rental." In a lecture given during the consecration celebration in August 2022, he drew on the Upanishadic distinction between a "good life" and a "pleasant life," urging devotees to choose the good life, as it would give a greater "return on investment" over the course of many rebirths. He also has remarked on numerous occasions that the performance of all forms of religious action performed at the Parashakthi Temple or for the benefit of the temple, where the Goddesses's *shakti* is at its strongest, is a means to making spiritual progress; through a variety of forms of action, especially when done with the right intent, one is able to effect self-transformation and progress on the spiritual journey to which the Goddess has called her human worshipers.

Grimes uses the term *ritualizing* to suggest the process of deliberately cultivating or inventing rites, and *ritualization* to refer to activity that is not always culturally framed as ritual (such as television watching) but that, in certain contexts, an observer may come to interpret as though it were ritual (Grimes 1990, 9–11). *Ritualizing*, for Grimes, is a term that is meant to refer to processes that "fall below the threshold of social recognition of rites" (10). Bell argues for thinking of ritual not in terms of discrete acts but instead as actions performed via strategies of "ritualization," which she understands to be "a way of acting that differentiates some acts from others" (Bell [1992] 2009, xv). Kumar articulates a similar perspective on the nature of religiously efficacious activity: he portrays mundane acts such as donating money to the temple, writing about the temple, volunteering to help with or blog about events, or taking photos at important temple functions, along with the performance of meditation, mantra recitation, and participation in temple rites, to all be spiritually meritorious actions that can contribute to one's spiritual evolution. As Grimes notes, the practical contexts of ritual criticism include "emic," or insider, discourse about the meaning of rites and other forms of religious practice in which individuals engage (Grimes 1990, 19). In the case of the Parashakthi Temple, Kumar and others articulate their own, indigenous understanding of what constitutes religious practice, the purpose of such practice, and the effects that such practice has on those who perform it.

Kumar and other temple officials also often invoke the theme of "sacrifice" when talking about meaningful religious action. The idea that religiously meritorious action constitutes a form of sacrifice permeates Parashakthi Temple discourse. In a public talk that Kumar gave during a festival in July 2013, for example, he noted themes pertaining to religious practice that I have heard numerous times over the years in which I have been involved in the temple:

> Grace comes by your devotion, by your worship, by coming and doing. Ultimately, it goes back to sacrifice. What's dearest to you, you give her, and she gives a thousand times more to you.... She always tells me, "I prepare the food. If anyone comes to my house, there the food is placed in front of them." But consumption comes from you. You have to take the food and put it in your mouth and consume it and digest it. That is purely up to you. That comes from sacrifice ultimately.... To consume it, you have to show your love, your devotion.

Kumar understands "sacrifice" here in a particular manner. Demonstrating one's love or devotion requires performing some type of action, and actions done to show love or devotion entail offering up something that you yourself value or find desirable. Only by performing such actions are you able to "consume" the Goddess's grace. While traditionally, sacrificial meals constituted the actual consumption of food, often food offered to deities before being consumed by humans, here the "food" is understood as the Goddess's grace, which provides spiritual, not material, nourishment to the sacrificer. Kumar has noted as well in public discourses that the Parashakthi Temple's spiritual power derives at least in part from the sacrifices that Kumar and the other founders made to build the temple as per Divine Mother's wishes.

Rites and other forms of religious practice are also types of performance. Taking a performative perspective on religious rites and other religious practices, Catherine Bell argues, suggests "active rather than passive roles" for participants, who may both rework and "reinterpret value-laden symbols as they communicate them" (Bell 1997, 73). Ritual "does not simply express cultural values or enact symbolic scripts but actually effects changes in people's perceptions and interpretations," and Bell wants scholars to attend more closely to these effects:

> Several basic concepts are central to most performance approaches. First, ritual is an event, a set of activities that does not simply express cultural values or enact symbolic scripts but actually effects changes in people's perceptions and interpretations. Closely involved with this perspective on ritual events is an appreciation of the physical and sensual aspects of ritual activity. . . . Such theories attempt to grasp more of the distinctive physical reality of ritual so easily overlooked by more intellectual approaches. (1997, 73–74)

Elizabeth Collins, similarly, observes that thinking of ritual as performance requires sophistication in thinking through agency. She notes, "The model of performance implies several different agents and different kinds of agency. There is the agency of the author of the text, but also the agency of the performers who choose to perform a particular ritual or a particular variant of a ritual text and who may even revise the text or tradition in their performance. There is the agency of those who participate as audience" (Collins 1997, 183–184). Similarly, Mary Hancock notes in her work on women's domestic rites that religious practices "are performances attributed with the power to transform participants" (Hancock 1999, 22). Rites and other forms of religious practice are "creative strategies" that humans may use either to reproduce or to reshape their social and cultural environments (Bell 1997, 76). In other words, they can help individual religious actors not only appropriate but also modify cultural values and ideals that mold social identity (Bell 1997, 73, 82). Following Ronald Inden's observation that "actions make what order there is in the human world" (Inden 1990, 26), William Sax notes regarding his own research on performance in India that religious rites are "an important site for the construction of identities: in ritual, communities ... define and represent themselves and their constituent parts, both to themselves and to others" (Sax 2002, 49).

I adopt here a hermeneutic that emphasizes performance and the agency of religious actors and attends to emic interpretive perspectives on the purpose, meaning, and experience of religious rites and other forms of religious activity. I highlight in this chapter practices that temple discourse portrays as fulfilling four essential functions at the Parashakthi Temple. First, religious practice serves as a method for the Goddess to reveal herself to her devotees and permit them to "explore and experience her," which is now part of the temple's mission. Through participation in temple rites and other forms of religious performance, devotees come to experience the Goddess as a real and immensely powerful, albeit sensorily imperceptible, presence in their lives. Second, religious practice at the temple enacts and helps fortify the Goddess's and the community's emplacement in her "seat" in Pontiac. Bodies that engage in religious practices are "essential to the process of emplacement; *lived bodies belong to places* and help to constitute them" (Casey 1996, 24; italics are original). At the Parashakthi Temple, devotees engage in religious practice as an act of neoterritorialization. Temple rites both establish and reinforce in the minds of devotees both the nature of the temple as a uniquely powerful divine space and the nature of devotees' identities as members of the Goddess's devotional community. Third, at the Parashakthi Temple, religious practice functions as a means of helping devotees pass spiritually from the mundane realm, the *bhuloka* (*bhūloka*), to the divine realm, the *devaloka*. I have often heard Kumar and others at the temple describe the Parashakthi Temple as the entrance to *devaloka*, so coming to the temple and participating in its rites initiates processes of spiritual transformation. Oftentimes, engagement in religious performance at or in relation to the Parashakthi Temple is said to function as a form of spiritual work that alone transforms the practitioner and, by extension, the devotional community; it enables humans to move forward in their spiritual journey, "making you aware of [the Goddess] and activating her grace" (Kumar, temple talk, August 2015). Finally, religious practice functions to increase the temple's *shakti* and continually enhance the temple's spiritual power and efficacy, making this power consistently available in increasing intensity to all those able to "consume" it. For human actors, performing the work they need to do to produce this increase in power is not always pleasant or easy but is done to fulfill the Goddess's wishes. Without practices that continually supply, replenish, and enhance the temple's *shakti*, the temple risks becoming "lifeless," to use the language of temple discourse, which is something the Goddess would not wish to happen. The Goddess's power at this temple enables her to help devotees and protect the entire world, so ritual actors must carefully maintain and continually restock it. This means that religiously powerful temple objects, too, must be continually "recharged" through religious rites.

While an emphasis on the role of religious activity in accomplishing the four functions I outline above is not necessarily unique to the Parashakthi Temple, taken all together they suggest a situated, embedded, emic perspective on the purpose and power of religious practice that temple discourse articulates and propagates and that is influenced by, among other things, both vernacular, "village" Hindu practices and Hindu tantra. The tantric world "is a world of power, a world permeated by the power of the deity who manifests and animates it, a power that can be mastered and manipulated through ritual" (Padoux 2017, 114). White understands tantric practice broadly to encompass religious action done "to gain access to and appropriate the energy or enlightened consciousness of the absolute godhead that courses through the universe, giving its creatures life and the potential for salvation." He observes further that in tantra, humans "are empowered to realize this goal through strategies of embodiment" that cause divine energy to concentrate into "one or another sort of template, grid, or mesocosm" (White 2000, 8–9). The meditative recitation of powerful mantras is, as I have noted, a basic form of tantric practice. Tantra also often ritualizes mundane activities. Parashakthi Temple discourse promulgated in newsletters, emails, and Kumar's lectures adopts a broad, often diffuse tantric understanding of the purpose of all religious activity that is not explicitly tied to any specific Hindu tantric lineage.

Kumar has identified his own path as one of tantric *kriya* (*kriyā*) yoga. His spiritual practice has been most influenced by both Shri Vidya meditative techniques and by Kashmiri Shaiva traditions, especially those expounded by Abhinavagupta, a Kashmir Shaiva *tantrika* and philosopher from approximately the tenth to twelfth centuries CE. Abhinavagupta founded a tantric yoga lineage, the Kaula lineage, that stresses direct experience over doctrine or religious speculation (Muller-Ortega 1989, 4). Kumar also incorporates techniques of Kriya yoga, a form of yoga that Parmahansa Yogananda popularized in the West in his book, *Autobiography of a Yogi,* first published in 1946 and reprinted many times over. Yogananda moved to the United States when he was twenty-seven years old and established his organization, the Self Realization Fellowship, in 1920. In his autobiography, Yogananda insists that because of certain yogic injunctions, he could not "give a full explanation of *Kriya Yoga* in the pages of a book intended for the general public" (Yogananda [1946] 1987, 275). But he describes Kriya yoga as a form of meditation and breath control that moves the practitioner quickly toward spiritual liberation or "self-realization," the experience of one's unity with the divine (Yogananda [1946] 1987, 278–279). In his temple talks, Kumar frequently mentions "self-realization" as the ultimate goal of human life.

Kumar has forged from these and other sources his own path of religious practice, which he calls *prayogam.* The term *prayogam* is not widely used for Hindu meditative practice as far as I have been able to discern. Kumar described his practice of *prayogam* by referencing its description by Swami Rama, a twentieth-century Indian yoga guru infamous for sexually abusing some of his followers but known also for his alleged ability to control his brain waves. Kumar described it to me as a state beyond ordinary consciousness where one is interacting and communicating directly with divine forces (interviews, July 2012, July 2013):

This path is not just tantric. You must bring the deity inside and then communicate. See, yoga means you're in the divine. Kriya yoga means you go into their space and interact with them. Yogis want to unite, but they don't want to communicate and do things. . . . *Kriya yoga* means you go to the devatas' space. You go to the higher consciousness level and then communicate, worship them, and ask for what you want. The only thing I want is for people to get grace. . . . It's yoga because I'm using mantra, I'm using yantra, I'm using tantra. But once I go to the space, it becomes pure bhakti. I sacrifice myself to them.

In a talk he gave in 2010, Kumar noted that *prayogam* practice is very intense and can be dangerous for those who do not have, as he does, a mantra of protection (*kavaca*); he claims that he received his protective mantra directly from the Goddess. He noted in his conversation with me during my visit in October 2010:

Yoga is "union;" *prayogam* is activity after union. And that activity is risky activity. If you go into that world, you meet all kinds of deities after attaining *turiya* (*turīyā*) state [the "fourth state" of meditative awareness in which one achieves spiritual liberation]. So, you go into *samadhi* [*samādhi*, a high state of meditation] and peacefully join with the highest form. Do not look this way or that way. You just keep going straight to the shining one. This way and that way are full of demons.

On numerous occasions, Kumar has noted that the key to spiritual progress is "mantra," "yantra," and "tantra." In a document called "Pearls of Wisdom" that is posted on the Parashakthi Temple website (Parashakthi Temple, "Pearls of Wisdom"), Kumar describes yantra as awareness of the structure of the universe; mantra as the sound form of a deity and a repository of divine power; and tantra as a combination of worship and yogic *sadhana*, religious practice, that enables one to expand one's consciousness. Any action done with the correct intention falls under the broad umbrella of yantra, mantra, and tantra. Religious action is about journeying forth spiritually from the earthbound, mundane realm of human existence toward the disembodied, subtle, divine realms that exist beyond the more tangible realms signified symbolically by earth, water, and fire.

I explore here two broad types of religious performance regularly undertaken at or in conjunction with the temple: temple rites, including the regular practice of various kinds of rites performed in temple space; and the pilgrimage journeys that Kumar undertakes frequently not on his own behalf, but on behalf of all devotees, to enhance the presence of *shakti* and the availability of the Goddess's grace at the temple. While both temple rites and pilgrimage journeys are mainstream forms of Hindu religious practice, they come to be interpreted at the temple through a tantric-vernacular lens that fits the overall religious framing particular to this temple and its devotional community. I conclude with a section exploring the week of religious activity surrounding the rededication of the temple, which draws together these two arenas of religious practice. Ritual functions at the Parashakthi Temple, like the air or wind element, to enable movement that lies beyond the gross bodily senses. In Samkhya philosophy, the air or wind element in the body is the source of motion, which is necessary to maintain life. At the temple, rites facilitate the movement of *shakti* across borders and boundaries and, like the wind element in the body, maintain the circulation and movement that keeps the temple alive.

Rites at the Parashakthi Temple

Axel Michaels has noted that Hindu traditions are characterized by "ritual affluence," by which he means a "very elaborated habitual preference for ritual forms of communication and action" (Michaels 2016, 3–4). Nowhere is this truer than in Hindu temples, which, in general, abound in the performance of temple rites. The Parashakthi Temple is no exception. The temple employs on a regular basis three trained temple priests who have been serving at the temple for various lengths of time. The longest-serving priest still on staff in 2023 had been with the temple since 2008. As at other Hindu temples both in India and the United States, these temple priests are available to the temple community to perform a variety of home and personal ritual events, such as weddings, house warmings, the performance of life-cycle rituals, and so forth (Parashakthi Temple, "Our Priests"). Their main responsibility, however, is the performance of temple rites that occur at the temple daily, weekly, monthly, annually, or on special occasions. Kumar and other temple officials are almost always present at important temple rites and are often active participants along with the temple priests. Devotees come by the temple all day and evening to sit and meditate, pay their respects to a particular deity or deities, or just be in the Goddess's presence. But the largest crowds come for weekly, monthly, annual, or unique, one-time celebrations.

Michaels observes that Hindu rites, including Hindu temple rites, share several characteristics across a variety of contexts. First, they are often framed, meaning they are separated temporally from everyday life. Second, they are often formal, scripted, and governed by specific rules that prescribe how they should be conducted. Third, they are repetitive; that is, they recur over and over (Michaels 2016, 311–313). Sahila Kulshreshtha outlines several such types of practice that occur regularly at Hindu temples, including the Parashakthi Temple. These include the ritualized worship of temple icons; temple festivals and annual celebrations; music, dance, and drama performances; food offerings and feasts; and temple processions (Kulshreshtha 2023, 102).

At the Parashakthi Temple, as at other Hindu temples, temple priests perform the most basic form of Hindu devotional rite, *puja*, several times throughout the day, while special *pujas* to specific deities may be performed once a week or once a month. *Puja* includes chanting of prescribed mantras accompanied by offerings, including water, flowers, food, cloth, and incense. *Puja* is also usually accompanied by sounds like ringing bells, drumming, and blowing a conch shell. Temple *puja* generally culminates in *arati* (*ārati*), the offering of flame, and often includes the performance of *abhishekam*, bathing of the deity image (*murti*) with not just water, but also valued substances such as milk, yogurt, and sandalwood paste. *Arcana* (*arcanā*), a briefer, often informal version of *puja* performed by or on behalf of an individual or family, takes place throughout the day as devotees stop by the temple to offer their respects. These rites are, in general, sensorily rich occurrences that make "full use of the senses," as Eck has noted:

One "sees" the image of the deity (*darśan*). One "touches it with one's hands (*sparśa*), and one also "touches" the limbs of one's own body to establish the presence of various deities (*nyāsa*). One "hears" the sacred sounds of the mantras (*śravana*). The ringing of bells, the offering of oil lamps, the presentation of flowers, the pouring of water and milk, the sipping of sanctified liquid offerings, the eating of consecrated food—these are the basic constituents of Hindu worship, *pūjā*. (Eck 1981, 11–12)

The Parashakthi Temple also hosts numerous weekly and monthly events. On Wednesday evenings, for example, devotees can come chant the thousand names of Vishnu. Thursday evenings are for the performance of *abhishekam* to the South Indian deity Guruvayurappan, while on Saturdays devotees may come to the temple to perform *arcana* for Saturn (Shani) specifically or the nine planets generally. On Sundays, devotees can sponsor an *abhishekam* to the deity Ayyapa. On the first Friday of every month, the temple performs an *abhishekam* for the eight Lakshmis, goddesses of prosperity and fecundity, while on the second Saturday of every month there is an *abhishekam* for the shaligrams I discussed in Chapter 3. These are just some of the rites that take place at the temple on a weekly and monthly basis, year in and year out. They took place even during the four years between the temple burning down and being rebuilt as temporary accommodations were made for all these practices.

The Parashakthi Temple is at its liveliest during festivals and special celebrations, including rites performed in conjunction with votive practices (*vratas*). The most fervently celebrated religious events are, not surprisingly, those dedicated to the Goddess, especially the autumn celebrations of Navaratri, the "nine nights" of the Goddess, and Diwali, the "festival of lights" dedicated primarily to the goddess Lakshmi. But, like other Hindu temples in the United States, the Parashakthi Temple also celebrates both North and South Indian Hindu festivals, including Thaipusam, Shivaratri, Pongol, Makarsamkranti, Vasant Pancami, Krishna Jayanti, Vaikunth Ekadashi, Kalashthami, Ayyappa Mandalothsavam, Skanda Sashthi, and more. For elaborate events, priests from elsewhere in the United States or India may also be called to the temple to assist. Festivals usually draw large crowds to the temple. On these occasions, many of the most committed devotees— almost all women, as far as I was able to observe—often use the temple kitchen to prepare and distribute meals to the crowds of attendees, who might spend twelve or more hours on temple grounds over the course of several days.

Deity consecrations are special occasions at the Parashakthi Temple and are frequented by devotees from all over the United States and even India. Temple rites surrounding each installation may continue for several days, and luminaries from Asia or from other Hindu temples in the United States are often invited to preside over the installations. For example, the temple brought over Sridhar Guruji, a South Indian guru and devotee of both the Goddess and Narasimha, the lion form of Vishnu, to preside over the installation of Lakshmi-Narasinha in 2007 and Venkateshvara in 2008. Shrivatsa Goswami, a well-known Gaudiya Vaishnava religious leader, was brought to the temple for a Krishna installation in 2011. In 2008, during the Venkatesvara installation, Shridhar claimed that he could see numerous celestial beings who had come to attend the installation at the temple and referred to the temple itself as Vaikuntha, Vishnu's heavenly realm.

Among the most practiced Hindu rites performed regularly at the temple is the one that caused the 2018 temple fire: *homa*. *Homa* practice is rooted in the traditions of Vedic fire sacrifice in ancient India but has been transformed in contemporary times into a much simpler rite. Michaels describes *homa* as the most common form of Indian ritual performed around the world today, not just by Hindus, but also by Mahayana Buddhists in Central and East Asia (Michaels 2016, 237). While *homa*s can be quite elaborate, the central practice of every *homa* is the placing of offerings, *ahuti* (*āhuti*), into a fire so that Agni, the deity of fire, can transform them into gifts to be offered to the universe or consumed by deities and other spiritual beings. There are several steps involved in the performance of a *homa*. First, ritual actors must construct a sacrificial arena or pavilion, or they must ritually prepare an existing arena, if one exists, before the *homa* can take place. Next comes the ritual preparation of the sacrificial ground, utensils, vessels, and performers. Third, deities and other beings who exist in subtle realms are invited to take part in the *homa* as guests before (fourth) the fire itself is kindled. The heart of the ritual, placing oblations, in the fire, comes next, and then finally, the *homa* is ended with concluding

Figure 4.1 A *homa* at the Parashakthi Temple in 2011

rites and the cleaning of the ritual arena (Michaels 2016, 239–240). The entire rite is accompanied by the chanting of mantras (see Figure 4.1).

Michaels observes that *homa* practice has transformed in the last decades such that it has been absorbed into the repertory of new religious practices available to both Hindu and non-Hindu spiritual seekers. Some contemporary religious actors perform *homa* to respond to political or social justice issues, with individuals or organizations sponsoring or performing *homa*s for world peace, environmental concerns, or issues of public welfare, for example. In some cases, *homa* performance has been severed from its South Asian roots and transformed into a universal ritual of blessing and healing. Michaels makes a note in this regard of the California Universal Church of Baba's Kitchen in Santa Cruz, California, which offers *homa*s to anyone. They can even be ordered online "in your own name, or someone else's" for the purpose of generating powerful healing energy (Michaels 2016, 245–246).

At the Parashakthi Temple, however, *homa*s are done in a traditional manner, and priests perform *homa* with great frequency. A cursory glance at the regular temple event schedule (Parashakthi Temple,

"Pooja Schedule") reveals that the temple priests perform *homa* on a regular basis one day a week and six additional days a month. New moon days are reserved for a special *homa* done at night for Varahi, the boar-headed goddess associated with demonic forces. Showing respect by folding one's hands in the folding (*añjali*) gesture normally used when standing before a deity, with hands pressed together and fingers pointed upwards, is forbidden in this *homa* since "we don't want to show respect" to those demons "because they would stay with us, and we don't want them to stay with us. So symbolically we take them out and let them go" (Devi Parashakthi Temple Temple, Facebook video 3, August 8, 2021, 1:45:50). But *homa*s occur also during festivals, deity installations, inauspicious planetary transition times, votive rite days, and the like. Oftentimes, *homa*s are ongoing all day or all evening and may be performed either indoors or outdoors. The offerings placed into the fire include various substances, such as grains, fresh or dried fruit, flowers, shawls, and saris. Temple discourse endorses the idea that a complete set of offerings, *purnahuti* (*pūrṇāhuti*), when given correctly into the fire leaves behind special blessings, also called *purnahuti* in temple discourse, that remain in the ash after all the offerings are burned. In a conversation we had in 2012, Kumar insisted that everything we offer to deities is *ahuti*. After a *homa* is complete, he insisted, the deities honored then leave for us their divine energy. He described *purnahuti* as the deities' "imprint," the part they leave behind when they disperse at the conclusion of temple rites. The "Pearls of Wisdom" document posted on the Parashakthi Temple website notes the following, offering the temple's own understanding of the nature of *purnahuti*:

> When we perform a *homa*, we invoke the cosmic forces with proper mantras granted by the Divine Mother; we receive them and honor them. The sacrificial offerings in the *homa*, such as ghee, fruits and other items, and our mantras are what we offer to them through the mediation of Agni or Fire, who is the *ādidevata* ("root deity") for Earth. In return, they give us our blessings in the form of *pūrṇāhuti* (the black ash from the *homa* pit). "*Pūrṇa*" means "after;" "*āhuti*" means "sacrifice." So, it is very important to receive *pūrṇāhuti* after a *homa*. (Parashakthi Temple, "Pearls of Wisdom," lightly edited)

This document then goes on to note that "sponsoring a *homa* when we go to the [Parashakthi] Temple is a thousandfold more effective in receiving divine grace than performing an *abhishekam*."

In a lecture he gave at the temple in July 2021, while the new temple was still under construction, Kumar made the claim that the temple indulges in a great deal of *homa* performance because "among all the methodologies of reaching her [the Goddess], *homa* is best." First, *homa* "draws down cosmic forces" more effectively than other kinds of rites. Second, because *homa* engages the most subtle of the gross elements—air, ether, and fire over water and earth—it is the most effective way to communicate with the divine realm, which includes but extends beyond the gross, material realm. The next powerful method, Kumar notes, is *abhishekam*, especially when done with liquids that have been energized directly during a *homa* performance so that Agni can still function as a mediator despite the liquid medium. After that, *alankara* (*alaṇkāra*), adorning the Goddess with material objects like flowers, clothing, and jewelry, is acceptable. *Alankara* is associated with the element earth as it entails the direct offering of embodied, material substances (lecture, July 2021). Hence, according to Kumar, the most efficacious forms of worship are those that utilize the gross elements that are closest to the divine realm. Kumar and other members of the temple board claim that *homa*s done at the temple not only benefit the entire world with their energy, but also offer special benefits to devotees involved in their performance by helping move devotees' consciousness away from "lower," material realms toward "higher" concerns and realms. Hence, *homa*s are uniquely efficacious in facilitating devotees' spiritual transformation.

The performance of *homa* and other rites at the Parashakthi Temple is always accompanied by the chanting of Sanskrit mantras. Mantras are "speech acts" whose power resides in the chanting and hearing of the mantra itself, not in its semantic meaning. As Michaels observes, "To be able to use the sacred power of mantras depends on (ritually correct) saying and hearing," not on understanding what the mantra means (Michaels 2016, 256). Mantra recitation is especially important in tantric forms of Hindu practice, where mantras function as a form of "verbal metalinguistic power" when recited properly (Padoux 2017, 107). At the Parashakthi Temple, mantra recitation plays a key role in many forms of religious practice. On some occasions, the congregation chants mantras collectively to increase the level of *shakti* in the temple. For example, during deity installations, devotees may chant the seed (*bija*) mantras of the deity whose *murti* is being consecrated for very lengthy periods of time, often over several days. Mantra recitation is vital according to Kumar, because it "feeds the gods" and "keeps the temple alive." While normally gurus bestow specific mantras on their disciples, at the Parashakthi Temple, temple discourse maintains that the Goddess herself reveals mantras to Kumar, who then shares the mantras with the entire congregation and even publishes them on the temple website. Kumar himself attributes the power of *homa* practice largely to the mantras that accompany the *homa*, noting that "mantra is what draws the gods" to the temple, where they "consume only the mantra." When the mantras stop, the gods leave, but "they leave their imprint" behind, which enhances the temple's spiritual potency (interview, August 2009).

The most chanted mantra at the Parashakthi Temple is the Gayatri (*gāyatrī*) mantra in its many variations. Gayatri is both a goddess and a verse from the Rig Veda Samhita (3.62.10), a collection of hymns dating from the Vedic period that were chanted during Vedic sacrificial performance (*yajna*, ca. 1500–600 BCE). It is a twenty-three-syllable mantra preceded by the *bija* mantra "Om" followed by the phrase "*bhūr bhuvaḥ svaḥ*," the *mahavyahriti* (*mahāvyāhṛti*) or "great utterance." The *mahavyahriti* has been interpreted in many ways but is often understood as an invocation of the earthly, middle, and heavenly realms. Following the invocation, one then recites the mantra itself: *tat savitur vareṇyaṁ// bhargo devasya dhīmahi// dhiyo yo naḥ pracodayāt*. The mantra has been translated in many ways but roughly means, "Let us meditate on that most excellent sun/light, divine glory, who inspires our intellect." The exactitude of the translation, however, is very much beside the point as the power of the mantra lies in its recitation. While the Gayatri mantra is invoked frequently at the temple, often it is not just the standard version that devotees chant. There are in fact numerous Gayatris dedicated to different deities. The temple has published on its website several of these Gayatris, including a Subramanya Gayatri, a Jagannath Gayatri, a Lakshmi Narasimha Gayatri, a Venkateswara Gayatri, a Garuda Gayatri, a Hanuman

Gayatri, a Shiva Gayatri, and many others (Parashakthi Temple, "Deities"). Devotees and priests alike often chant the appropriate Gayatri mantra during *puja* and other temple rites.

Brian Hatcher notes that the Gayatri mantra, which is attributed to the legendary Hindu sage Vishvamitra, is "the most widely known and recited mantra of Vedic religious life" (Hatcher 2019, 241). Early Vedic scripture refers to it as the "mother of meters" and "mother of the Veda," and in the Upanishads, Gayatri is called the "source of all that is" and a mantra that protects "this entire creation" (Hatcher 2019, 241). The Gayatri is important in the postclassical, premodern, and modern eras as well. Traditionally, reciting the Gayatri was the privilege of male Hindus of higher castes who received the mantra, and recited it for the first time, during a rite of ritual initiation, called the *upanayana*, when they received a thread or garment signifying, among other things, the start of their education. Today, however, a wide variety of Hindus and non-Hindus alike chant the Gayatri for its reputed physical, emotional, and mental benefits. Hindu reform movements of the nineteenth and twentieth centuries encouraged women and lower-caste individuals to recite the Gayatri, and in the twenty-first century, the internet thoroughly democratized its usage. The All World Gayatri Pariwar ("Gayatri Family"), for example, founded in the middle of the twentieth century, elevated the performance of fire sacrifice and the chanting of the Gayatri mantra by all people above all other religious practice for the purpose of reforming "the individual, the family and social values of mankind and to change the current ideologies and concepts of morality and social structure for a better tomorrow" (All World Gayatri Pariwar, "Origin of Mission"). Anyone can now find on YouTube videos explaining the scientific basis of Gayatri and teaching you how to chant it (e.g., "The Power and Benefits of Gayatri Mantra | Dr. Hansaji Yogendra" 2021) or you can set your screen so the Gayatri plays repeatedly in the background while you go about your daily business (e.g., "Gayatri Mantra 108 Times with Lyrics - chanting by Brahmins" 2014). Numerous websites and YouTube videos expound on the miraculous efficacy of chanting Gayatri. Nick Tackes notes, for example, that the Gayatri Pariwar posted videos on YouTube during the COVID-19 pandemic calling for a "daily collective chanting of the Gayatri Mantra worldwide to provide relief from the ills of COVID-19" (Tackes 2021, 1026). Meditativemind.org claims that chanting the Gayatri mantra helps reduce asthma symptoms, keeps your heart healthy, removes toxins from the body, and improves overall immunity, among its many other benefits (Meditative Mind, "10 Amazing Benefits of Gayatri Mantra Chanting"). Devotees at the Parashakthi Temple also have reported to me that they chant the various Gayatris that the temple makes available to them to attain both bodily and mental boons along with the spiritual benefits the mantra is alleged to offer.

Michaels notes that while Hindu rites are rule-governed, nevertheless, "one can play around with them, vary them, repeat them, transform them, and imitate them. Once can put them together in different ways like bricks" (Michaels 2016, 313). At the Parashakthi Temple, such variation is on display in several ways, including in the ways that the temple has adopted American celebrations. The Parashakthi Temple is not unique in this regard as many Hindu temples in the United States have adapted American holidays and rites. At the Parashakthi Temple, the Goddess's cosmic birth-giving capacity has come to be celebrated annually on Mother's Day, an American holiday that has been transformed at the temple into a day of religious ritual. Before Mother's Day in 2014, which fell on Sunday, May 11, an email announcing a special Mother's Day *abhishekam* emphasized the nature of the Goddess as the one who gives her child "the highest knowledge, the Brahma Vidya" (meaning "knowledge of God") and describes motherhood as "the symbol of love, compassion, and forbearance" (temple email, May 10, 2014). Devotees bring roses to the temple to offer Divine Mother as they would do for their own mothers, and pregnant women—or those desiring to become pregnant—are especially encouraged to participate since they are said to be special recipients of divine, maternal favor on this day. Mother's Day often also coincides with a fundraising sari sale in which saris worn by the *murti* of the Goddess in the temple are auctioned, and devotees are encouraged to purchase them as "a wonderful, blessed gift of sarees adorned by Divine Mother for a special mother, grandmother or aunt in your life" (email, May 10, 2014).

Parashakthi Temple religious practices help create the temple as a sacred space. The temple's constant performance of sumptuous rites generates perceptions of the temple as a spiritually potent spot. Religious practice repeatedly and richly engages the bodily senses at the Parashakthi Temple, ensuring that people experience the temple as sensorily and spiritually powerful and leave its grounds feeling transformed. Temple rites make available strongly experienced "intersensory perceptual processes" that occur only in temple space (Feld 1996, 98). As Feld notes, "senses make place," meaning that "the perceptual engagements we call sensing" play a critical role in our "conceptual constructions of place" (Feld 1996, 91). The "feelingful sensuality" (Feld 1996, 98) that temple rites engage then continually reaffirms perceptions of the temple as a unique, *shakti*-filled abode that has been specially blessed by the Goddess. One devotee articulated to me very clearly that being at the temple and participating in temple rites facilitates the movement of one's consciousness from the gross realm to the subtle realm and helps a person on their path to spiritual enlightenment (interview, 2012). Another devotee who paused to speak with me during the temple reconsecration in August of 2023 declared that participation in temple rites is a form of spiritual journeying. According to this devotee, temple rites performed at the Parashakthi Temple "activate Divine Mother's vibrations," releasing the immense stores of divine energy available at the temple and thereby activating the Goddess's grace, moving it from the unmanifest to the manifest realm. Those who are physically present at the temple during these rites are then necessarily swept along on the waves of grace and spiritual energy that the rites unleash.

Pratinidhi Pilgrimage: The Ingathering of *Shakti*

In October of 2010, Kumar gave a lecture, which I was invited to attend, about the temple and the plans that were in the works at that time for construction of the *rajagopuram*. He gave the lecture during a board meeting attended by members of the temple board and invited donors and guests. During his talk, Kumar made note of a recent journey he had undertaken to India as well as the journey's importance to the larger temple community. At the Parashakthi Temple, most devotees and board members do not undertake pilgrimage journeys to India or other places on a regular basis for a variety of reasons, including lack of time or financial resources. Kumar, however, undertakes them constantly.

In Chapter 3, I noted that Kumar journeyed to India to secure the two shaligram stones that he then brought back to Michigan for the benefit of the temple community. The purpose of such types of journeys is to collect divine power from other places in the world to bring back to the Goddess's home in Michigan, where they can then provide spiritual and protective energy to devotees and, beyond that, to the Western world and the world at large. Kumar often undertakes this type of journey multiple times in any given year. In a lecture he gave to the temple community in 2021, Kumar explicitly described one such pilgrimage journey, which he had recently undertaken to the Himalayas, as a *pratinidhi* journey. A news email sent to members of the temple's email list in June of 2021 stated the following:

> Dr. Krishna Kumar, M.D, our Temple's Founder and Spiritual Director, travels (Pratinidhi Yatra) on behalf of all the Temple Devotees, to the Himalayas and performs proper rituals with Manthras given by the Divine Mother Parashakthi to bring the energy and grace of the Divine and the Himalayan Masters (Maharishis and Siddha Purushas) who are in Jeeva Samadhi. Thus, they are eternally present at our Temple for Devotees to receive their blessings. (Temple email, June 17, 2021).

The term *pratinidhi* here refers to a proxy or a person who is acting in the place of someone else.

Kumar refers to these journeys as *yatras* (*yātrās*) or, when he uses English, as pilgrimage journeys. There is a vast literature on pilgrimage that is beyond the scope of this chapter, but there are a few points of consensus regarding the nature of pilgrimage, and of Hindu pilgrimage in particular, that bear mentioning. Alan Morinis defines pilgrimage as "a journey undertaken by a person in quest of a place or a state that he or she believes to embody a valued ideal." Pilgrimage destinations function as an "intensified version of some ideal that the pilgrim values but cannot achieve at home" (Morinis 1992, 4). In his discussion of Hindu pilgrimage practices, Knut Jacobsen argues that the "salvific power of place" and "salvific sites as deities" are the two most "remarkable characteristics" of Hindu pilgrimage traditions (Jacobsen 2013, 19). For Hindus, pilgrimage is a form of journeying that is explicitly tied in some way to religious goals; it is "travel for a religious purpose toward a place believed to have a divine presence or possess salvific power." The sites to which Hindu pilgrims journey are called *tirtha*s (*tīrtha*s), "crossing over" places, or, if they are goddess-related sites, *pitha*s. Such sites function as bridges between the mundane world and the subtle, spiritual worlds that lie beyond the mortal realm. James J. Preston has identified a number of qualities that he associates broadly with pilgrimage sites: spiritual magnetism, that is, the power of a pilgrimage site to attract devotees; the perception of occurrences of miraculous cures, especially those involving sources of water that are perceived to have special healing capabilities; apparitions of supernormal, or, to use the language of the Parashakthi Temple, "supersensual" beings, that is, beings that exist beyond the perceptual capacities of human bodily senses; often, dramatic features in the landscape of the site; and difficulty of access (Preston 1992, 33–38). Jacobsen notes that Hindu pilgrimage sites are places "of divine or extraordinary power that is believed to have a particular ability to fulfill wishes and grant salvation" (Jacobsen 2013, 22). Much of the scholarly literature on pilgrimage focuses on the effect of the pilgrimage journey on the pilgrim, for whom the journey is intended to be in some way transformational.

Kumar's pilgrimage journeys to India and other parts of the world deviate to at least some extent from these patterns, however. First, Kumar undertakes these pilgrimage journeys to places not of his own volition, and not to fulfill his own wishes or to achieve his own salvation, but instead to carry out the Goddess's command to journey to places she has identified to make the power inherent in these places available to him. He claims that the Goddess decides when and where Kumar must journey; he does not make these decisions for himself. Furthermore, the sites that he visits are not always specifically Hindu pilgrimage spots, and often, the site to be visited is kept secret from everyone, sometimes even from Kumar, until the journey has already begun. Furthermore, Kumar undertakes these pilgrimage journeys not because they are transformational for him or for others undertaking the journey with him—temple board members, devotees, family members, ANK, or close Indian friends sometimes accompany him on these journeys—but instead because they act as vehicles of transformation *for the temple*, its community of devotees, and, ultimately, the world at large. The goal of these journeys is to secure the *shakti* that is especially available at the sites to which the Goddess sends Kumar to transport it back to the Parashakthi Temple, thereby augmenting the power available to temple devotees and the larger world. *Pratinidhi* pilgrimage, in which a pilgrim undertakes a journey on behalf of someone else—often, but not always, an infirm family member who cannot make the journey because of physical limitations—is an accepted Hindu practice, but I have not before encountered a pattern of *pratinidhi* pilgrimage done for an entire religious institution or community.

In October of 2010, Kumar told me during one of my visits to the temple that he had just returned from a journey to India during which he went to Rishikesh, where the Goddess had instructed him to go to spend time at a site associated with Raibhya, a legendary Hindu sage, or *rishi*. Vedic Hindu texts present *rishis* as the composers of the Vedic hymns, but later Hindu traditions engage the term *rishi* to refer more broadly to a spiritually enlightened person, a sage, or a *siddha*. Hindu *rishis* and *siddhas* often play a significant role in the founding stories (*sthalapuranas*) of many Hindu temples. As noted in Chapter 1, for example, the *rishi* Agastya, widely understood in Tamil Nadu to be the founder of the Tamil *siddha* tradition (Venkatraman 1990, 40), is said to have founded the Karumariamman Temple in Thiruverkadu. Regarding his trip to Rishikesh in 2010, Kumar noted:

> Every few months, she [Divine Mother] will tell me, "Come to me in [such and such] temple. And there is a *rishi*. Each temple has a *rishi*. And [she tells me,] 'Take the *rishi* [from India] to your temple [in Michigan]. Energize my place [in Michigan] with those *rishis*.' . . . Because she is the highest level, she is the source of everything, and she must transcend [the material realm]. The best medium for us is the *rishi* or the sage or the yogi who has given life to a particular aspect of her through a mantra. (Interview, October 2, 2010)

Kumar claims he had never heard of Raibhya until the Goddess instructed him to go and perform religious rites at the specific place she told him to visit. Kumar says that he went to this site, which he did not name, three times to perform *homa*s there. In a talk he gave to the temple congregation describing his pilgrimage to this site, he went on to note, "See, it is done for all of you. Not for me. I happen to be the medium. . . . It is done for all of you. And for the world" (temple talk, October 2, 2010). Kumar continued his talk by noting that in the mid-2000s, the temple mission changed such that it went from being a place to worship Divine Mother and access her grace and powers of protection to being a place to "explore and experience her," which Kumar insists "is an act of tantra" and "the highest form of interaction" (interview, July 2012). He claimed in 2010, now "the *rishis* have started coming" to the temple, including Agastya, Raibhya, and the guru of Dikshitar's lineage, Vishvamitra.

Often, when Kumar felt called to go on pilgrimage, he says Divine Mother would reveal to him where to go, what energy he should seek, and the mantra he should use to invoke the energy. But this would not always happen. In 2010, for example, he went with other members of the temple board on a pilgrimage journey to the Kamakhya Temple in Assam because the Goddess had called him to go there to meditate and sponsor *homa*s on behalf of the temple community. Kumar claims that for that journey, the Goddess gave him no prior information. He says he discovered when he was at the Kamakhya Temple that all seven of the Vedic *rishis* were present in subtle form at the site to protect the world from new demonic forces. The Kamakhya Temple is an important tantric *shakta pitha*, a Goddess pilgrimage site, where tantric practices are still performed. The Kamakhya Temple presents itself as the site where Sati's *yoni*, her womb or vagina, fell and took root when Vishnu followed Shiva and sliced off pieces of Sati's corpse, which Shiva was carrying around out of grief at losing his beloved wife. Kumar claims that he experienced there the seven *rishis* preventing terrible demonic emotions from entering creation by guarding the symbolic entrance to the universe, the Goddess's vagina, so they could not enter our world. He says he discovered their presence when he was at the Kamakhya Temple and realized that the Goddess had sent him there to tap into that intense protective energy to bring it back to Michigan (interview, October 2010).

While many of the pilgrimage journeys Kumar and other board members undertake for the purpose of gathering energy are to India, not all are. During that same 2010 visit, Kumar told me he had gone recently also to Pompei, Italy, to meditate, again at the Goddess's behest. While the figurine of a yakshi (*yaksī*) or courtesan from India was found in the ruins of ancient Pompeii, indicating a trade connection between India and Rome ("Figurine of a Yakshi or Courtesan"), this connection was not front and center in Kumar's understanding of why the Goddess sent him there. Rather, Kumar said there were specific "left-over" energies inherent in the Pompei landscape that he needed to gather and bring back to the temple from there because of the "intense emotions," presumably of those who had died in place when Mount Vesuvius erupted almost 2000 years ago, that had left significant spiritual energy at the Italian site. Intense emotions draw deities (*devatās*) who stay in such places, so one can go there to "draw the energy from them." It is notable that in this case, the energy that Kumar sought to bring back to the temple was grounded in an event that was tragic and sad. In fact, negative spiritual energies also play a vital role at the temple along with the helpful, positive energies that religious performance is meant to cultivate.

When I returned to the temple in 2019 for a visit about a year after the temple fire, Kumar revealed that he had just returned from a pilgrimage to a site in India where the *rishi* Dadhici (Dadhīci) allegedly died. Dadhici is a *rishi* famous in the Puranas for sacrificing his life so that the deity Indra could use his bones to make the weapon, or *vajra*, that Indra needed to kill a serpentine demon, Vritra, who was hoarding life-giving water. Kumar claims that the Goddess called him to the very place where Dadhici died, where his subtle body "is still hanging around" and where Dadhici's life force remains "in Jiva samadhi," that is, as living spiritual power that remains behind at the spot where he passed away. Although the spot was not marked, Kumar assured me that before he went, the Goddess had told him that he would know the spot by feeling it on the subtle plane. Sure enough, he told me, he was in the middle of a wilderness area when he saw the energy "as a flame."

So, I feel the heat, the energy, then I go and sit, and I feel the flame. But not on the gross (*sthula*) level. Only on the subtle level (*sukshma*). Anyone else who comes would not see it. (Interview, October 2019)

He stayed in the spot to which, he told me, the Goddess had guided him to meditate so that he could gather up demonic energy from that spot to bring back to the temple. As he explained it to me:

When deities slay demons, they do not slay them 100 percent. They slay them 99.99 percent. The reason is that some of that negative energy needs to be kept here for other life forms, so they (too) can evolve—so they can feel that [negative energy] and fight it. If you are completely pure, there can be no [spiritual] evolution. So, the gods leave a little bit behind. People don't know that. They think, "We do the Candi *homa*, we slay the demons," but no, it is not like that— only 99.9 percent [of the negative energy is slain.] Some of it must be kept, just mitigated. It [the demonic energy left behind] then will become like a vaccine for humans and for other life forms. (Interview, October 2019)

Here Kumar refers to a specific *homa*, the Candi *homa*, that involves reciting the entire Devi-Mahatmya text, celebrating the Goddess's victory over demonic forces. His argument here is that the Goddess wants at least a bit of demonic energy to remain behind so that "life forms," including humans who are on a spiritual path, can learn how to confront and overcome negative, "demonic" forces in the world. His job in this case was to bring some of that mitigated negative energy back to the Parashakthi Temple community so it could be used in this way.

In a 2021 temple talk, Kumar made an explicit connection between the journeys that he undertakes at the Goddess's command and the spiritual growth of the temple community. Noting that the Goddess had called him to undertake a pilgrimage to Gauri Kund, a site in North India, he announced that the Goddess had instructed him to go there specifically because creation itself started at Gauri Kund. He described the goddess Gauri as the primordial mother in the form of primordial consciousness, which was the only entity present at the time of creation:

I am supposed to go to that place where she started the whole cycle. I will go to that place in July on your behalf. You [all] will be there. I will go on your behalf as a *pratinidhi* and do the rituals she [the Goddess] wanted [me to do]. [The place is] Gauri Kund. "Kund" means lake. It probably formed four and a half or five million years ago years ago. . . . At that time meteors came here and hit the earth, and one of them formed that Gauri Kund. It formed a high vibratory energy where she [the Goddess] meditated. She did meditation for a very long time because she had to create a trillion trillion forms of life. Trillion, not million. Many forms. We [humans] happen to be the [most] highly advanced [life forms] on this earth, but there are so many galaxies—billions and billions of galaxies. . . . She had to create many, many forms—forms which we can't even comprehend. But they are there. (Parashakthi Temple, "Importance of Gouri Kund and Its Relevance to Creation" 2021)

After he returned from that pilgrimage journey that July, he gave another temple talk, now posted on the Parashakthi Temple Facebook page, following a long *homa* and describing his experience:

That place had intense energy. She went there and did a wonderful sacrifice to create us, meaning all life forms—trillions and trillions of life forms. . . . So that is the significance of that *yatra*. She wanted me to go on your behalf. It was a wonderful *yatra* and a very intense, powerful active *yatra*. Many, many yakshinis [spirit beings] came, and [now] they are here [at the Parashakthi Temple] for you to receive, so you will get them all. They will be part of the temple. . . . I was given the privilege to represent you, go on your behalf and do very powerful, very mystical, intense rituals for world protection, the purpose being to protect the world from this *asuric* era. Now is the *asuric* era—you see the signs of it already. COVID is just one small aspect of it. There will be many, many more attacks by *asuric* energies. . . . She said to go there and do this ceremony on behalf of all of you. . . . I go there as your *pratinidhi* and do exactly what she wants me to do: very mystical, very deep, and significant rituals. . . . Many miraculous things happened while I was there, and I brought [the energies] back on your behalf. . . . [The Goddess's] job is to create us, to create life forms, and give us a chance to act out so we take advantage of this time and evolve to higher form of consciousness. So, this *yatra* helps us to meet that goal, which is self-realization, realizing who we really are: not this mind/body/intellect/ego; it is temporary. We use it to "go up." But the real us is her, a piece of her, part of her.... Through the process, we evolve, and hopefully we realize our true self, which is Divine, and go to that world from the human. . . . We will go into a higher form until we become part of her and go back to the source.... And these rituals we do, these *homa*s, these *yatra*s, all of it helps. (Devi Parashakthi Temple, Facebook Video 2, July 9, 2021)

The physical journeying that Kumar and others undertake makes the entire devotional community's spiritual journeying possible. As Kumar put it:

Since many of you will never be able to go [on pilgrimage], she makes one person among us [go]; she gives me the opportunity to represent you. So, I go on your behalf. Each time I do that—I've been doing it for thirty years now—each time, she makes me do one thing. It's a very profound, meaningful, divine-seeking job. She tells me what to do.... She won't give me the details—where to go, when to do, on what *tithi*[1] to perform [rites], what to perform—she won't give me the details. Nobody will know--only she will know. And then she kindly grants us the ability to know where to go, when to go, what *tithi* to perform, what to perform. These are secrets. Only she knows.... To be able to do that [the trip to Gauri Kund]—it was a hard journey, a hard trip, but it was a great privilege. Many, many actors were participating, not only human . . . . All the divine beings participate. (Devi Parashakthi Temple, Facebook Video 1, July 7, 2021)

By carrying out the Goddess's wishes, Kumar and others who accompany him on these pilgrimage journeys are able to transport a variety of subtle, spiritual energies back to the Parashakthi Temple and make them available to others. Hence, *pratinidhi* pilgrims facilitate the kinds of spiritual transformation that devotees come to the Parashakthi Temple to seek.

Collins articulates two distinctive approaches to the contemporary study of ritual: one that emphasizes what ritual does to people and another that emphasizes what people do with ritual (Collins 1997, 17). The first approach elicits a hermeneutics of suspicion, seeking to elucidate ways that ritual practices affirm and reproduce larger relations of social power, often without the conscious assent of ritual actors. The second approach emphasizes instead the ways people use rites to pursue their own individual and collective interests, appropriating and sometimes modifying rituals when convenient or desirable (Collins 1997, 178). While the first approach Collins outlines stresses the nature of ritual actors as (frequently unwitting) recipients of larger ideological and hegemonic structures, the second stresses their nature as agents who may creatively deploy ritual for their own purposes. This second approach is the one I have tried to demonstrate here. In adopting a performative perspective on Parashakthi Temple rites and pilgrimage journeys, I have tried to emphasize the ways that temple actors—both human and divine, at least according to Kumar and other devotees—dynamically create, mold, reinvent, and interpret their religious practices.

In her work on contemporary Hindu religious practice in Bengaluru (Bangalore), South India, Tulasi Srinivas notes the existence of an ongoing dynamic between what she refers to as the iterative and creative dimensions of modern Hinduism (Srinivas 2018). Srinivas describes the world of contemporary Hindu rites, at least as she has observed it, as comprised of "iterative, strategic, and creative improvisation within and around Hindu rituals" (Srinivas 2018, 15). Leela Prasad observes a similar dynamic in the way Hindu individuals in the Hindu pilgrimage town of Sringeri, South India, where she has conducted her research, construct "the normative," invoking traditions sources like scripture (*śāstra*), custom (*paddhati*), proper conduct (*ācāra*), tradition (*sampradāya*), and rules pertaining to restraint or religious conduct (*niyama*) (Prasad 2006, 1). She argues that in Sringeri, a "lived grammar of the normative" includes a wide field of discourse and practice that includes an interplay among all these concepts and reconstitutes them in a way that is dynamic and emergent, simultaneously situated in contexts that are both local and larger than local (Prasad 2006, 4–5). At the

Parashakthi Temple, this "lived grammar of the normative" is on display in the ways that temple actors both conduct and make sense of a variety of religious activities.

Rising from the Fire: Divine Mother Returns Home

When the temple roof and much of its structure were destroyed in the 2018 fire, the only forms said to survive unscathed both materially and spiritually were the main *murti* of the Goddess and the *rajagopuram*, with the *shakti garbha* safely tucked beneath it. When I returned to the temple in October 2019, I met with Kumar and a handful of key devotees to ask them specifically about this issue. Kumar told me that the Goddess made sure the *rajagopuram* was constructed entirely in inflammable stone and consecrated in 2015 so that the *shakti* that was present in the temple would have somewhere sacred to which it could retreat while the fire took place. The implication was that the Goddess foresaw in 2015 that the 2018 fire would occur and had in fact planned for it. This narrative has been put to service in explaining why the fire occurred in the first place. Every person I spoke with during my October 2019 visit told me that the fire could not have happened if the Goddess had not wanted it to happen. There were two primary reasons given for her desire to destroy the temple in existence at the time. The predominant claim I heard was that the temple functioned well for the twenty years it lasted but was not powerful enough for the future given the demonic (*asuric*) energy that the universe is soon going to face, so the Goddess had to destroy it to make way for a more powerful structure. Another claim I heard is that small but religiously significant mistakes were made in the construction of the original temple, leading the Goddess to burn it down so it could be recreated in a stronger way. In all cases, everyone I spoke with seemed very sure that the structure to come would be even more powerful than the one it would replace. For that to occur, however, almost all the *murtis* would have to be replaced, for two reasons. First, even if the physical structure of specific *murtis* had emerged from the fire unscathed, the subtle energy that they embodied had not; it had been transformed by the fire-energy that had touched it. Second, the fire was the result of divine intervention, an intervention that had occurred precisely because of the need for a more powerful structure, which meant that more spiritually powerful *murti*s would be needed to replace the ones that were no longer up to the job.

To begin the rebuilding process, temple officiants had to move the energy that had been present in the *murti*s into drawings and wooden figures that the temple's main architect had constructed specifically for this purpose. When a Hindu temple is being renovated or rebuilt, the divine power resident in the *murti*s of the temple must be transferred into a water pot, a wooden image, or a drawn picture to render the space mundane so that anyone can enter it in any state, even a state of ritual impurity, to complete the construction work needs to be done (Shridharan 2019, 80). This transfer of power took place over several months during 2018–2019. While I was not present for this process, a devotee later described it to me, noting that the temple priests had to go to every shrine, do an *abhishekam*, perform the energy transfer, and move on to the next *murti* until the energy transfer was complete. The drawings, wooden figurines, and the main *murti* of the Goddess were all moved to a shed that was built expressly for this purpose next to the main temple site, which is where I saw them during return visits in 2019, 2020, and 2022 (see Figure 4.2).

A devotee later told me that when Kumar went to India in 2020 and meditated in the Himalayas, the Goddess revealed to him that from that point forward, she wanted the existing *murti* to remain separate from the new temple structure to keep the whole area energized, so she wanted the shed to be turned into a permanent structure. This wish was carried out, and a brand new *murti* of the Goddess was consecrated in the main temple structure during the 2022 *kumbhabhishekam*, the rite of temple consecration. Kumar and others told me that because the fire had not touched the original *murti* of the Goddess, even on the subtle level, it could be retained, but now the Goddess wanted her own space. With several new *murti*s coming to be installed in the new, main temple structure, the Goddess would continue her role as chairperson of the (divine) board "to make sure the *homa*s performed there [at the main temple] are performed properly, everything is done properly—she'll be monitoring it" ("Significance of Devi Mahamariamman"

Figure 4.2 The drawings and paintings containing divine energy that were moved to the shed in 2018

2022). But she preferred to perform this role from a distance, at her new "office."

When I returned to the temple for a visit in 2020, the rebuilding effort was well underway. Kumar told me that even after the energy from the *murtis* had been moved to the shed, the temple priests had continued doing rituals, especially *homas*, in the now physically empty space where the temple had stood right behind the *rajagopuram* "because when you stop doing rituals, the energies might dissipate." These *homas* and other rites helped maintain the divine power in place and kept it active and alive. Kumar noted:

> These [supersensual beings], *yakshinis, gandharvas* (celestial musicians), *vidyadaras* (supernatural beings with magical powers)—all the cosmic energies, they are all very active at the temple. But these cosmic energies are very, very fickle. If you don't keep the highest energy continually there, with proper *homa*, with mantra, yantra, tantra—everything must continue—if you don't, they dissipate. I have seen that many times.

Even though the temple structure had been destroyed, either by fire or by the bulldozers that tore down the remaining structure, the subtle, divine energies that constituted temple space and rendered it powerful were continually "fed" so they would remain present in the location where the temple had stood for almost nineteen years. In an important way, the temple was never destroyed; only its material shell was destroyed. Through the practice of ongoing rites, the energies that had always constituted the temple as a living, powerful place and not just a "lifeless" structure were made to remain in place. Hence, I was told the temple continued to protect its community and the world even during those years when it was, technically speaking, no longer there. While the new, much larger temple building was being planned and then constructed between 2019 and 2022, Kumar told me, he and others often sensed the presence of the subtle bodies of deceased temple priests and religious leaders who had spent time at the temple. Kumar told me they were hanging about because they missed the temple as much as the community of living, human devotees missed it, and they were coming by to check on the progress of the rebuilding effort.

Between a fall 2020 visit and my return to the temple for its grand reopening in August 2022, I followed temple happenings online, especially through the temple's YouTube channel and website, but I did not return to visit the temple in person. The COVID-19 epidemic and family entanglements kept me away, but I knew I would have to return for the *kumbhabhishekam*. A blast email that I have lightly edited, sent out on August 7, 2022, described the pending consecration of the new temple as follows:

> Devi Parashakthi Temple is Devi's own abode, and all Her transcendent cosmic angels are intensely manifest at our temple for world protection during *Kali Yuga* (difficult times). We are very fortunate and blessed to be given a very powerful place of worship by Divine Mother that is a high vortex of energy as confirmed by many mystics and *siddha*s in India. Divine Mother has given us the opportunity to explore and experience "Her," which is something even the greatest of gurus like Vashista (Guru of Lord Rama) tried to achieve after severe penance; She has given this privilege to us at our temple. Divine Mother, out of extreme kindness and affection, has designed and chosen the most effective and important intense cosmic energies to be placed [here] to protect the world from the *asuric* energies so that the world can continue to evolve and keep the *asuric* energies under control. This will let life forms continue to evolve and go back towards the realm of Divine so that Divine Mother can watch and enjoy our ascension to the higher worlds back to the origin where we came from. Let us enjoy the journey and become one with Divine Mother Adi Parashakthi Karumari Ambika. We request all of you to participate in this divine venture. Sacrifice is essential for the soul to be pleased. Let us become part of the magnificent venture of the protection of the universe as predicted by various *siddha*s.

The plan for the temple is eventually to have thirty-three new *murti*s installed, although only a handful of those were completed, paid for, shipped from India, and ready to be installed at the time of the August 2022 *kumbhabhishekam*. Kumar maintains that the Goddess revealed to him directly the names and forms of these thirty-three new deity *murti*s, which, he says, will render the Parashakthi Temple one of the most, if not the most, spiritually powerful and protective temples on earth. Invoking the "degenerate age" or *kali* (*kāli*) *yuga*, the fourth of four progressively degenerate eras of history enumerated in the Puranas, as the age in which we live, and the sanctuaries or *sannidhanams* in which each of the planned deity *murti*s will be placed, Kumar noted the following:

> Mother said this is *kali yuga*. These are dangerous times, and the world will go through various crises. One we are facing right now is the COVID crisis, and that won't end that soon. . . . So, she said, "We need many of my aspects to fight each *asuric* aspect that is causing this [confluence of crises]." This is one example. There are many other examples. There will be many other attacks. . . . So many attacks are in for us, but we will be protected because Divine Mother is giving us this wonderful temple with various *sannidhanam*s of her, aspects designed by her, energized by her, so they will have the ability to protect us from this onslaught in this *kali yuga*. ("Dr Krishnakumar Speech about Upcoming New Shrines and Its Significance on Vasantha Navarathiri 2021" 2021)

Most of the rites that took place before and during the Parashakthi Temple's consecration are standard for the dedication or rededication of a Hindu temple. I describe them here, however, to offer a sense of what it was like to be present for the week of activity that surrounded the effort to restore the Goddess to her American abode. I have left out many details, although some readers will surely think I have included too many. Not every temple consecration or reconsecration is identical as there are regional and lineage-based variations. The progression of rites that preceded and led up to the reconsecration of the Parashakthi Temple, therefore, is not necessarily the same progression as one might see at the consecration of another Hindu temple, but most of the elements are at least similar from context to context.

The Parashakthi Temple executed several purificatory rites over several months preceding the *kumbhabhishekam*. Before temple *murti*s can be established as living images through *prana-pratishtha* rites, there are several preparatory rites that must be completed to purify both the *murti*s themselves and the place where the *murti*s are to reside. The Parashakthi Temple's reconsecration process included, for example, rites of spatial purification (*puṇyahavācanam*); the assignment of duties to the priests and the offering to them of new garments (*ācārya ṛtvik varṇam*); the transfer of deities' power into water kept in special pots, called *kalasha* (*kalaśa*) *or kalasa*, which have a wide base and a narrow mouth (*kalaśa sthāpana*); establishing the firepits to be used to perform the consecration *homas* (*agni pratiṣṭhā*); the rite of seeking blessings from Vastu Purusha, the lord of the home (*vastu puja* and *homa*); and the sowing of nine kinds of seeds in pots (*ankurārpaṇam*). As the date of the temple consecration grew near during July and August of 2022, several rites specifically for the ritual cleansing of the new *murti*s also took place. These included the immersion of new temple *murti*s in water (*jalādivāsam*) and grains (*dhanyādivasam*); offerings of flowers, gold, and milk; and finally, the dressing of the deity images in new clothing and putting them down to rest (*shayanādivasam*) (temple email, August 5, 2022; Parashakthi Temple, "Prana Pratishtha").

The week leading up to the *kumbhabhishekam* began on the morning of Monday, August 22, 2022, with a Ganesha *homa* in the small temple that the Goddess had commandeered as her new "away" space. By late summer of 2022, the temporary shed constructed to house her *murti* was replaced with a permanent structure. Since Ganesha is the deity of obstacles, the temple community needed to seek his blessings before launching the rest of the week's activities. That evening, packets of nine jewels, the *navaratna*, were collected from devotees and transferred to the main temple to be placed under the *murti*s the next day. Collection of the *navaratna* packets continued daily throughout the week, in fact, until the final installation. The second day began at 9 a.m. with a *homa* to the nine planets in the new, small temple, followed by *abhishekam* to the nine planets and the Goddess herself. In Hindu practice, the *navagraha* or "nine planets" are heavenly bodies that can influence human life on the earthly plane, so devotees propitiate them also to avoid misfortune. That evening, a group from Kerala, South India gathered in the temple to sing *bhajan*s, devotional songs, while a small number of devotees milled about informally. On the morning of the third day, August 24, the temple priests started at 10 a.m. with a *sudarshana* (*sudarśana*) *homa*, a *homa* done to eradicate negative, demonic energy. There was a lull in the afternoon until 6:00 p.m., when the priests performed *abhishekam*, *alankara*, and *puja* to several of the deities residing there, followed by a dance troupe's performance of classical Indian dance from the state of Odisha.

Starting around 8:30 on the morning of August 25, the fourth day of consecration week, the temple architect performed the eye-opening ceremony for the *murtis* that were ready to be installed on the actual *kumbhabhishekam* day. The opening of the eyes is accomplished when *shilpi*s carve the pupil on the eye of a deity's granite image, which opens that deity's eyes. Temple priests and devotees also began to complete and decorate the sacrificial "hall" or "arena," the *yagashala* (*yajñaśālā*), in which temple priests and officials would construct nine ritual fires that would be used in the days directly preceding the *kumbhabhishekam*. These fires are used to perform fire rites that are like *homa* but much more elaborate and based on ancient, Vedic ritual traditions. The *yagashala* had been built outdoors near the temple and was covered with a canvas roof. In the evening of August 24, 2022, temple priests performed a *homa* outside the doors of the main temple for about an hour before performing a purification ritual, *vastu shuddhi* (*vāstu śuddhi*), that entailed setting fire to a straw effigy and dragging the burning effigy around the new temple complex to remove all evil energies from the temple grounds.

On the fifth day, August 26, the morning's festivities began at 8:00 a.m. with the ritual "charging" of the yantras and *navaratnas* that were to be placed under the *murtis* before installation. The temple priests performed this rite in front of the Goddess's small temple *murti* before bringing the yantras and *navaratnas* to the temple and placing them in the *sannidanam*, the main shrine that was slated to house the new *murti* of the Goddess. Immediately following this rite, a trailer from a local farm and petting zoo pulled into the temple parking lot and released two cows for the performance of cow *puja* (see Figure 4.3). The two cows were coaxed inside the main temple building, where they circumambulated the new *sannidanam* before being brought back outside to circumambulate the *yagashala* three times before being put back in their trailer and driven around the entire temple complex.

Figure 4.3 Cows and devotees inside the temple in August 2022

After an afternoon break of about six hours, the activities resumed at 6:00 p.m., with many devotees coming by to purchase and place their *navaratna* packets on deity pedestals in preparation for the next day's *murti* installation.

The first *yaga* (*yajña*) took place that night outdoors in the *yagashala* while the temple hosted a cultural program of Carnatic classical singing. Fires were lit in the nine firepits established earlier in the week. The weekend's rites required six additional priests beyond those already resident at the Parashakthi Temple, so several had flown in from other Hindu temples in the US and from India. Included among the visiting priests was Dr. Thanga Bhattar, a very elderly priest from the Minakshi Temple in Madurai who claims to have presided at over 800 *kumbhabhishekams*. The pots (*kalasha*) of water into which the divine energy had earlier been transferred were brought to the *yagashala* and adorned with mango leaves and a coconut. The water in the pots would come to be charged with divine energy through the hours of mantra chanting and fire rites that would take place all weekend. Hundreds of *kalasha*s, most of which devotees had sponsored with a financial donation, surrounded the *yagashala* on all sides. I left the temple at around 10:00 p.m., while rites were still underway.

Temple activity began to escalate significantly on the morning of Saturday, August 27. So did the temple crowds as increasing numbers of devotees flocked to the temple for the weekend's festivities. I was later told that about 2,000 people attended the *kumbhabhishekam* that weekend. Many of the attendees were local temple regulars, but there was a surprising number who were not. As I circulated among the crowds asking people to tell me about themselves and their relationship to the temple, I met several Indian Americans who had come from other states, including California, Florida, Illinois, Connecticut, and New Jersey. Some of Kumar's friends had flown in from India to attend the grand reopening, and there were a few curious Euro-Americans who had learned about the temple from videos posted on the temple's YouTube channel and website who felt drawn to it. One such man, a musician named Steven, for example, had come across Kumar's lectures on YouTube and found them so inspiring that he decided on a whim to fly up from Miami, Florida for the *kumbhabhishekam* weekend. He had never been to a Hindu temple before the day I met him, looking dazed and overwhelmed, standing outside the Parashakthi Temple's *rajagopuram*. Kumar, always a gracious host, kept introducing me to people he thought I should meet and interview, so I got caught up in several conversations and missed some of the morning rites.

By the time I made it into the main temple, I saw that several of the *murti*s had been placed on their pedestals overnight and were ready for consecration, including the new *murti* of the Goddess flanked by Ganesha on one side and Subramanya (Karttikeya) and his wives on the other. Those of us present for the morning's activities were invited to dab these three *murti*s with sesame oil, which many Hindus believe repels demonic forces. After the application of sesame oil, the temple priests sat in front of the new goddess *murti* chanting Sanskrit mantras and purifying themselves with ritual gestures (*mudras*). By late morning, we were all ushered out to the *yagashala* for about three hours of fire rites using all nine firepits.

The mantras chanted in the *yagashala* that morning and afternoon included 1,008 names of the Goddess and long repetitions of a variety of Gayatri mantras. When the water in the *kalasha*s had been sufficiently charged with divine energy, they were ready to be brought to the temple to transfer that energy to the *murti*s. Kumar, the nine priests, major donors, and members of the board scooped up several of them and carried them ceremoniously to the main temple building. Kumar climbed onto a crane that lifted him about twenty or thirty feet up into the air and over the *sannidhanam*s of Ganesha, the Goddess, and Subramanya. Over the course of about thirty minutes, navigating the small, unstable space above the deity shrines, Kumar, the temple priests, members of the temple board, and invited major donors dabbed each of the *murti*s with water, sprinkled them with flower petals, and sealed up the very top entry point to each shrine with cement as the congregation below yelled and clapped (see Figure 4.4).

When this task had been accomplished, Kumar went to the smaller temple where, exhausted from the week's activities, he stopped at the base of the Goddess's shrine and gave the consecrating waters to close devotees to pour on the Goddess's *murti*. When all these rites were completed, Kumar announced to those in àttendance that, by virtue of attending the *kumbhabhishekam*, we would all now be connected

Figure 4.4 Consecrating the deities and their *sannidhanams* in August 2022

to Divine Mother forever. He also pleaded with the congregation "to be kind and calm for the next two days because we are all semi-divine for now."

After a three-hour break, rites restarted at around 6:00 p.m. The evening began with the replacing of the energized yantra and *navaratna*s under the goddess *murti* in the small temple. The Goddess's yantra had by then been ritually cleansed, ritually prepared, and recharged, so it was ready to be replaced under the *murti* of the Goddess that would now inhabit the small temple. The temple priests then performed a *puja* to the Goddess. Devotees were then moved to the main temple for a talk by Kumar about the temple and its significance. There was another long evening of fire sacrifice performed in the *yagashala*, followed by a dance performance in the main temple. I left, exhausted from the week's activities, at around 11 PM, while the fire rites and dance were ongoing.

The day of the actual temple consecration was Sunday, August 28, 2022, with fire rituals that began at 8:00 a.m. I slept in a bit and arrived late, at around 9:00 a.m., so I had to park in a remote lot and walk to the temple, arriving around 9:30 am while the rites were already in progress. When I arrived at the edge of the *yagashala*, one of the most involved devotees, whom I shall call Madhav, pulled me into the arena and told me to sit right next to one of the sacrificial fire pits and assist the priest in performing the ablutions. I understood and appreciated that I was being given a great honor, although I could not help but wonder what the hundreds of Hindu devotees crowding around the *yagashala* made of me being given this special pride of place.

When it was time to begin the final consecration rites, the procession of *kalashas* from the *yagashala* to the main temple began. Hundreds of devotees processed into the temple carrying *kalashas* and handed them to volunteers, who placed all the *kalashas* in front of the Goddess's new *murti*. By the time the procession ended, the temple was packed, with everyone crowding in shoulder-to-shoulder while some devotees had to watch from outside the temple doors. The priests then poured all the water from the *kalashas* onto the new *murti* of the Goddess as well as the *murtis* of Ganesha and Subramanya. The curtains were then closed for about an hour while the priests, aided by Kumar, performed the necessary consecration rites. When the curtains reopened, the temple priests performed a long *abhishekam*. The audience was chanting and singing *bhajans*, and the atmosphere

Figure 4.5 The Parashakthi Temple in August 2022

was electric. After the *abhishekam*, the priests performed a *puja* to the newly installed goddess *murti*. Divine Mother had come home (see Figure 4.5).

Robert Orsi has observed that religion entails an "ongoing, dynamic relationship with the realities of everyday life. . . . People appropriate religious idioms as they need them, in response to particular circumstances. All religious ideas and impulses are of the moment, invented, taken, borrowed, and improvised at the intersections of life" (Orsi 1997, 7–8). To examine lived religion means to focus on religion "as it is shaped and experienced in the interplay among venues of everyday experience" (Orsi 1997, 9). Orsi observes further that inherited religious idioms combined with the cultural structures and particular historical moments "give rise to religious creativity and improvisation" and insists that "it is the historicized and encultured religious imagination by means of which, in Marx's famous expression, the frozen circumstances of our worlds are forced to dance" (Orsi 1997, 16–17).

The 2018 fire at the Parashakthi Temple, taking place at the specific historical moment at which it occurred and in the context of the temple community's inherited religious idiom, sparked an act of religious creativity "made necessary and possible by particular circumstances in the world" (Orsi 1997, 8). This act of creativity, in the minds of the temple community, was shared between divine and human realms. Both the Goddess and the community that reveres her worked together to create out of the ashes of the temple's destruction a new temple that would better serve the needs of the contemporary world.

5

Divine Crossings/Space

Frontiers and Maps

In *Friction*, Tsing highlights the complexity of the concept "frontier" and the numerous ways that frontiers are constructed. Speaking of a context entirely different from the one that is the subject of this book, she notes that frontiers are "projects in making geographical and temporal experience" (Tsing 2005, 28–29). She observes further that a frontier is not just a place, but also an imaginative project "capable of molding" places (Tsing 2005, 32). Frontiers, like other landscapes, "are simultaneously natural and social, and they shift and turn in the interplay of human and nonhuman practices" (Tsing 2005, 29). Frontiers are, says Tsing, at the "edge of space and time: a zone of not yet—not yet mapped, not yet regulated" (Tsing 2005, 28).

I do not know if Tsing would approve, but I borrow her understanding of "frontier" here as a way of gaining perspective on the nature of the Parashakthi Temple and its goddess, both of which, I would argue, lie metaphorically at a frontier of Hindu religious life. The Goddess of the Parashakthi Temple resides in a religious imaginary that is, to borrow Tsing's words, "not yet mapped, not yet regulated" and that continues to "shift and turn in the interplay of human and non-human practices" (2005, 28). Even before its founding, the Parashakthi Temple was constructed on a vision of the Goddess that was grounded in, but not limited by, traditional Hindu texts and traditions. The Goddess's boundary-crossing nature transpires simultaneously in multiple registers.

Like many of her US-based devotees, the Goddess in Pontiac is, on one level, a transmigrant. Nina Glick Schiller, Linda Basch, and Cristina Szanton Blanc describe transmigrants as having an identity dependent on "multiple and constant interconnections across international borders" whose public identifiers "are configured in relationship to more than one nation-state" (Glick Schiller et al. 1995, 48). Glick Schiller, Basch, and Blanc describe transnational migration as "the process by which immigrants forge and sustain simultaneous multi-stranded social relations that link together their societies of origin and settlement" (48) and that "migration is one of the important means through which borders and boundaries are being contested" (Glick Schiller, Basch, and Blanc 1995, 50). The Goddess and her temple in Michigan operate in a translocal register in which "new forms of (post) national identity are constituted, and not simply one in which prior identities assert themselves" (Mandaville 2002, 204). The Goddess does not just move from one place to the other but emerges in a new paradigm suitable for the new context and the new role she is to play in this context.

The Goddess's persona in Pontiac reflects her translocal, trans-migrant status. Like Laura, whose story I offer in Chapter 2, others closely involved in the establishment of the temple have also told me that the original plan was to build the temple as a monument to the Divine Feminine in all religions, with shrines to Mary and goddesses from other traditions, but plans changed when the Goddess appeared to Kumar in a dream and told him that she did not want that initial plan fulfilled. The temple as it now stands is the embodiment of the Goddess as the totality of *shakti* ingathered from India and other nations and continents and mixed with the power of Native American shamanic spirits on American land to generate a home on the frontier lands of her shaktiscape. The temple website declares further that its Goddess is supreme consciousness and the eternal, divine mother who has been worshipped "in all cultures, the world over, since earliest of times . . . known to us from the ancient written records of Egypt, Mesopotamia, Greece, Rome, and India:"

> Mahadevi Parashakthi has been worshipped as Isis, Sophia, Shekina and with many other names. She manifests in various historical religions of the world, including the most ancient living religious tradition of Hinduism. In the early Church, the Holy Spirit was experienced as feminine, as seen from the writings of some church Fathers. In early Judaism, the figure of wisdom is experienced as feminine and the theology of "Shekina" and other references in the book of

Isaiah as to the Motherhood of God are well known. Ever since the resurrection of Christ, the grace of Christ has always manifested itself in the form of Mother Mary. Now, in today's world, there is a new realization to view God as the Mother. It is in this regard that Shakthi worship in Hinduism, which dates back to several thousand years in India, can make a significant contribution toward betterment of humanity and uplifting of spirituality. (Parashakthi Temple, "Mahadevi Parashakthi Sannidhi")

Here the Goddess assumes a hybrid identity that is "a product of intermingling and fusion, a product of movement" (McDowell 1999, 212). Temple discourse maintains that she dwells completely both in Pontiac and in Thiruverkadu; her American manifestation has chosen this moment to make herself known and make her power available in the American Midwest because this is the time and place where it is needed.

In this chapter, I focus on the various forms that the Goddess assumes, and the registers in which she acts, at the Parashakthi Temple. I examine both "official" temple discourse, including website statements along with Kumar's temple talks and published remarks, and the experiences and understandings that devotees reported to me. Official temple discourse attributes to the Goddess both esoteric and exoteric dimensions, as is true in many traditional Hindu *shakta* and tantric contexts as well. At the highest level, the Parashakthi Temple represents the Goddess as pure light-sound vibration, *spanda*, expanding out to create the material universe and infuse it with her vibrating presence. Here the temple embraces the kind of tantric themes that have, as I have tried to show in earlier chapters, been part of the temple's history since before its founding. Burchett observes that yoga, *bhakti*, and tantra are "not properly bounded entities" but are instead "forever intertwined, often blurring into one another in practice" (Burchett 2019, 308). They are certainly thoroughly intertwined at the Parashakthi Temple. But from 2007 to 2022, I noticed an increased stress in official temple discourse on the transcendent, abstract, esoteric dimensions of the Goddess and the role of the temple in facilitating individual spiritual growth over the Goddess's nature as a beneficent, miracle-working deity to be worshipped, although both emphases have endured. The shift in emphasis paralleled an increasing integration of tantric and Kriya yoga themes into temple discourse and identity along with themes of devotion. Kumar told me in a conversation we had in July 2012 that while he avoided discussing tantric themes for the first ten years or so of the temple's existence, he had then begun integrating such themes increasingly into his talks and noted that the Goddess "is communicating with devotees more, so they understand."

The form that the Goddess takes at her temple in Michigan is also, however, that of the singular Divine Mother, the Great Goddess, who has come to the West for the benefit of all beings. The Goddess is simultaneously emplaced, neoterritorialized in her home in Pontiac, and thoroughly beyond place. In this regard, the theology of the Goddess promulgated at the temple adopts and adapts prevailing Hindu *shakta* theologies that portray the Goddess as the "matter-energy that underlies all reality" as well as a deity who is "accessible, immanent, and worldly" (Erndl 1993,158, 162). The Goddess is transcendent and immanent, simultaneously "beyond form" or *nirguna* (*nirguṇa*) and "with form" or *saguna* (*saguṇa*), supersensual but also a living presence attentive and available to her devotees. She is supreme, pure *shakti*, the totality of all matter (*prakriti*), and the Divine, loving Mother who helps devotees in need, assisting them in both their material and spiritual journeys.

The Impersonal Goddess: Goddess as Space, Vibration, Light, and Sound

In November of 2009, I travelled from Chicago to Pontiac to attend the consecration of the temple's *drishti pitha* (*dṛṣṭi pīṭha*), a small temple placed at that time at a short distance from the main temple. The purpose of this small temple was to provide a place of concentrated energy to remove the ill effects of the evil eye (*dṛṣṭi*). It was very cold outside that day, and there were dozens of us packed together inside the very small temple. I was given the honor of sitting next to Kumar, who was absorbed in meditation during the lengthy rites that the temple priests were busy performing. Following the installation, I was approached by a Euro-American woman who told me she was attending the temple for the first time and asked me to explain to her what was taking place. She also told me she sensed vibrating energy in her body but was not sure what to make of it. I hesitated. I, too, felt that day strong, vibrating energy radiating off Kumar's body as I sat next to him, but I was not sure I should share that information. So, I let the woman know that many devotees had reported to me that they also felt such vibrating energy when on temple grounds, and they considered the energy to be the living presence of the Goddess. A devotee sitting near us and listening in on our conversation chimed in: "That is Mother! She has called you here and is now gracing you with her presence!"

Official temple discourse has come to feature more prominently than it did in the past descriptions of the Goddess as the vibratory power that has sparked the universe into being and continues to permeate the universe. But devotees' descriptions of experiencing the Goddess physically in one's body as vibration have long been a part of temple discourse. One of the board members, a South Indian male in his sixties, for example, told me when I interviewed him in June 2010:

> As you enter the temple, you feel like you are blessed. I cannot explain this. It is the feeling that you get, a vibration, that you are not in the same world when you come here. You forget everything. When you come, you get the vibration. You won't get it in any other place. . . . When you go to other temples you don't get that kind of feeling when you are there. You see, when you are in the right temple, when the temple is filled with vibrations you feel that, but when you go to other temples you don't get that kind of feeling.

One regular devotee told me in March 2012 that she sensed the most spiritual movement at the temple during deity installations, which she claimed always brought special, intense energy to the temple; she told me she could feel the Goddess's vibrations causing changes in her body and her psyche when she was present during these installations.

In a talk that Kumar gave at the temple in 2012, he explains the evolution of material creation in terms that he attributes to direct revelation: Divine Mother has, he recounts, narrated to him directly and clearly who she is and how the created universe came about. He has rearticulated outlines of this version of cosmogony, sometimes in a shortened or different version, in many contexts over the years. A shortened version is also posted on the Parashakthi Temple website (Parashakthi Temple, "Temple History"). The Goddess's ultimate, transcendent nature is "highest (Parā-) Brahman," which exists as divine, pure, eternal consciousness. Highest Brahman gives rise to *nirguna* Brahman, which is her nature with attributes but no form. From *nirguna* Brahman evolves *saguna* Brahman, the Divine with form, from which arises her form as *maya*, or Mahamayi (Mahāmayī). As Mahamayi, the Goddess both conceals her higher dimensions and projects forth the material universe. Because she wishes to experience herself, Mahāmayī then becomes Brahman as sound, *nada* (*nāda*), which then condenses into *nada bindhu*, the "point" of potential creation consisting of "sound and spiritual light." Shiva and Shakti evolve from this "point" as *purusha* and *prakriti* (Parashakthi Temple, "Temple History"). The temple's website further equates *nada bindhu* with the mantra "Oṁ" and the "Big Bang" that gives rise to the *trimurti* (*trimūrti*), the deities Vishnu, Shiva, and Brahma, and then to all the other deities. *Nada bindhu*, which consists of light and sound, begins to oscillate; it is so immensely powerful that it creates a trillion degrees of heat, cooling down rapidly to form multiple universes (Parashakthi Temple, "Sri Chakra Nava Āvarana representation on our Rājagopuram"). This heat energy transforms itself into matter, and that is the start of the physical universe, culminating in the production of the five gross elements. Kumar has on several occasions likened the oscillating or vibrating heat energy of cosmogenesis to the birth contractions of the laboring maternal body.

Many aspects of this account of creation overlap with accounts of creation found in South Asian Hindu texts and contexts, especially Hindu tantric cosmologies. Tantric texts frequently present the information they contain as a product of direct, divine revelation. Similarly, Kumar insists that the Goddess has revealed the process of cosmogenesis directly to him, so he does not attribute it to any textual or otherworldly authority. André Padoux observes that "the Tantric vision is that of a world issued from, upheld and completely permeated by divine energy (*śakti*)" (Padoux 2017, 16). In Shri Vidya theology, for example, the "initially unified Absolute" evolves into a "dyadic divinity" with both masculine and feminine elements, which then evolves further; creation is presented as a process of self-expansion "in which the universe is considered identical to *and* different from the Absolute" (Brooks 1992, 60). Such could also be said of Kumar's account. In a conversation we had in July of 2012, Kumar stated that, while he did not realize at first what was taking place when he helped found the temple, he realized over time that the Goddess wanted the main principles of Shri Vidya demystified, so she called Kumar to her service to accomplish this goal through his role at the temple.

An emphasis on the divine as vibration, called *spanda*, finds its fullest expression in medieval Kashmir Shaiva Tantric traditions, including the works of the philosopher Abhinavagupta, who has been an important influence on Kumar and hence the temple more broadly. Kashmiri Shaiva Tantra encompasses numerous different texts and schools of thought and practice, but, as Mark D. G. Dyczkowski, one of the foremost Western scholars of Kashmir Shaivism, observes, *spanda* as a concept represents "an important point of contact between them" (Dyczkowski 1989, 23). Dyczkowski argues that the emphasis on *spanda* that permeates Kashmir Shaiva tantra is a unifying "Doctrine of Vibration" that "eventually came to represent a focal point of synthesis" of all the various schools of Kashmir Shaivism. Hence, "*spanda* presents in general and essential terms the whole of Kashmiri Shaivism" (Dyczkowski 1989, 23).

The *spanda* tradition presents the Goddess, Shakti, as supreme consciousness and Shiva's creative energy as well as the immediate source of creation. Shiva is identified as Brahman and is said to be eternally united with *shakti*. As creation unfolds, Shakti expands and manifests herself from the highest to the lowest levels of creation. Everything in the created world is seen to be an emanation or vibration, *spanda*, of *shakti*; hence, the world and the human body function not as impediments to spiritual progress and ultimate enlightenment, but instead, as aspects of divinity and channels to such (Dyczkowski 1989; see also White 2000, 10). One of the most important texts of the *spanda* tradition, the Spandakarika or "Stanzas on Vibration," stresses the importance of experiencing the divine directly (Dyczkowski 1989, 21). Dyczkowski describes the spiritual goal of the Doctrine of Vibration as "the contemplative experience the awakened yogi has of his true nature as the universal perceiving and acting consciousness. Every activity in the universe, as well as every perception, notion, sensation or emotion in the microcosm, ebbs and flows as part of the universal rhythm of the one reality" (Dyczkowski 1989, 21).

While Kashmir Shaiva traditions stress Shiva's superiority over Shakti, the Parashakthi Temple does the opposite. Like the Shri Vidya tradition, this temple stresses the nature of the Goddess as, on the highest level, genderless, formless, supreme consciousness and the highest power in the universe, even though language of the Goddess as "vibration" or *spanda* is more prevalent in Kashmir Shaiva traditions than it is in Shri Vidya. In a talk he gave at a board meeting in 2010, Kumar asserted that the Goddess herself intervened in the construction of her own *murti* when she was first brought to the temple to communicate her desire to emphasize the feminine pole over the masculine one:

> The deity [the Goddess's *murti*] was made by the most distinguished Muthiah Stapathi—he makes most of the *murtis* in American temples, so I asked him to make it, and we installed it. My guru-ji [Dikshitar] saw it and said, "Something is not right because the legs are put wrongly. If you look at her, she has the left leg down and the right leg up." Then I also thought, that's a mistake he made. And I called the *sthapati*, I said it's a wrong installation. We missed it completely." When I called him, he said, "How could that be? I made it right." I said, no, it's wrong." Then my guru was very upset at him. But Mother came at night [in a dream], and she said [to me], "No, I want it to be a *shakti* first. Because this is a protective temple. I want my *shakti* aspect manifest first, and then I'll come as Shiva." So, when the left leg is down, it stresses the *shakti* aspect. When the left leg is up, it shows the Shiva aspect. All this I learned after a major mistake that was not a mistake, because it was designed by her [the Goddess].

The emphasis on *spanda* as the mark of divine presence permeates temple discourse. Objects, structures, and rites all function to capture the divine vibrations that emanate from and constitute the Goddess and make it available to her devotees for spiritual growth as well as for protection and mundane boons. Because the Goddess wants humans to be aware of her presence at the highest level and learn to "explore and experience" her, as the temple's mission statement proclaims, she "descends" into forms that are more available to humans and hence easier for humans to "consume" in the form of her grace. Kumar has published on the temple website, for example:

> During deep kundalini meditation the Divine Mother communicates and conveys certain mystical information to me. One of the points of information which She shared with me, is to explain that the various "Shakthis" are Her aspects with different vibratory energy which make Them more conducive for our receptivity of Their grace and energy. In other words, She descends from the highest vibratory level to a more human vibration so that Her grace can be received by us. (Parashakthi Temple, "Sri Devi Raaja Maathangi")

Kashmir Shaiva texts describe the Divine at the highest level as pure consciousness. Mark Dyczkowski notes that in Kashmir Shaiva texts, the Divine takes the form of pure, unchanging, infinite energy, which is modeled on the element of space (Dyczkowski 1989, 63), the most subtle of the five elements and the one that is most difficult for humans to grasp with their senses. The Divine as pure space is also equated with light, the "pure luminosity" that constitutes the essence of all phenomena (Dyczkowski 1989, 60), Brahman, which is the foundation of all being. Light also serves as a metaphor for spiritual cognition, "seeing the light," so to speak. Furthermore, Kashmir Shaiva texts equate light with "the mass of sounds (śabdarāśi) that "makes the universe manifest and contains all things within itself" (Dyczkowski 1989, 198). Identifying the Divine with sound is common in tantra, especially given the vital role of *bija* mantas in tantric practice; sounds are the sonic form of divinity. Shri Vidya theology emphasizes the manifestation of the Goddess as Tripurasundari in and as the Shri Cakra, promoting her presence in the form of geometric shapes. These emphases on representing the Divine abstractly as not just vibration, but also sound, light, and shape are also in evidence at the Parashakthi Temple. The webpage dedicated to explaining the Shri Cakra, for example, proclaims:

The abstract Divine Mother is the interplay of sound and light which was experienced by Ancient seers (Rishis) as sound (mantras) and light forms as yantras that is given the form of energized linear, triangular, circular, pentagrams, hexagrams, octagrams etc constituting various yantras. These various geometric patterns offer us an abstract form of worship and if deciphered and understood properly with Divine Mother's grace and our own Bhakthi (Devotion), we will be able to understand them and receive Eternal Divine Grace to wake up the "Divinity in us"... . Visiting and praying at Her Temple activates our Pranic flow towards self-realization. Worshipping Her through Sri Chakra at active energy centers like the Parashakthi Temple channels energy of our soul or self towards Cosmic union with "Her." (Parashakthi Temple, "Sri Chakra Nava Avarana representation on our Rajagopuram")

While Shri Vidya and Kashmir Shaiva Tantric traditions have shaped the Parashakthi Temple in profound ways, the temple does not identify itself thoroughly with either of those lineages. It is a Karumariamman temple. Douglas Brooks notes a certain disregard for intellectual territorial boundaries among Shri Vidya tantrics, who, he claims, "appropriate concepts and values articulated in other systems without concerning themselves with what others may say about the consequences of embracing those views" (Brooks 1992, 16), so it seems that Kumar is in good company. However, the specificity of deity forms at the temple is important because each is said to embody a particular vibration that can be captured and transmitted only by that form. In a conversation I had with him when I visited the temple in October of 2019, for example, Kumar reported the following regarding the reason that the Goddess came to Pontiac in the form of a South Indian village goddess (*amma*):

She wanted to come to this temple as *amma* because there is an *amma* in every village. What would *amma* want? She would want to grace everyone—not just rich people or poor people. Everyone. Even those who don't have access to go to a temple. That is her wish. She wants to be touched. She wants to be consumed. She wants your

soul to connect with her soul. To do that, she must be available eve-
rywhere. So, it is not because she is an insignificant person sitting in
Thiruverkadu. (Interview, October 2019)

In the same October 2019 conversation, Kumar described to me the
larger significance of Karumariamman in particular, emphasizing the
need for the Goddess to assume a *saguna* form in order to have a relationship with devotees. Here he emphasized the nature of the Goddess
as "dark energy":

Karumari to me is a very scientific aspect of mother, because 95 percent is dark energy. She represents that. The universe is what I am
talking about. Only five percent is visible—all the galaxies, everything clumped together is less than five percent that is by gadgets
or whatever. The rest of this is dark energy. That is where she remains: dark mass, and dark energy. . . . So, she's called Karu. Karu
means "dark," the dark energy aspect of the universe, which only
continues the creation of the supernovas or the black holes, they
all come from dark energy. Mari is transformation, from *nirguna* to
saguna. We can only have a relationship with *saguna*. So, she changes
from attributeless energy into attributeful energy.

Merging Tantric and vernacular *amma* traditions, the temple website
declares the name "Karumariamman" to be a form of the one, supreme,
vibrating energy that creates and permeates the universe and calls
devotees to spiritual ascension. The site describes each syllable of the
name as a *bīja mantra* embodying a male/female pair of deities: "Ka"
is a *bīja mantra* for Brahma/Saraswati; "ru" is a *bīja mantra* for Rudra
and Rudrini; "ma" is a *bīja mantra* for Vishnu/Lakshmi; and "ri" is
a *bīja mantra* for the "microcosmic divine consciousness vibrating in
the heart region" (Parashakthi Temple, "Shakthi Worship"). Hence,
according to temple discourse, the name "Karumariamman" is "the
name of the supreme divine eternal consciousness" and a "mantra
for supreme deities" (parashakthi Temple, "Shakthi Worship"). The
temple site elides Karumariamman's identity as an *amma* with Tantric
conceptions of *shakti*:

The concept of Divine Mother-Amman is ancient, and this indicates that supreme divine consciousness as transcended from the highest plane to the lowest in the material plane and can be reached by humans as Divine Mother-Amman. We are most fortunate and blessed to have the privilege of worshipping this supreme divine consciousness as our Divine Mother at our temple, where "SHE" has manifested actively due to the nature of the origin of our temple, which is deeply mystical. She is the mother of Kundalini Shakthi. A minute part of her has manifested as Purusha (Shiva) and Prakrithi (Shakthi), which together have materialized into various universes (the multiverse) as living and non-living entities through maya shakthi. (Parashakthi Temple, "Shakthi Worship," lightly edited)

Like tantric Hindu traditions, the Parashakthi Temple presents the Goddess as assuming a variety of non-material forms at the highest level of her existence, including primordial pure energy, space, sound, light, and pure consciousness. But she transforms into the matter that constitutes the created world and all its forms.

Goddess as Metaphor

Kumar has stated plainly in temple talks that gods—even the Goddess as Divine Mother—do not really exist as such. Instead, they are metaphors for psychological or spiritual realities, experiences, and processes. In a talk he gave at the temple in August of 2012, for example, Kumar looked directly at the audience and stated with conviction: "Let me tell you something. I am an atheist. I will tell you why: because I don't accept 'God' as we understand the term." He continued:

We made God finite, humanized with all the human emotions, punishment, anger, cursing people, all this. God would not do that. No. "God" is pure creative force, consciousness; the pure, undivided consciousness from which all of us came. (Temple talk, August 2012)

Here Kumar's understanding of the divine as, at the highest level, pure consciousness aligns with concepts promulgated in tantric and

some Hindu philosophical contexts, such as Samkhya. The Goddess
or "Divine Mother" is, therefore, not really a Goddess or mother at
all. At a board meeting in October 2010, for example, Kumar noted
that at the highest level, there is no gender, only one supreme power
who is the source of everything. The temple calls this supreme power
"Divine Mother" or "Goddess" because it is creative, kind, generous,
and forgiving. But that is just a way of speaking. In fact, Kumar—and
by extension, the Parashakthi Temple more broadly—has little use for
mythology except as metaphor. Kumar frequently speaks of deities
as representations of cosmological, physical, psychological, or spiritual phenomena. The below claim, for example, is posted on the
Parashakthi Temple website:

As you know Hinduism is deeply metaphorical, symbolical and alle-
gorical and our rishis in their deep meditative states have understood
and appreciated the various attributes of the Supreme-Cosmic-
Consciousness that is manifested in the material world as various
deities. (Parashakthi Temple, "Deities: Sri Devi Raaja Maathangi")

The site states further that "the Vigrahas of the deities in our temple
are designed by mystical sculptors and the various symbolic and metaphorical meanings are engraved in the various aspects of the Vigrahas."
Regarding Sri Devi Raja Mathangi, the deity to whom this webpage
is dedicated, she is said to be the power of grace that "gives us the
wisdom to connect to the 'creative forces'" that constitute the Goddess
as Divine Mother. She is the power that connects "the microcosmic
representation of the divine in us" with the "macrocosmic manifestation of the Divine" from which we all descend (Parashakthi Temple,
"Deities: Sri Devi Raaja Maathangi").

Thinking of deities as, at least on one level, metaphors for or
symbols of psychological or spiritual processes or states is deeply
entrenched in a variety of Hindu and Buddhist streams of thought
and practice in Asia and has been adopted by Kumar and the larger
Parashakthi Temple community. In October 2014, for example, during
the celebration of Navaratri, the "Nine Nights" of the Goddess, Kumar
gave a talk in conjunction with two events that occurred at the temple
that day: the *alankara* of Annapurna, the goddess of food, and the

installation on the *rajagopuram* that day of the *vigraha* of Vaishnodevi, a goddess at the center of an important pilgrimage site in North India. Kumar noted in his talk that Annapurna has to do with much more than food. He described her as the source of nourishment for all five of the *koshas*, the five "sheaths," of the body that I discuss in the introduction. He remarked on a journey to Kerala, South India that he had recently undertaken:

> There is a famous temple in India, in Kerala. It is called Sri Randu Murti Temple, "Two Murti Temple." Very strange, very ancient—Mother [the Goddess] asked me to go there. . . . And they have Mahishasuramartini [One Who Destroys the Demon Mahisha] and Annapurna—Mahishasuramartini to slay the evil, the highest evil. . . . and Annapurna feeds our body and soul. . . . Annapurna is much more than a food-giving deity. She is a very, very high vibratory energy. . . . all the spiritual energy in us . . . she sustains it. . . . So, this temple which I visited, which is very unique, in those ancient days, they figured it out: you need to slay evil so that your spiritual journey can start, so you can start to feel how to be immortal. So that starts with the slaying of evil, and Mahishasuramartini did it. So, right next to her is Annapurna in that ancient temple. (Parashakthi Temple, "Dr Krishna Kumar Spiritual Talk During Navaratri Celebrations")

Kumar's talk on this occasion repeated several common temple themes: the need to destroy the evil tendencies within oneself, the Goddess's call to devotees to evolve spiritually, and the metaphorization of deities and demons. Deities are not deities as such but forces or energies that have been ascribed form. Similarly, in a lecture he gave in November of 2021, on the anniversary of the installation of Bhuvaneshvari, one of a group of ten tantric goddesses (the Mahāvidyās), Kumar emphasized her nature not as a deity, but as the element of pure space, the most subtle of the five elements that appear in many Hindu textual and vernacular contexts. David Kinsley writes that Hindu texts describe Bhuvaneshvari as a "cosmic queen" who embodies the five gross elements—earth, water, fire, wind, and space—as the created universe. But she simultaneously transcends the world "as its source and its container at dissolution" (Kinsley 1997,

133, 142). In his talk, Kumar emphasized Bhuvaneshvari's form also as pure space:

> Bhuvaneshvari Ambika is the empress of the universe. She is space. Kali is time. The universe is between time and space and causation. That is all there is in the universe: time, space, and causation. Nothing else is real. Everything else is our own creation. . . . What is space? Space here; space inside me; space beyond the solar system; space beyond the galaxies; space around the creation; space everywhere. There are various types of spaces. She represents all space. (Parashakthi Temple, "Devi Bhuvaneshvari and Space Element")

Kumar continued to note that we cannot see most of what is in outer space as it consists of dark matter and dark energy, claiming again that "Mother is dark energy." Hence, we cannot perceive the Goddess as she exists at the most abstract level as she is beyond both comprehension and perception. In discussing Yama, the god of the underworld, in a Mother's Day talk in 2022, Kumar again asserted that gods are not really gods:

> All these mythological stories do have a meaning. Do you really see him (Yama)? No. There are no cosmic beings. You don't see Yama. You see a picture. But you do see the presence of that cosmic entity, which gives you what you feel. . . [But] we have come here for only one thing: to realize ourselves and go back to Her. ("Mothers Day Talk by Dr. Krishna Kumar" 2022)

Kumar has emphasized on several occasions that the numerous deities housed at the temple are, ultimately, "just cosmic energies. They do not have any form. But we give them form" (Kumar temple talk, January 1, 2012). He has on several occasions referred to Einstein's thoughts about religion, and he aligns his views with those of the renowned scientist:

> Einstein says we are in eternal illusion. He says that religion as it is now, there is no hope [for it]. There has to be a new movement. So, he foresaw what we are doing here. The whole concept [of this temple]

is not the usual religious concept. (Temple talk, January 1, 2012; see also Parashakthi Temple, "Mahadevi Parashakthi Sannidhi")

Kumar has asserted that, like many other American citizens from a variety of religious backgrounds (Fuller 2001), he is "spiritual" but not "religious," and he understands the Parashakthi Temple to be the foundation of a new, spiritual movement that transcends the parameters of religion, at least as he understands it to exist in traditional terms (interview, March 2008). The Goddess is at the highest level an impersonal force that transcends materiality, but the temple is needed because it creates a "vortex" of *shakti* that not only protects the world but also facilitates devotees' quest to reach "her" and experience profound spiritual transformation. It enables the impersonal divine to become, in the language of the temple, personal.

The Personal Goddess: Goddess as Healer, Caretaker, and Spiritual Guide

Many temple devotees engage with and experience the Goddess less as pure consciousness, light, sound, space, or metaphor, and more as a personal deity who intervenes in their lives on both material and spiritual planes as they negotiate the subtle realms of the Divine Mother's shaktiscape. While Karumariamman operates on multiple levels at the Parashakthi Temple, many congregants experience her most substantially as a form of "living energy," as Waghorne puts it, that offers her devotees comfort and assistance in their daily lives, aspects of her that are characteristic broadly of local South Indian deities. Kumar has noted on numerous occasions that the "impersonal" Goddess becomes "personal" at the Parashakthi Temple in ways she does not do in other places. One of the reasons for the temple's existence is, in fact, to facilitate this transformation. Kumar noted in his 2021 New Year's speech, for example, that the new temple was being built "so that you can receive her because she is personal:"

Come and worship and your troubles will be taken care of; she will wake up in you and communicate with you. . . . By showing your love, you develop a personal relationship. That is a great privilege, the divine telling us to develop a personal relationship with her. At this temple, she said, "I want my children to be able to take me at any time they want, and I will be with them." And that is a unique aspect of our temple. (Parashakthi Temple, "Dr Kumar's Speech on New Year 2021" 2021)

As a personal deity, the Goddess has many roles. She is a guru who communicates with many of the temple devotees through the "faster cable" that the temple provides; she is the temple's divine architect and CSO—Chief *Shakti* Officer—who tells devotees what to do so they can carry out her wishes and continue to increase the temple's potency; she is the dispenser of spiritual blessings who invites devotees to her "house" (the temple) and offers there her grace to those ready to "consume" it; she guides her "children" on a spiritual path, using Kumar, the temple community, and the physical structure of the temple itself as her instruments; and she intercedes in the lives of devotees to help with the mundane obstacles and difficulties that exemplify the human condition.

The image of the Goddess as a miracle worker who intervenes directly and helpfully in the lives of dedicated devotees has been a strong part of the temple's identity since it was established in 1999. Corinne Dempsey (2008a, 2) notes that members of a modern, rational, educated Indian elite, a demographic to which many devotees at the Parashkathi Temple belong, often "have little time for or interest in miracles" and therefore may experience their own encounters with miracle events as "conundrums." I have not found this to be the case at the Parashakthi Temple, particularly for the devotees with whom I have had contact and who often accept the Goddess's miraculous interventions as a common occurrence. Davis observes that miracles are "social acts" that may function as "signs or communications, the signifying practice of God" and constitute "claims to religious authority" (Davis 1998, 5–6). Miracle reports at the Parashakthi Temple generally conform to this model and serve as evidence of the Goddess's power and supernormal abilities. These miracles are, furthermore, acts that are grounded in place: they emanate from the Goddess's power spot, the Parashakthi Temple, which serves as the means of transmission that makes these miracles possible.

Kumar and other temple officials frequently encourage devotees to share on their webpage, under "testimonials" (Parashakthi Temple, "Testimonials"), any experiences that they consider to be the result of miraculous divine intervention, reporting that this occurs commonly in devotees' lives once they become involved in temple life. The third issue of *Om Shakthi*, the temple's newsletter, contained a page dedicated to reports of miracles that took place after a devotee visited the temple. Below are two of the reported healing miracles in that newsletter, which I have edited slightly for grammar and sense:

Mr. R. B. was admitted at Williams Beaumont Hospital intensive care unit with serious illness involving multiple organ failure, and various consultants taking care of him said the situation was hopeless. Family members of Mr. R.B. asked one of our board members to do an *arcana*, and the holy powder [from that *arcana*], vibhudi [ash], was sent to Mr. R.B. Within a day, the patient made a dramatic recovery and gradually returned to work as a CEO of a large private company.

T.K., a devotee, had a serious illness and was hospitalized at William Beaumont Hospital. He had a cardiac arrest and was resuscitated and was placed on life support. One of the family members requested our trustee to pray for him and offer a special *arcana*. A special Kundalini prayer was offered to Divine Mother. At the same time that the prayer was being offered, T.K. woke up and felt two snakes entering into his nostrils and giving him Divine breath of life. Rapidly, he recovered from his long hospitalization and a serious illness. He is recuperating at home. (*Om Shakthi* 2, no. 1, n.d., 9)

Such reports from temple devotees continue to be commonplace.

Some of the most fervent devotees I encountered at the Parashakthi Temple insist that the Goddess brought them there so that they could establish a relationship with her and enjoy her continuing intervention in their lives. I conclude this chapter by offering here the stories of three such devotees, all of whom were drawn to the temple after it was constructed and consecrated, and who agreed to speak with me, at some length, about their own experiences of the Goddess. All three were born in South India and spent the first years of their lives there, emigrating to the United States when they were young adults. They first came to the temple in a variety of ways and for a variety of reasons, but they have all become steadfast members of the congregation. They report experiencing the Goddess's grace as transformative energy, feelings of comfort, favorable outcomes with jobs or family, healings from illness, or spiritual guidance. In all three cases, the Parashakthi Temple played a significant role in connecting these individuals to the Goddess and her power. While none of the kinds of experiences I describe below are unique to this temple or these individuals, their stories speak collectively of the ways in which the Parashakthi Temple's Goddess appears in devotees' lives as a caring, loving, "personal" deity demonstrating, per Waghorne's observations, how the concrete world "becomes a site for divine powers to interact with human devotees" in order to heal bodily pain and emotional anguish, help devotees achieve financial success, and shower auspicious blessings on those who put their faith and trust in her (Waghorne 2004, 181).

Rohan

Like many first-generation Indian American immigrants, Rohan moved from India to the United States for higher education and then stayed for a job. By the time I interviewed him in 2011, he had been in the United States for sixteen years and had settled into the Pontiac/Detroit area in a secure professional position in a private company. He had a house, a wife, a child, and American citizenship. He was also then, and remains, a regular devotee at the Parashakthi Temple.

Rohan told me that when he was growing up in India, he was "a little bit religious." When I asked him what he meant by "a little bit religious," he told me, "Well, religion is basically a kind of blind faith. You know, you just go to a temple, and you do certain rituals because you see other people doing it. And you think, 'Okay, if my father does it, if my grandfather does it and if all these people over here do it, there must be something to it.' So, you just do it based on faith." Like Kumar and countless other Americans of various backgrounds (see, for example, Fuller 2001), Rohan drew a distinction between "religion" and "spirituality," characterizing spirituality as "faith with understanding and belief." He noted further that according to his understanding, "in spirituality, God is not outside. God is within you. So, there are no [external] constraints," such as caste, gender, ethnicity, and so forth. Rohan reports that when he first came to the United States in the late 1990s, he was still "a little bit religious." He was living in with roommates in a dorm room, where he kept some small images of Hindu deities and sometimes "put some holy ash and all that" on the images. By 1999, his mindset had changed, and he had become "a total atheist," which he remained until 2005.

After he married in the early 2000s, he and his wife started exploring the United States and then the area around Detroit, going out every evening to get out of the house. He said that at a certain point, he said to his wife, "Okay, we've seen all the malls, we've seen all these restaurants. Let's go to temples." He admits that his wife was not religious, either, but going to temples gave them something to do and a way of connecting with other Indian Americans.

One day in 2002 or 2003, after they had explored other Hindu temples in the area, Rohan told his wife, "Okay, there's this temple, the Parashakthi Temple. Let's go there." He reports that he is good with directions and knew how to get to the temple, but even though he was driving right by it, he could not see it:

> So, I was driving like a half hour, forty minutes, all around this neighborhood. Then I gave up. It was almost like somebody didn't want me to come to the temple. I said, "Okay, we have to go home now, so let's go." I remember this because I have never tried to get to a place and not gotten there.

Rohan's story conforms to a larger temple narrative that only those whom the Goddess calls to the Parashakthi Temple are allowed to be there. In retrospect, Rohan told me, he was not yet ready, so the Goddess would not allow him to find the location of her "house."

In 2005, Rohan was between jobs, and his wife was pregnant with their first child. He and his wife were under financial stress and had to sell their house and move into an apartment, which they found difficult. Rohan's wife, meanwhile, wanted to find a Hindu priest to perform a traditional Hindu sacramental ritual performed in the last trimester of pregnancy (*sīmantam*). Rohan reports: .

> So, I said, "Okay, you know, I don't believe in all this, but I want my son to be good so, you know, let's do it." Then I started calling. I called a couple of temples—this was last minute, right? We must do it tomorrow, and today I'm calling around. And then something told me, okay, let's try the Parashakthi Temple. Or maybe I was just calling all the temples so maybe I'll call this temple. Jayakumar [one of the temple priests] picked up the phone. So, he said, "Yeah, I'll be there tomorrow; I'm free."

Rohan reports that Jayakumar went to Rohan's apartment the next day and performed the necessary rites. Since Jayakumar did not have a car, Rohan had to pick him up and drop him off at the temple. There is a residential building on temple grounds about a hundred feet or so from the main temple where the temple priests live. When he returned to the temple to drop Jayakumar off, Rohan reports:

> I said to myself, "I'm just here to drop this guy off." And then, you know, I think I probably went into the temple because I was not really in control of my life. So, I thought, "Okay, let's go to the temple." Normally, when you go to a temple, you're a little bit scared, right? That's God, and, you know, you're supposed to do the rounds [honoring all the deities] and move. But when I came here the feeling was very loving. When I saw [the *murti* of the Goddess], it felt like it was my own mother, but my divine mother, not my physical mother. I had that feeling of motherly love plus something more profound than that. I couldn't believe it. I felt totally loved and protected. I didn't want to leave that place, and I'm an atheist. It is totally personal, you know. And then I sat there for some time.

While he was in the temple that day, he told me, he joined a couple that was performing *arcana*. Swami Mama, who was alive and working at that time as a temple priest, saw him, smiled, and said, "I was waiting for you." After the *arcana*, Swami Mama came to give Rohan *prasad* in the form of food that had been offered to and blessed by the Goddess and told him, "Yeah, you got it. She gave it to you." The "it" in question is a specific job for which Rohan had applied. Rohan insists that he had never met Swami Mama before that moment and that Swami Mama only knew that he was anxious about a job application because the Goddess had communicated this information directly to Swami Mama.

After that episode, Rohan insisted, "I've never looked back. I'm a total devotee of the temple." He reports that on the way home from that first visit, he thought to himself, "Now I am ready to come to this temple. That is why she [the Goddess] let me. You can only come here if you are invited." At that point, Rohan did not know about Kumar or any of Kumar's teachings, but he felt transformed by the visit. He also told me, "There are so many temples in South India, and they are powerful, but you don't get this kind of feeling there."

Rohan did indeed get the job he was seeking at that time and attributes this happy outcome to the Goddess. He has remained closely involved with the temple to this day. He told me that the Goddess has also helped him get through family illnesses and difficult emotional situations, reporting that she has been responsible for "several miracles" in his life. He takes great comfort in his relationship with the Goddess, as he told me:

> Sometimes, when I'm standing outside my house in the night, I feel—I can't describe it but, like Doctor Kumar says, life on earth is so uncertain, right? And there are so many things that could happen. I feel it sometimes, you know. But she protects us so much we don't even know [how much].[1]

Dempsey observes that at the Shri Rajarajeshwari Temple, a Sri Vidya temple in Rush, New York, miracles are often associated with "worldview shifts." She describes an event that Aiya, the head priest of this temple, narrated to her about his own experience of the Goddess. Aiya reports that she appeared to him in human form as a Dalit woman in a temple in Sri Lanka, then disappeared but left behind traces of herself as *vibhuti* ash. According to Dempsey, this event instigated a "'reorientation' of Aiya's perception, resulting in him feeling a "complete change within me and without me" (Dempsey 2008b, 120–121). Rohan's encounter with the Goddess at the Parashakthi Temple instigated a similar reorientation, one that effected a complete change in his perception of the world and made the Goddess's ongoing miraculous intervention in his life possible. The same is true of Chandran and Padmini, whose stories I recount below.

Chandran

I had seen Chandran at the temple during the week the new temple was consecrated in August of 2022, but I did not get a chance to interview him at length until the day after the temple consecration was completed. Chandran had come from Arizona to attend the events of the final three days and was scheduled to head home the evening following the *kumbhabhishekam*, but he was happy to talk to me while he was waiting to meet with Kumar. He was working at the time for an IT company as a project manager.

Chandran hails from Tamil Nadu but came to the United States for work in the 1990s. He told me that in 1996, he had lived in Detroit for several months. He was a partner at a company and then, because of a professional disagreement, he left his place of employment. He told me he was aware at that time that there was a group that was building the Parashakthi Temple. He felt an emotional connection to the Goddess and had hoped to visit the temple when it was completed but did not get the chance to do so before he relocated to Arizona. He remained somewhat religious during his first decade in Arizona and "used to get dreams of being in temples or being a monk." Over ten years later, he needed to return to the Detroit area for work and resolved to come to the Parashakthi Temple. He first entered the temple on January 29, 2010, during the celebration of Thaipusam, an important Tamil festival dedicated to Murugan/Subramanya and celebrating divine victory over demons. He reports:

> I left my footwear [at the front door] and entered the temple and went to the front desk. And suddenly, I turned around, and I'm standing right in front of her [the *murti* of the Goddess]. An electric shock went through me. I was rooted in that spot. I didn't know

what to do. I was like, rooted, and I think I was shaking. Then I went inside the temple. After I got out of that initial shock. I went in and stood in front of her, And I started crying. My whole body started shaking like this. [He demonstrates by shaking his whole body.] I am not exaggerating. I was stunned. Then I moved away from her to Ganesha, and I became normal. Then I moved from Ganesha to Devi, and it started again, same thing. Then I moved to Lord Murugan and again became normal. That power—you have to be able to handle it right. That was the thing then. From that time, you know, I started getting connected to Devi.

In 2011, Chandran received *diksha* from a religious teacher affiliated with the Venkata Krishna temple in Tempe, Arizona. This guru later sent a message that Chandran should focus during this lifetime on the Goddess. During this period, he started a practice of waking up at 3 a.m., bathing, and performing mantra meditation, a practice that he attributes to the Goddess's influence in his life.

Chandran returned to the Parashakthi Temple in December 2012 for the *rajagopuram bhumi* (*bhūmi*) *puja*, a rite performed to bless the ground and eliminate negative spiritual energy at the *rajagopuram*'s construction site. At that time, he had been unemployed for about three years. He reports that he had only about $700 left in his bank account, and the round-trip ticket to Detroit was more than $600. He prayed to the Goddess, asking her to send him a sign if she wanted him to attend. He prayed to her on a Saturday, and the following Tuesday, he had an overwhelming urge to check his mailbox. There he found a parcel from the Parashakthi Temple containing a sari. He opened it and found a note saying, "Please accept this *prasad* from Mother." There was a name and signature on the note. So, he called the temple to ask why they had sent him the sari as he had not sponsored it. He gave the name of the person who had signed the note and was told that no such person worked or volunteered at the temple. Chandran interpreted this chain of events to mean that the Goddess herself had sent him the sari to encourage him to come to the temple for the *bhumi puja*. He went right out and bought a plane ticket so he could attend the function.

On December 9, 2012, during a Candi *homam* that the Parashakthi Temple performed following the *rajagopuram bhumi puja*, Chandran reports that Kumar told him the Goddess wanted him to focus on Candi as his chosen deity, his *ishtadevata* (*iṣṭadevatā*). Candi is a fierce form of the Goddess who destroys evil forces. Chandran was concerned that he needed a guru to participate in the Candi *homam*, but Kumar told him that Divine Mother would be his guru until a human guru appeared. Chandran reports that such a guru appeared six months later at the Ganapati Temple in Maricopa, Arizona during a Candi *homam* that is performed there annually.

Chandran tried to return to the Parashakthi Temple in 2013, but he says the Goddess would not allow it. His next visit occurred on February 27, 2014, which was both his birthday and Shivaratri, the "night of Shiva," which is a Hindu festival held in honor of the deity Shiva. He then returned for the *rajagopuram* installation in 2015, where he met and took *diksha* from an Indian guru, Swami Divya Cetanananda, one of the Hindu spiritual teachers that Kumar had invited to partake in the *rajagopuram* installation rites. Divya Cetananada, who passed away in 2021, was a tantric practitioner in the Shri Vidya tradition who came to the Parashakthi Temple for several functions over a period of about ten years and acquired during his lifetime a sizeable following in the United States.

Chandran found a respectable job following his experiences with the temple in January 2010, but he says he is not especially wealthy or high-up in his professional organization. In his conversation with me, he invoked the distinction between a "good life" and a "pleasant life" that Kumar has also invoked in his temple talks. Chandran says he is destined during this lifetime to strive for a good life, so the Goddess has intervened in ways that enable him to follow such a path. He helps run a variety of *seva* groups that take care of daily *puja* at Goddess temples in India. And he returns regularly to the Parashakthi Temple to attend important functions.

Padmini

I was sitting at my desk answering emails in October of 2022 when Padmini texted me just to say hello. I met her at the Temple earlier that year during the rededication of the Parashakthi Temple. She is a devotee who immigrated to the United States from Chennai in the 1990s and now lives in the Chicago area. We started a text conversation, and she revealed that she had been in meditation that morning when Divine Mother told her to send me a text so I could complete my interview with her.

Padmini and her husband Raju are followers of a guru from Chennai called Kamakshi Swamigal. In August 2014, he was visiting the Chicago area and stayed with Padmini and her family, who hosted a small gathering during his stay. One of the core devotees at the Parashakthi Temple, Davesh, had come to Chicago to see the guru and came to that gathering. He told Padmini and her husband about the Parashakthi Temple and insisted they should come and visit sometime. Davesh offered to send Padmini a photo of the Goddess. In October, a friend of Davesh's came to Chicago for a concert and delivered the photo to a colleague of Raju's who was attending the same concert. The colleague then passed the photo onto Raju. As Padmini told me, "Amma entered our home" (in the form of the photograph) on the second day of Navaratri in October 2014. Padmini reports that she was "mesmerized" by the photo of the Goddess when it arrived and provided it with a special place in her home *puja* room.

Padmini reports that one day, while sitting in the *puja* room, a voice told her, "Why don't you talk to Dr. Kumar?" She told me:

> I didn't know who was asking me to talk to Dr. Kumar, who is Dr. Kumar, and why did I need to talk to him? I had no clue about all this. I didn't pay much attention to it. But this kept going on within me; [the voice] kept saying, "You should get in touch with Dr. Kumar." So, I sent a text to Davesh and asked him, "Who is Dr. Kumar?" And he told me, "He is the person in charge of the temple," and he gave me a description of what Kumar is and who he is and everything. And Davesh said, "Why are you asking about him?" I told him, "There is some voice that says I need to talk to Dr. Kumar." I am clueless about what I am to talk to him about. I am totally unaware of what is happening.

Davesh told Padmini that the voice was Amma, the Goddess, guiding her. Davesh then spoke to Kumar on Padmini's behalf and arranged for them to talk on the phone.

In 2015, Padmini had to go to Detroit for a wedding and decided to visit the Parashakthi Temple while she was there. She reports that when she first entered and saw the *murti* of the Goddess, she was struck by its beauty. She sat down before the image, chanted verses from an important *shakta* text, the Lalita Sahasranam ("Thousand Names of the Goddess Lalita"), and then began to weep uncontrollably. She reports that she was unable to stand and was thinking to herself, "What is happening here? What is the energy that is pulling me in? I couldn't get up." She decided to just sit and let whatever was happening to her body happen. The next day, she and her husband met with Kumar, who gave them information about the temple and its origins. When she returned to Chicago, she called Davesh and told him that the meeting was not enough, so Davesh arranged to have Kumar call her. She told him the voice was now telling her the word "*diksha*" ("initiation") over and over. According to Padmini, Kumar consulted with the Goddess, who, according to Padmini, gave Kumar instructions to give Padmini the Dakshina Kali mantra, thereby initiating her into Kali worship. Dakshina Kali is a benevolent, maternal form of the goddess Kali.

When Padmini returned to the temple after the *rajagopuram* was installed, she was sitting and meditating in a spot between the Dakshina Kali *vigraha* on one side of her and the Lalita *vigraha* on the other side. Another woman was also present and sitting in front of Padmini. A voice told Padmini that this other woman was bothered about something and had questions, so Padmini should go and tell her the answer to her questions. Padmini resisted, worried that the woman would think she was crazy, but the voice kept urging her on. Padmini did not tell me what the questions or answers were, but the implication was that the Goddess was communicating directly with Padmini. She asked Kumar what she should do, and Kumar told her the voice was that of Divine Mother, and she should follow the Goddess's instructions. On another occasion when Padmini was visiting the temple, she was meditating when a different woman sat near her. The voice told Padmini to open her purse, pull out some Kumkuma *prasad* and an envelope that were both in there, and give them to the woman. Kumkuma is a type of powder that many Hindu temples, especially Goddess temples, offer as *prasad* to devotees. Padmini had a habit of collecting the powder when she would visit temples in India and had not remembered that she still had a container of Kumkuma powder in her bag. She had visited Chennai earlier that year and had also picked up an envelope from the Dakshina Kali temple there, which is why she had it in her purse. The envelope had an image of Dakshina Kali on the front and some advertisements on the back, including the name and address of a local jewelry shop. The voice told Padmini to put the Kukuma *prasad* inside the Dakshina Kali envelope and hand it over to the woman sitting in front of her because "she needs this." Padmini approached the woman and told her that the key to what she was seeking would be in that envelope, which Padmini gave her. Padmini reports that the woman told her that the temple and jewelry shop were two of the places she had wanted to go to in Chennai. Following that experience, Padmini's husband was given a consulting assignment in Detroit, and for three years, he would travel to the Detroit area every Monday and stay there until Thursday evening. He became a regular at the Parashakthi Temple. Padmini reports that the image she keeps in her *puja* room continues to offer her instruction in the form of a divine voice. It told Padmini how to establish in her *puja* room three coconuts in pots (*kalasha*) as the Goddess's forms. Padmini continued to keep in touch with Kumar by phone and in person when she was able to visit the Detroit area. She continues to share with him her spiritual experiences.

Padmini insists that the Goddess housed at the Parashakthi Temple "is not an ordinary deity. It is a talking deity. She answers all your questions." Padmini says that the Goddess continues to offer her guidance in both spiritual and mundane matters. For example, in March 2020, following her father's death in Chennai a year earlier (in March 2019), Padmini and her sister needed to return to India to complete ancestral rites. The Goddess told her to leave Chicago on March 7 and return from India on March 21, so she booked flights for those dates. Her flight in March was the last flight from India to the United States as the COVID-19 epidemic began to cause the world to shut down international air travel. When Padmini asked the Goddess for a sign of her presence in the *murti* and coconuts that Padmini had established in her home *puja* room, her gardener rang the bell and told her a man had dropped off a bangle for her. Like Chandran's sari, Padmini's bangle acted as a means of communicating the Goddess's reality and loving care for her devotee.

When Padmini came out to Detroit for the *kumbhabhishekam* in August 2022, Kumar introduced me to the congregation, so she was aware that I was writing a book about the temple. Padmini reports that the Goddess told her to come and talk to me. She was reluctant to do so, but the Goddess kept urging her on, so she did. As Padmini says, "I just came and said hello to you, and we clicked. It was Amma [Divine Mother] who pushed me to do it." Then, in October, the Goddess came to Padmini when she was meditating and said, "You haven't spoken to Tracy in a long time. Send a text to Davesh to get her number." She then texted me, and that is how her story ended up being part of this book.

Postscript

On the Parashakthi Temple as a "Diaspora" Temple

As Edward S. Casey notes, "There is no knowing or sensing a place except by being in that place, and to be in a place is to be in a position to perceive it" (Casey 1996, 18). Knowledge of a place is necessarily experiential, bodily, and sensate. It is, as Casey calls it, "placial," which entails knowing a place "by means of our knowing bodies" (Casey 1996, 45). One cannot really know the Parashakthi Temple from reading this book, which is a woefully inadequate substitute for placial knowledge. Nevertheless, I hope I have given readers a sense of the richly layered texture of the kinds of experiences the temple provides. At the Parashakthi Temple, representations and perceptions of the Goddess's various dimensions and the reach of her power cross boundaries of time, space, religion, sectarian division, geography, and ethnicity. The Goddess manifests at all levels of the universe, from the highest levels of abstract space to the small voice that speaks to a single, shy devotee. The temple that this Goddess has claimed as her home promotes a vision of itself as a uniquely powerful, mystical place from which the Goddess acts in the mundane realm for the spiritual and material benefit of both individual devotees and the world at large.

Religion has "never obeyed political or ethnic boundaries" and hence is and has always been the ultimate border crosser (Levitt 2007, 12, 17). Religious people may think of themselves as living in an "alternative topography" that has nothing to do with nation-states but is instead delineated by "the sacred" as they understand it (Levitt 2007, 83). This topography is inconstant; it resides in a state of perpetual transformation as it responds to both local and global pressures and shifts. The Parashakthi Temple and its community exist in this kind of alternative topography, one that presents the world as a stage for the

Goddess's shaktiscape and the temple as a node in the networks of divine power that extend throughout the layers of creation. This is why I have resisted referring to this temple as a "diaspora" Hindu temple (Pintchman 2023).

The term "diaspora" originated as a way of describing settlements of Jews outside of the traditional Jewish homeland of Palestine after the Babylonian exile. Hence, in origin, the term described a people who were exiled from their native soil but who shared a common religious and cultural heritage. The term has proliferated in academic settings and across disciplines, however, offering academics a "useful concept through which to reorganize their research interests" but not always with a clear sense of what, exactly, the term indicates outside of its original context (Vertovec 2004, 275–276). Stephen Vertovec makes note of Kachig Tölöyan's observation that recent decades have seen a rapid increase in both "the number of global diasporas" and in "the range and diversity of the new semantic domain that the term 'diaspora' inhabits" (Vertovec 2004, 276 citing Tölöyan 1996, 3). Not everyone is a fan. Kim Knott and Seán McLoughlin note that some scholars describe "diaspora" as "an exhausted concept emptied of meaning by overuse and lack of precise and agreed definition" (2010, 2). Vertovec makes note of Colin A. Palmer's assertion in the opening plenary of the American Historical Association in 1999 that the term "diaspora" "is a problem that invites a great deal of methodological fuzziness, ahistorical claims, and even romantic condescension" (Vertovec 2004, 276, citing Palmer in Winkler 1999). Vertovec himself observed that the seeming overuse and under-theorization of the term "diaspora" threatens its "descriptiveness and usefulness" (Vertovec 2004, 278).

In many academic settings in the social sciences, "diaspora" is deployed to refer broadly to the "scattering" of peoples in general. Jonathan Grossman notes that the term "diaspora" commonly refers to "a transnational community whose members (or their ancestors) emigrated or were dispersed from their original homeland but remain oriented to it and preserve a group identity." He observes further that members of a diaspora community reside "outside the homeland due to dispersal or immigration. Group identity is among the things that render them a community. Their homeland orientation involves transnational exchanges" (Grossman 2019, 1267–1269). It is important to

note here the "homeland orientation," since the use of the term "diaspora" presumes a center-periphery stance toward place, identifying a
principal location toward which other locations and communities are
oriented and in relation to which they occupy a marginalized position.

Definitions of "diaspora" like Grossman's, however, focus exclusively
on the experience of human communities. Thinking about diaspora
religion becomes more complex if we take seriously such communities'
discourse about the experience of their deities. In the case of the
Parashakthi Temple, for example, how accurate is it to think of India as
the Goddess's homeland? The discourse of the temple maintains that
the Goddess is just as fully present, if not more present, in Pontiac as
she is in the Indian landscape. Michigan is not a place of "scattering"
but a place of "gathering in" of the Goddess's energy. As I have tried to
show in Chapter 1, translocality as a frame of reference provides a way
of thinking about Hindu spaces and practices outside of India in ways
that are potentially more fertile than those offered by the ubiquitous
but unnuanced and limited dichotomy of homeland and diaspora. Yet
translocality as a frame does not capture all the movement, change,
and invocations of transcendence and transtemporality that characterize the Parashakthi Temple's religious life. In this regard, Tsing's
invocation of "gaps" is also apposite here. Tsing notes that "gaps are
conceptual spaces and real places into which powerful demarcations
do not travel well" (Tsing 2005, 175). Much of what takes place at the
Parashakthi Temple seems to fall into such conceptual gaps.

The term "diaspora" is, of course, helpful in many situations.
However, the dynamics of religious life at the Parashakthi Temple require us to push our understanding of the complexities and diversities
of "diaspora" Hinduism beyond the conventional boundaries of
Western scholarly discourse. Homi Bhabha's thinking about cultural
processes of change through the lens of hybridity is also helpful here.
Bhabha suggests a vision of cultural worlds as bearing "the traces
of those feelings and practices which inform it" in a way that "gives
rise to something new" and "displaces the histories that constitute
it" (Bhabha 1990, 211). This "something new" he deems to be a kind
of third space beyond the perceived "here" and "there" that constitute it. In his discussion of Third Space theory in relation to culture,
Bhabha imagines third spaces as "interventions" that "challenge our

sense of the historical identity of culture as a homogenizing, unifying force" (Bhabha 1994, 54). For Bhabha, what is at issue in Third Space theorizing is "the regulation and negotiation of those spaces that are continually, *contingently*, opening out, remaking the boundaries" (Bhabha 1994, 313). He further describes "third spaces" as those that facilitate the articulation of postmodern identities in terms of "relocation and reinscription" (Bhabha 1994, 277). For Bhabha, hybrid "third spaces" also function to establish new structures of authority (Bhabha 1990, 211).

The Parashakthi Temple, I would argue, operates in a translocal, iterative/creative, "third space" register that bears "the traces" of both American and Hindu religious and cultural worlds but "gives rise to something new" in a way that "displaces the histories that constitute it." The Parashakthi Temple participates in a perceived web of divine power and a network of religious sites that extend back to South India. But this web extends forward as well, expanding into the networks of people and power that have come to shape her presence and her future in Michigan. The aim of this book is to tell the story of the Goddess, the temple, and its devotional community's experiences in ways that best illuminate their underlying dynamics; doing so requires engaging the ever-changing, multiscalar, and multidirectional flows that circulate between and among the sites, landscapes, communities, individuals, and discourses that help constitute them (Burawoy 2000, 29). This is the approach I hope I have shown here. To present the Parashakthi Temple only as a diaspora Hindu temple would be to miss all the nuance and complexity that give it life.

Endings

On an oddly sunny, warm afternoon in late February 2024, I drove out to Michigan one last time to see the temple, take some additional photos, and touch base with Kumar as I was finishing up details on this book. We had arranged to meet on temple grounds the following morning. Asha was spending a lot of time with out-of-town family and was no longer involved in temple life, so I booked a room for one night in a generic hotel off a busy road in Auburn Hills, an area not too far from the temple grounds. I called my husband and both of my children, Molly and Noah, now young adults living and working in the Washington, DC suburbs, to let them know I had arrived safely. My kids both asked me how it felt for me to be back in Michigan knowing that the project was done. I told them I was not really sure. My daughter Molly remarked that she could not remember a time in her life when I was not working on my book about the Parashakthi Temple.

The weather changed dramatically overnight while I was asleep at the hotel, so it was windy and snowing when I got up the next morning to head over to the temple. On the drive, I noticed more than I had in past years the poor neighborhoods with their dilapidated, boarded-up homes and businesses that surrounded the temple grounds. I was struck, not for the first time, by how well the temple's location fit its narrative of the Goddess as a being who wants her *shakti* to reach everybody, regardless of status. I arrived at the temple parking lot, pulling my car into a spot that was close to the temple entrance. Not knowing that the temperature would drop so precipitously, I had brought with me only a light jacket, not a winter coat, so I braced myself for the walk from my car to the temple entrance. I saw that some new outdoor shrines and a place for car *puja* and been added since I had last been there, with several other smaller construction projects underway around the temple's perimeter. The shell of a new building for the *drishti pitha*, much larger than the previous one, was also in process. The outside of both the main temple and the smaller one now housing the original *murti* of the goddess had been finished with aesthetically pleasing flourishes.

I took several photos and went inside the main temple, leaving my shoes at the entrance, as is customary in a Hindu temple. I sat for a moment, taking in the temple's quiet beauty. It was almost empty at 10:30 a.m. on a cold and snowy Wednesday morning, but a few devotees were milling about. I saw that a *dhvajastambha*, a flagstaff, had been installed inside the temple since I had last been there. A *dhvajastambha* is said to channel divine energy into a Hindu temple. One of the temple priests was busy performing *arcana* to the Goddess for a smartly dressed female devotee, with another woman looking on. The temple was preparing for a *kumbhabhishekam* in late March for two new deity *murti*s: Lakshmi-Hayagriva, Lakshmi joined with a horse-headed form of Vishnu; and Pancamukha Anjaneya, a five-headed form of Hanuman. The *jaladhivasam* ritual for these *murtis* had been completed ten days before my arrival, so I came upon the *murtis* immersed in water and resting comfortably in two large blue-and-white inflatable children's swimming pools. Parts of the temple were blocked off for the coming deity installations, and a sign placed in front of the cordoned-off pools announced that the pre-installation program for these two deities was underway.

I walked back to the temple entrance, fetched my shoes, and went over to the priests' quarters to meet up with Kumar and his fiancée, Pam Costa, the devotee I cited in Chapter 1. Kumar had been divorced from his first wife, Margaret, since before I had started coming to the temple, and Margaret had passed away in 2020. Kumar and Pam had been a couple for many years. Now in his early 80s, Kumar had retired from his medical practice to devote himself full-time to the temple. He had been quite ill before my visit and had been hospitalized for a month, so he was not his usual energetic, ebullient self. We talked, among other things, about this book, about all the changes to the temple that had taken place over the years, and about the coming deity installations. He and Pam invited me to lunch at their favorite Indian restaurant, so we got in our cars and drove through the blowing snow to a strip mall. There were just a handful of customers in the restaurant, so we were served quickly and made small talk over lunch.

As we got up to leave after finishing our meal, I wished them both good health, and we hugged goodbye. I zipped up my jacket, pushed open the restaurant door, and ran through the icy wind to my car.

Notes

Introduction

1. Corinne Dempsey tells of a similar hesitation, which resulted in her writing a book about an American Hindu Goddess temple (Dempsey 2006).
2. In the Hindu philosophical school of Advaita or "non-dualist" Vedanta, for example, Brahman alone is fully real; the manifest world of multiplicity conceals the true unity of Brahman and hence functions a kind of illusion that Brahman generates through the power of *maya*. Advaita Vedanta texts tend to portray *maya* as a cause of spiritual ignorance (*avidyā*), that is, an inability to perceive Brahman's oneness and transcendence, which in turn keeps one bound to the cycle of birth and rebirth.
3. The other *tattva*s are pure consciousness: intellect (*buddhi* or *mahat*), egoity (*ahaṁkāra*), mind (*manas*), five sense capacities (*buddhīndriya*s: hearing, touching, seeing, tasting, and smelling), five action capacities (*karmendriya*s: speaking, grasping, walking, excreting, and procreating), and five subtle elements (*tanmātra*s: sound, contact, form, taste, and smell),
4. These are, in order from most material to most subtle, the physical (*annamaya*) body; breath or life-force (*prāṇamaya*); mind or, as Kumar described it, conscience or moral awareness (*manomaya*), intellect or knowledge (*vijñānamaya*), and the "bliss" layer (*anandamaya*).

Chapter 1

1. Margaret Trawick (1984) has argued that since the eradication of smallpox, tuberculosis has come to be a symbol of the goddess's affliction; William Harman notes that she has come to be associated with tuberculosis, cholera, and typhoid, all of which continue to afflict people living in South India (Harman 2010, 189).
2. Perundevi Srinivasan reports in her dissertation (2009, 160–161) that she was able to interview him. According to Srinivasan, he claims

the same ancestry as Mariammal and also functions as a medium of Karumariamman.

3. This video is in English. There are also Tamil language YouTube videos of the same temple. See, for example, https://www.youtube.com/watch?v=ialTbw72sQs and https://www.youtube.com/watch?v=GXsOf5_cypM.

4. See Dempsey 2006. For an overview analysis of Hindu temples in the United States, see Kurien 2007, 86–116.

5. For more on this temple, see Younger 1995.

Chapter 4

1. A *tithi* is a lunar day in the traditional Hindu calendar.

Works Cited

Abu-Lughod, Lila. 1993. *Writing Women's Worlds: Bedouin Stories*. Berkeley and Los Angeles: University of California Press.

All World Gayatri Pariwar. "Origin of Mission." Available at http://www.awgp.org/about_us/mission_vision/history. Accessed June 15, 2023.

Allen, John, and Allan Cochrane. 2007. "Beyond the Territorial Fix: Regional Assemblages, Politics, and Power." *Regional Studies* 41, no. 9: 1161–1175.

Appadurai, Arjun, ed. 1986. *The Social Life of Things: Commodities in Cultural Perspective*. Cambridge: Cambridge University Press.

Appadurai, Arjun. 1990. "Disjuncture and Difference in the Global Cultural Economy." *Theory, Culture & Society* 7, nos. 2–3: 295–310.

Appadurai, Arjun. 1996. *Modernity at Large: Cultural Dimensions of Globalization*. Minneapolis: University of Minnesota Press.

Appadurai, Arjun. 2001. "Grassroots Globalization and the Research Imagination." In *Globalization*, edited by Arjun Appadurai, 1–21. Durham, NC: Duke University Press.

Augé, Marc. 2008. *Non-Places: An Introduction to Supermodernity*. 2nd Eng. ed. London and New York: Verso.

Bell, Catherine. (1992) 2009. *Ritual Theory, Ritual Practice*. Reprint, New York: Oxford University Press.

Bell, Catherine. 1997. *Ritual: Perspectives and Dimensions*. New York: Oxford University Press.

Bell, Catherine. 1998. "Performance." In *Critical Terms for Religious Studies*, edited by Mark Taylor, 205–224. Chicago: University of Chicago Press.

Bhabha, Homi. 1990. "The Third Space: Interview with Homi Bhabha." In *Identity: Community, Culture, Difference*, edited by Jonathan Rutherford, 207–221. London: Lawrence and Wishart.

Bhabha, Homi. 1994. *The Location of Culture*. New York: Routledge.

Brickell, Katherine and Ayona Datta. 2011. "Introduction: Translocal Geographies." In *Translocal Geographies: Spaces, Places, Connections*, edited by Katherine Brickell and Ayona Datta, 3–20. Farnham: Ashgate.

Brooks, Douglas Renfrew. 1990. *The Secret of the Three Cities: An Introduction to Hindu Śākta Tantrism*. Chicago: University of Chicago Press.

Brooks, Douglas Renfrew. 1992. *Auspicious Wisdom: The Texts and Traditions of Śrīvidyā Śākta Tantrism in South India*. Albany, NY: State University of New York Press.

Brown, C. Mackenzie. 2002. *The Song of the Goddess: The Devī Gītā: Spiritual Counsel of the Great Goddess*. Translation with introduction. Albany, NY: State University of New York Press.

Burawoy, M. 2000. "Introduction: Reaching for the Global." In Michael Burawoy, Joseph A. Blum, Sheba George, Zsuzsa Gille, Teresa Gowen, Lynne Haney, Maren Kawiter, Steven H. Lopez, Seán Ó Riain, and Millie Thayer, *Global Ethnography: Forces, Connections and Imaginations in a Postmodern World*, 1–40. Berkeley and Los Angeles: University of California Press.

Burchett, Patton E. 2019. *A Genealogy of Devotion: Bhakti, Tantra, Yoga, and Sufism in North India*. New York: Columbia University Press.

Cabezon, José. 2006. "The Discipline and Its Other: The Dialectic of Alterity in the Study of Religion." *Journal of the American Academy of Religion* 74, no. 1: 21–28.

Casey, Edward S. 1996. "How to Get from Space to Place in a Fairly Short Stretch of Time." In *Senses of Place*, edited by Steven Feld and Keith H. Basso, 13–52. Santa Fe, NM: School of American Research Press.

Castree, N. 2004. "Differential Geographies: Place, Indigenous Rights and 'Local' Resources." *Political Geography* 23: 133–167.

Clifford, James. 1997. *Routes: Travel and Translation in the Late Twentieth Century*. Cambridge, MA: Harvard University Press.

Coburn, Thomas. 1991. *Encountering the Goddess: A Translation of the Devī-Māhātmya and a Study of Its Interpretation*. SUNY Series in Hindu Studies. Albany: State University of New York Press.

Coburn, Thomas. 2001. "What is a 'Goddess' and What Does It Mean to 'Construct' One?" In *Seeking Mahādevī: Constructing the Identities of the Hindu Great Goddess*, edited by Tracy Pintchman, 213–225. Albany, NY: SUNY Press.

Collins, Elizabeth Fuller. 1997. *Pierced by Murugan's Lance: Ritual, Power, and Moral Redemption among Malaysian Hindus*. DeKalb: Northern Illinois University Press.

Costa, Pamela. 2001. "Mystical Origins." *Om Shakthi*. 1, no. 1 (Jan-March): 12.

Craddock, Elaine. 2001. "Reconstructing the Split goddess as Śakti in a Tamil Village." In *Seeking Mahādevī: Constructing the Identities of Hindu Great Goddess*, edited by Tracy Pintchman, 145–169. Albany: State University of New York Press.

Daniel, E. Valentine. 1984. *Fluid Signs: Being a Person the Tamil Way*. Berkeley and Los Angeles: University of California Press.

Davis, Richard H. 1997. *Lives of Indian Images*. Princeton, NJ: Princeton University Press.

Davis, Richard H. 1998. "Introduction: Miracles as Social Acts." In *Images, Miracles and Authority in Asian Religious Traditions*, edited by Richard Davis, 1–22. Boulder, CO: Westview Press.

Dempsey, Corinne G. 2006. *The Goddess Lives in Upstate New York: Breaking Convention and Making Home at a North American Hindu Temple.* New York: Oxford University Press.

Dempsey, Corinne G. 2008a. "Introduction: Divine Proof or Tenacious Embarrassment? The Wonders of the Modern Miraculous." In *Miracle as Modern Conundrum in South Asian Religious Traditions,* edited by Corinne Dempsey and Selva Raj, 1–22. Albany, NY: State University of New York Press.

Dempsey, Corinne G. 2008b. "The Science of the Miraculous at an Upstate New York Temple." In *Miracle as Modern Conundrum in South Asian Religious Traditions,* edited by Corinne Dempsey and Selva Raj, 119–138. Albany, NY: State University of New York Press.

"Devi Bhuvaneswari and Space Element." Devi Parashakthi - Eternal Mother Temple. November 15, 2021. YouTube video. https://www.youtube.com/watch?v=jKdAIgl_vDE.

Devi Parashakthi Temple. Untitled 1. Facebook video. July 7, 2021. https://www.facebook.com/watch/live/?ref=watch_permalink&v=16160775 6035930.

Devi Parashakthi Temple. Untitled 2. Facebook video. July 9, 2021. https://www.facebook.com/EternalMotherPontiacMITemple/videos/18568261 3526970.

Dei Parashakthi Temple. Untitled 3. Facebook video. August 8, 2021. https://www.facebook.com/EternalMotherPontiacMITemple/videos/225372614 4/5/815/.

"Dr Krishnakumar Speech about Upcoming New Shrines and Its Significance on Vasantha Navarathiri 2021." Devi Parashakthi - Eternal Mother Temple. March 26, 2021. YouTube video. https://www.youtube.com/watch?v=fivm mebJU8M.

"Dr Krishnakumar's Speech on New Year 2021." Devi Parashakthi - Eternal Mother Temple. January 1, 2021. YouTube video. https://www.youtube.com/watch?v=u-IeDThWNg0.

"Dr Krishna Kumar Spiritual Talk During Navaratri Celebrations, Oct, 2014." Devi Parashakthi - Eternal Mother Temple. June 7, 2020. YouTube video. https://www.youtube.com/watch?v=oC_GONrKFKo.

Dyczkowski, Mark D. G. 1989. *The Doctrine of Vibration: An Analysis of the Doctrines and Practices of Kashmir Shaivism.* 1st Indian ed. Delhi: Motilal Banarsidass.

Eck, Diana. 1981. *Darśan: Seeing the Divine Image in India.* Chambersburgh, PA: Anima Books.

Eck, Diana. 2000. "Negotiating Hindu Identities in America." In *The South Asian Religious Diaspora in Britain, Canada, and the United States,* edited by Harold Coward, John R. Hinnells, and Raymond Brady Williams, 219–237. Albany, NY: State University of New York Press.

Eck, Diana. 2012. *India: A Sacred Geography*. New York: Harmony Books.

Egnor, Margaret Trawick. 1984. "The Changed Mother, or What the Smallpox Goddess Did When There Was No More Smallpox." *Contributions to Asian Studies* 18: 24–45.

Erndl, Kathleen. 1993. *Victory to the Mother*. New York: Oxford University Press.

Escobar, Arturo. 2001. "Culture Sits in Places: Reflections on Globalism and Subaltern Strategies of Localization." *Political Geography* 20: 139–174.

Faure, Bernard. 2004. *Double Exposure: Cutting Across Buddhist and Western Discourses*. Stanford, CA: Stanford University Press.

Feld, Steven. 1996. "Waterfalls of Song: An Acoustemology of Place Resounding in Bosavi, Papua New Guinea." In *Senses of Place*, edited by Steven Feld and Keith H. Basso, 91–135. Santa Fe, NM: School of American Research Press.

"Figurine of a Yakshi or Courtesan." https://www.metmuseum.org/art/collect ion/search/761644. Accessed February 16, 2024.

Flood, Gavin. 2006. *The Tantric Body: The Secret Tradition of Hindu Religion*. London: I. B. Taurus.

Flueckiger, Joyce. 2006. *In Amma's Healing Room*. Bloomington: Indiana University Press.

Flueckiger, Joyce. 2020. *Material Acts in Everyday Hindu Worlds*. Albany: State University of New York Press.

Fuller, Robert C. 2001. *Spiritual but Not Religious: Understanding Unchurched America*. New York: Oxford University Press.

"Gayatri Mantra 108 Times with Lyrics - Chanting by Brahmins - गायत्री मंत्र Peaceful Chant." Rajshri Soul. July 30, 2014. YouTube video. https://www.youtube.com/watch?v=6Kb0q9J8lPA.

Geertz, Clifford. 1996. "Afterword." In *Senses of Place*, edited by Steven Feld and Keith H. Basso, 159–262. Santa Fe, NM: School of American Research Press.

Glei, Reinhold and Nikolas Jaspert, eds. 2016. *Locating Religions: Contact, Diversity, and Translocality*. Leiden: Brill.

Glick Schiller, Nina, Linda Basch, and Cristina Szanton Blanc. 1995. "From Immigrant to Transmigrant: Theorizing Transnational Migration." *Anthropological Quarterly* 68, no. 1 (January): 48–63.

Greiner, Clemens, and Patrick Sakdapolrak. 2013. "Translocality: Concepts, Applications and Emerging Research Perspectives." *Geography Compass* 7, no. 5: 373–384.

Grimes, Ronald. 1990. *Ritual Criticism: Case Studies in Its Practice, Essays on Its Theory*. Colombia: University of South Carolina Press.

Grintz, Yehoshua M., and Harry Freedman. 2007. "Ark of the Covenant." In *Encyclopaedia Judaica*, edited by Michael Berenbaum and Fred Skolnik, 2nd ed. Detroit: Macmillan Reference USA. ii: 466–469. Gale Virtual

Reference Library. http://go.galegroup.com/ps/i.do?id=GALE%7CCX258
7501318&v=2.1&u=loyolau&it=r&p=GVRL&sw=w&asid=b7efae443b6fd
ad50f4dbd008dde9f7f.

Grossman, Jonathan. 2019. "Toward a Definition of Diaspora." *Ethnic and Racial Studies* 42, no. 8: 1263–1282.

Gubrium, Jaber F., and James A. Holstein. 2008. "Narrative Ethnography." In *Handbook of Emergent Methods*, edited by Sharlene Nagy Hesse-Biber and Patricia Leavy, 241–264. New York: Guilford Press.

Hancock, Mary Elizabeth. 1999. *Womanhood in the Making: Domestic Ritual and Public Culture in Urban South India*. Boulder, CO: Westview.

Harman, William. 2004. "Taming the Fever Goddess: Transforming a Tradition in Southern India." *Manushi* 140: 2–16.

Harman, William. 2010. "Possession as Protection and Affliction: The Goddess Mariyamman's Fierce Grace." In *Health and Religious Rituals in South Asia: Disease, Possession, and Healing*, edited by Fabrizio Ferrari, 188–198. Hoboken, NJ: Taylor and Francis.

Hatcher, Brian. 2019. "Rekindling the Gāyatrī Mantra: Rabindranath Tagore and 'Our Veda.'" *International Journal of Hindu Studies* 23: 239–258.

Hawley, John S. 1996. "Prologue: The Goddess in India." In *Devī: Goddesses of India*, edited by John S. Hawley and Donna Marie Wulff, 1–28. Berkeley: University of California Press.

Hedberg, Charlotta and Renato Miguel do Carmo. 2012. "Translocal Ruralism: Mobility and Connectivity in European Rural Spaces." In *Translocal Ruralism: Mobility and Connectivity in European Rural Spaces*, edited by Charlotta Hedberg and Renato Miguel do Carmo, 1–9. Dordrecht: Springer.

Heesterman, Jan C. 1967. "The Case of the Severed Head." *Wiener Zeitschrift zur Kunde des Sud-und Ostasiens* 11: 22–43.

Hicks, Mark. 2015. "New tower at Pontiac temple draws devotees." *Detroit News*. August 30. https://www.detroitnews.com/story/news/religion/2015/08/29/new-hindu-temple-pontiac/71390586/.

Horton, Scott. 2008. "A Political Prosecution Goes Under the Microscope." *Harper's Magazine*, January 25. https://harpers.org/blog/2008/01/a-political-prosecution-goes-under-the-microscope/.

"Importance of Gouri Kund and Its Relevance to Creation." Devi Parashakthi - Eternal Mother Temple. March 26, 2021. YouTube video. https://www.youtube.com/watch?v=u7pXAX714cM&t=1190s.

Inden, Ronald. 1990. *Imagining India*. Basil Blackwell: Oxford.

Irwin, John C. 1982. "The Sacred Anthill and the Cult of the Primordial Mound." *History of Religions* 21, no. 4 (May): 339–360.

Jacobsen, Knut. 2013. *Pilgrimage in the Hindu Tradition: Salvific Space*. London: Routledge.

Kaviyogii Shop. http://kaviyogishop.weebly.com/lineage.html. Accessed June 15, 2023.

Keane, Webb. 2008. "On the Materiality of Religion." *Material Religion: The Journal of Objects, Art and Belief*, Vol. 4, No. 2. (July): 230–231.

Khan, Miriam. 1996. "Your Place and Mine: Sharing Emotional Landscapes in Wamira, Papua New Guinea." In *Senses of Place*, edited by Steven Feld and Keith H. Basso, 167–196. Santa Fe, NM: School of American Research Press.

Kinsley, David. 1986. *Hindu Goddesses: Visions of the Divine Feminine in the Hindu Religious Tradition*. Berkeley and Los Angeles: University of California Press.

Kinsley, David. 1997. *Tantric Vision of the Divine Feminine: The Ten Mahāvidyās*. Berkeley and Los Angeles: University of California Press.

Knott, Kim, and Seán McLoughlin. 2010. "Introduction." In *Diasporas: Concepts, Intersections, Identities*, edited by Kim Knott and Seán McLoughlin, 1–18. New York and London: Zed Books.

Kopytoff, Igor. 1986. "The Cultural Biography of Things: Commoditization as Process." In *The Social Life of Things: Commodities in Cultural Perspective*, edited by Arjun Appadurai, 64–91. Cambridge: Cambridge University Press.

Kramrisch, Stella. 1976. *The Hindu Temple*. Delhi: Motilal Banarsidass.

Kulshreshtha, Salila. 2023. "Introduction to Temples and Rituals." In *The Routledge Handbook of Hindu Temples: Materiality, Social History, and Practice*, edited by Himanshu Prabha Ray, Salila Kulshreshtha, and Uthara Suvrathan, 99–110. London and New York: Routledge.

Kumar, Dr. G. Krishna. 2001. "Personal Note from Dr. G. Krishna Kumar." *Om Shakthi* 1, no. 1 (Jan-March): 4.

Kurien, Prema A. 2007. *A Place at the Multicultural Table: The Development of an American Hinduism*. Piscataway, NJ: Rutgers University Press.

Lauerman, Kerry. 2000. "The Man Bush Blames for Michigan." *Salon*, February 24. https://www.salon.com/2000/02/24/fieger/.

Levitt, Peggy. 2007. *God Needs No Passport: Immigrants and the Changing Religious Landscape*. New York: The New Press.

Livius, Thomas. 1893. *The Blessed Virgin in the Fathers of the First Six Centuries*. London: Burns and Oates.

Mandaville, Peter. 2002. Reading the State from Elsewhere: Towards an Anthropology of the Postnational. *Review of International Studies* 28, no. 1 (January): 199–207.

Massey, Doreen. 1999. "Spaces of Politics." In *Human Geography Today*, edited by Doreen Massey, John Allen, and Phil Sarre, 279–294. Hoboken, NJ: Wiley Press.

McDowell, Linda. 1999. *Gender, Identity and Place: Understanding Feminist Geographies*. Minneapolis: University of Minnesota Press.

McKay, D. 2006. "Translocal Circulation: Place and Subjectivity in an Extended Filipino Community." *The Asia Pacific Journal of Anthroplogy* 7, no. 3: 265–278.

McDannell, Colleen. 1995. *Material Christianity*. New Haven, CT: Yale University Press.

Meditative Mind. "10 Amazing Benefits of Gayatri Mantra Chanting." Available at https://meditativemind.org/10-amazing-benefits-of-gayatri-mantra-chanting/. Accessed June 15, 2023.

Michaels, Axel. 2016. *Homo Ritualis: Hindu Ritual and its Significance for Ritual Theory*. New York: Oxford University Press.

Michell, George. 1997. *The Hindu Temple: An Introduction to its Meaning and Forms*. New York: Harper and Row.

Mignolo, Walter D. 2009. "Epistemic Disobedience, Independent Thought and De-Colonial Freedom." *Theory, Culture & Society* 26, no. 7–8: 1–23.

Mignolo, Walter D., and Madina V. Tlostanova. 2006. "Theorizing from the Borders: Shifting to Geo- and Body-Politics of Knowledge." *European Journal of Social Theory* 9, no. 2: 205–221.

Morgan, David. 2008. "The Materiality of Cultural Construction." *Material Religion: The Journal of Objects, Art and Belief*, 4, no. 2 (July): 228–229.

Morgan, David. 2018. *Images at Work: The Material Culture of Enchantment*. New York: Oxford University Press.

Morgan, David. 2021. *The Thing about Religion: An Introduction to the Material Study of Religions*. Chapel Hill: The University of North Carolina Press.

Morinis, Alan. 1992. "Introduction." In *Sacred Journeys: The Anthropology of Pilgrimage*, edited by Alan Morinis, 1–28. Westport, CT: Greenwood Press.

"Mothers Day Talk by Dr. Krishna Kumar." Devi Parashakthi - Eternal Mother Temple. May 8, 2022. YouTube video. https://www.youtube.com/watch?v=kwfUfd5JJzQ&t=119s.

Muller-Ortega, Paul. 1989. *The Triadic Heart of Śiva: Kaula Tantricism of Ahbinavagupta in the Non-Dual Shaivism of Kashmir*. Albany: State University of New York Press.

"Mystical nature of temple land: Parashakthi Temple." Devi Parashakthi - Eternal Mother Temple. January 27, 2022. YouTube video. https://www.youtube.com/watch?v=mB5QFQf9zU0&t=155s.

Narayan, Kirin. 1997. "Sprouting and Uprooting of Saili: The Story of the Sacred Tulsi in Kangra." *Manushi* no. 102: 30–38.

Narayanan, Vasudha. 1992. "Creating South Indian Hindu Experience in the United States." In *A Sacred Thread: Modern Transmission of Hindu Traditions in India and Abroad*, edited by R. B. Williams, 147–196. Chambersburg, PA: Anima Publications.

Narayanan, Vasudha. 2005. "Heterogenous Spaces and Modernities: Hindu Rituals to Sacralize the American Landscape." *Journal of Vaishnava Studies* 13, no. 2 (January 14): 127–148.

Narayanan, Vasudha. 2006. "Sacred Land, Sacred Service: Hindu Adaptations to the American Landscape." In *A Nation of Religions: The Politics of Pluralism in Multi-religious America*, edited by Stephen Prothero, 139–159. Chapel Hill: University of North Carolina Press.

Om Shakthi. 2, no. 1. N.d. Newsletter produced by the Parashakthi Temple.

Orsi, Robert. 1997. "Everyday Miracles: The Study of Lived Religion." In *Lived Religion in America: Toward a History of Practice*, edited by David D. Hall, 3–21. Princeton, NJ: Princeton University Press.

Padoux, André. 2017. *The Hindu Tantric World: An Overview.* Chicago: University of Chicago Press.

Parashakthi Temple. "Deities." https://www.parashakthitemple.org/deities.html. Accessed June 15, 2023.

Parashakthi Temple. "Deities: Sri Devi Raja Maathangi. https://www.parashakthitemple.org/deities/sri-devi-raaja-maathangi. Accessed June 30, 2023.

Parashakthi Temple. "Mahadevi Parashakthi Sannidhi." https://www.parashakthitemple.org/shaktham-mahadevi.html. Accessed August 15, 2023.

Parashakthi Temple. "Our Priests." https://www.parashakthitemple.org/our-priests.html. Accessed June 15, 2023.

Parashakthi Temple. "Pearls of Wisdom." parashakthitemple.org/download-pdf/PearlsofWisdom.pdf. Accessed June 15, 2023.

Parashakthi Temple. "Pooja Schedule." https://www.parashakthitemple.org/pooja-schedule.html. Accessed June 15, 2023.

Parashakthi Temple. "Prana Pratishta." https://www.parashakthitemple.org/prana-prathishta.html. Accessed June 15, 2023.

Parashakthi Temple. "Shakthi Garbha or Ark of the Covenant." http://www.parashakthitemple.org/t/shakthi-garbha. Accessed November 21, 2017.

Parashakthi Temple. "Shakthi Worship." http://www.parashakthitemple.org/shakthi_worship.aspx. Accessed June 14, 2023.

Parashakthi Temple. "Sri Chakra Nava Avarana representation on our Rajagopuram." https://www.parashakthitemple.org/sricharkra-gopuram.html. Accessed June 15, 2023.

Parashakthi Temple. "Sri Devi Raaja Maathangi." https://www.parashakthitemple.org/deities/sri-devi-raaja-maathangi. Accessed June 30, 2023.

Parashakthi Temple. "Temple History." https://www.parashakthitemple.org/temple-history.html. Accessed June 15, 2023.

Parashakthi Temple. "Testimonials." https://www.parashakthitemple.org/testimonials. Accessed July 15, 2023.

"Parashakthi Temple Rajagopuram Opening on August 17th in USA: TV5 News." TV5 News. July 8, 2015. YouTube video. https://www.youtube.com/watch?v=mO0V5liHUKM.

Parker, Samuel K. 2009. "Sanctum and *Gopuram* at Madurai: Aesthetics of *Akam* and *Puram* in Tamil Temple Architecture." In *Tamil Geographies: Cultural Constructions of Space and Place in South India*, edited by Marth Ann Selby and Indira Viswanathan Peterson, 143–172. Albany: State University of New York Press.

Pintchman, Tracy. 1994. *The Rise of the Goddess in the Hindu Tradition.* Albany: State University of New York Press.

Pintchman, Tracy. 2014. "From Local Goddess to Locale Goddess: Karumariamman as Divine Mother at a North American Hindu Temple." In *Inventing and Reinventing the Local Goddess: Contemporary Iterations of Hindu Deities on the Move,* edited by Sree Padma, 89–103. Boulder, CO: Lexington Books.

Pintchman, Tracy. 2015. "The Goddess's Shaligrams." In *Sacred Matters: Materiality in Indian Religions,* edited by Tracy Pintchman and Corinne Dempsey, 115–133. Albany, NY: State University of New York Press.

Pintchman, Tracy. 2018a. "The Divine Mother Comes to Michigan." In *The Oxford History of Hinduism: The Goddess,* edited by Mandakranta Bose, 304–321. New York: Oxford University Press.

Pintchman, Tracy. 2018b. "Shakti Garbha as Ark of the Covenant at an American Hindu Goddess Temple." In *Between Dharma and Halakha,* edited by Ithamar Theodor and Yudit Greenberg, 35–49. Boulder, CO: Lexington Books.

Pintchman, Tracy. 2018c. "Hindu Goddess Traditions: Cosmological, Devotional, and Social Perspectives." In *The Oxford History of Hinduism: The Goddess,* edited by Mandakranta Bose, 17–28. New York: Oxford University Press.

Pintchman, Tracy. 2023. "Rethinking *Diaspora* in the American Hindu Landscape: The Translocal Śaktiscape of the Hindu Goddess in Pontiac, Michigan." *Journal of the American Academy of Religion* 91, no. 1 (June): 121–135.

Prasad, Leela. 2006. "Text, Tradition, and Imagination: Evoking the Normative in Everyday Hindu Life." *Numen* 53, no. 1: 1–47.

Preston, James J. 1992. "Spiritual Magnetism: An Organizing Principle for the Study of Pilgrimage." In *Sacred Journeys: The Anthropology of Pilgrimage,* edited by Alan Morinis, 31–46. Westport, CT: Greenwood Press.

"Rajagopuram Devi Parashakthi Temple." N.d. Booklet distributed at the time of the Mahakumbhabhishekam for the Parashakthi Temple *rajagopuram,* August 16–23, 2015.

Ramanujan, A. K. 1989. "Is there an Indian Way of Thinking? An Informal Essay." *Contributions to Indian Sociology* 23, no. 1 (January–June): 41–58.

Reetz, Dietrich. 2010. "'Alternative Globalities? On the Cultures and Formats of Transnational Muslim Networks from South Asia." In *Translocality: The Study of Globalizing Processes from a Southern Perspective,* edited by Ulrike Freitag and Achim van Oppen, 293–334. Leiden: Brill.

Richardson, E. Allen. 2019. *Hindu Gods in an American Landscape: Changing Perceptions of Indian Sacred Images in the Global Age.* Jefferson, NC: McFarland & Company.

Sax, William. 2002. *Dancing the Self: Personhood and Performance in the Pandav Lila of Garhwal.* New York: Oxford University Press.

Shapiro, Allen. 1987. "Śālagrāmaśilā: A Study of Śālagrāma Stones with Text and Translation of Śālagrāmaparīkṣā." PhD diss. New York: Columbia University.

Shridharan, Shriya. 2019. "The Contemporaneity of Tradition: Expansion and Renovation of the Vedanta Desikar Temple in Mylapore, Chennai." In *The Contemporary Hindu Temple: Fragments for a History*, edited by Annapurna Garimella, Shriya Shridharan, and A. Srivathsan, 74–83. India: Tata Trust.

Shulman, David Dean. 1980. *Tamil Temple Myths: Sacrifice and Divine Marriage in the South Indian Śaiva Tradition*. Princeton, NJ: Princeton University Press.

"Significance of Devi Mahamariamman." Devi Parashakthi - Eternal Mother Temple. February 13, 2022. YouTube video. https://www.youtube.com/watch?v=cK99LM_5N4s.

Silburn, Lilian. 1988. *Kuṇḍalinī: The Energy of the Depths*. Albany: State University of New York Press.

Singh, Rana B. 2009. "Goddesses and Spatial Ordering in Kashi: Shaktiscape." In *Cosmic Order and Cultural Astronomy: Sacred Cities of India*, ed. Rana B. Singh, 186–208. Cambridge Scholars Publishing: Newcastle upon Tyne.

Sinha, Vineeta. 2014. "Bringing Back the Old Ways: Enacting a Goddess Festival in Urban Singapore." *Material Religion* 10, no. 1: 76–103.

Sircar, Dineshchandra. 1973. *The Śākta Pīṭhas*. New Delhi: Motilal Banarsidass.

Srinivas, Tulasi. 2018. *The Cow in the Elevator: An Anthropology of Wonder*. Durham, NC: Duke University Press.

Srinivasan, Perundevi. 2009. "Stories of the Flesh: Colonial and Anthropological Discourses on the South Indian Goddess Mariyamman." PhD diss., George Washington University.

Srour, Némésis. 2015. "Deterritorialization of the Image: Dissonances in the Imagery of Arab Identity?" In *Dislocating Globality: Deterritorialization, Difference and Resistence*, edited by Samas Paunksnis, 77–96. Leiden: Brill.

Tackes, Nick. 2021. "First Responders: The Gayatri Pariwar and the Immune Ritual Body." *Journal of the American Academy of Religion* 89, no. 2 (September): 1006–1038.

Tamil Nadu Tourism. "Devi Karumariyamman Temple, Thiruvadisoolam, Chengalpattu." December 17, 2016. https://Tamil Nadu-favtourism.blogspot.com/2016/12/devi-karumariyamman-temple.html.

"The Power and Benefits of Gayatri Mantra | Dr. Hansaji Yogendra." The Yoga Institute. June 13, 2021. YouTube video. https://www.youtube.com/watch?v=vOvigqv8Vkg.

Thiruvadisoolam. Facebook page. https://www.facebook.com/Thiruvadisoolam/.

Thiruvadisoolam [@aathithiruvadi]. Twitter page. https://twitter.com/aathithiruvadi?lang=en.

Thiruvadisoolam SarvaSaktiPeedam [@thiruvadisoolam]. Instagram page. https://www.instagram.com/thiruvadisoolam/?hl=en.

"Thiruvadisoolam - VISWAROOPA DARSHAN - English - Video 14." Thiruvadisoolam. May 8, 2017. YouTube video. https://www.youtube.com/watch?v=5ugU5Lzs5d4.

Tölöyan, Kachig. 1996. "Rethinking Diaspora(s): Stateless Power in the Transnational Moment." *Diaspora* 5, no. 1: 3–36.

Tsing, Anna Lawenhaupt. 2005. *Friction: An Ethnography of Global Connection*. Princeton, NJ: Princeton University Press.

Tweed, Thomas A. 2006. *Crossing and Dwelling: A Theory of Religion*. Cambridge, MA: Harvard University Press.

United States Department of Justice. 2007. "Michigan Attorneys Indicted for Alleged Campaign Finance Violations." Press release. August 24. https://www.justice.gov/archive/opa/pr/2007/August/07_crm_655.html.

Urban, Hugh B. 2003. *Tantra: Sex, Secrecy, Politics, and Power in the Study of Religion*. Berkeley and Los Angeles: University of California Press.

Urban, Hugh B. 2010. *The Power of Tantra: Religion, Sexuality, and the Politics of South Asian Studies*. London: I. B. Tauris.

Venkatraman, Ramaswamy. 1990. *A History of the Tamil Siddha Cult*. Madurai: Ennes Publications.

Vertovec, Steven. 2004. "Religion and Diaspora." In *New Approaches to the Study of Religion, Vol. 2: Textual, Comparative, Sociological, and Cognitive Approaches*, edited by Peter Antes, Armin W. Geertz, and Randi R. Warne, 275–303. Berlin: De Gruyter.

Waghorne, Joanne Punzo. 2004. *Diaspora of the Gods: Modern Hindu Temples in an Urban Middle-Class World*. New York: Oxford.

White, David Gordon. 2000. *Tantra in Practice: Mapping a Tradition*. Princeton, NJ: Princeton University Press.

White, David Gordon. 2003. *Kiss of the Yoginī: "Tantric Sex" In Its South Asian Contexts*. Chicago: University of Chicago Press.

Winkler, Karen J. "Historians Explore Questions of How People and Cultures Disperse across the Globe." *Chronicle of Higher Education*. January 22, 1999. https://www.chronicle.com/article/historians-explore-questions-of-how-people-and-cultures-disperse-across-the-globe/.

"Yantra sthapanam and kundalini ascension." Devi Parashakthi - Eternal Mother Temple. August 30, 2022. YouTube video. https://www.youtube.com/watch?v=bTycV_ZMRso.

Yogananda, Paramahamsa. (1946) 1987. *Autobiography of a Yogi*. 11th ed. 9th reprint, Los Angeles: Self-Realization Fellowship.

Younger, Paul. 1995. *The Home of Dancing Śivaṉ: The Traditions of the Hindu Temple in Citamparam*. New York: Oxford University Press.

Index